AF644381

ELEMENTARY PSYCHOLOGY

ELEMENTARY PSYCHOLOGY

S.M. Mohsin
M.A. (Patna), Ph.D. (Edinburgh)

MOTILAL BANARSIDASS PUBLISHERS
PRIVATE LIMITED • DELHI

First Edition : Mumbai, 1967
Second Edition : Mumbai, 1976
Third Revised Edition: Delhi, 1983
Reprint: Delhi, 1988, 1997, 2001

© 1988 MOTILAL BANARSIDASS PRIVATE LIMITED
All Rights Reserved

ISBN: 81-208-0499-6 (Cloth)
ISBN: 81-208-0500-3 (Paper)

Also available at:

MOTILAL BANARSIDASS

236, 9th Main III Block, Jayanagar, Bangalore 560 011
41 U.A. Bungalow Road, Jawahar Nagar, Delhi 110 007
8 Mahalaxmi Chamber, Warden Road, Mumbai 400 026
120 Royapettah High Road, Mylapore, Chennai 600 004
Sanas Plaza, 1302 Baji Rao Road, Pune 411 002
8 Camac Street, Kolkata 700 017
Ashok Rajpath, Patna 800 004
Chowk, Varanasi 221 001

Printed in India

BY JAINENDRA PRAKASH JAIN AT SHRI JAINENDRA PRESS,
A-45 NARAINA, PHASE-I, NEW DELHI 110 028
AND PUBLISHED BY NARENDRA PRAKASH JAIN FOR
MOTILAL BANARSIDASS PUBLISHERS PRIVATE LIMITED,
BUNGALOW ROAD, DELHI 110 007

PREFACE

SOME justification is perhaps necessary for the addition of yet another elementary text-book of psychology to the fairly long list of those already available. This, the author feels, is to be found in the particular technique of presentation he has adopted to ensure understanding of the basic facts and theories of psychology in the background of real-life situations, equipping the student with the ability to transfer the knowledge gained from the reading of the book to his everyday experiences. Well before a new term or concept is introduced, the reader is prepared in advance to understand and accept it. The language of definition has been scrupulously avoided. For example, while learning, motivation and personality form the core of our knowledge of man's behaviour today, unfortunately, for the average student, a treatise on learning is little more than a multitude of anecdotes about rats, cats, and chimpanzees, which seldom have any bearing he can recognize on his life and behaviour and that of his fellows. An attempt is made in the present work to bring the topic of learning much closer to the readers' life and endeavours and to integrate it with his day-to-day experiences of the world around him. In this treatment of motivation and personality, the author has drawn liberally upon his knowledge of psycho-pathology and the facts of social behaviour without which an understanding of the underlying dynamics of behaviour is not possible.

An additional special feature of the book is the chapter on intelligence and aptitudes which prepares the student for a full-dress discourse on techniques of test construction at a later stage in his study of the subject. It also explains the elementary statistical concepts, not in a vacuum, but in the concrete context of intelligence tests so that the value of statistics in psychology is fully appreciated.

Since the book assumes no previous knowledge, it is hoped it will be found useful also by a layman interested in the subject. Frequent references to familiar events and situations will, it is hoped, enliven his interest and lend him some insight into the currents, cross-currents, and under-currents of human behaviour.

I am grateful to some of my colleagues in the Department of Psychology, Patna University, to whom I read out chapters of this book before it was completed and from whose suggestions and criticism I have greatly benefited. It was they who encouraged me to have the work published.

Patna University, S. M. M.
December 1, 1966.

REVISED EDITION

Some changes have been made in the revised edition of the book. The first chapter has been completely revised to make the approach of the book upto date. Some additions have also been made in a few chapters.

Patna, S. M. M.
June 1982.

CONTENTS

CHAPTER I

SUBJECT MATTER AND DEFINITION OF PSYCHOLOGY

Subject Matter of Psychology

Psychology studies man in his environment. From the very moment of his birth man lives and grows in an environment of objects and persons. Other living beings also live and grow in in an environment. But the environment in which they live is much simpler. The environment in which man lives is very complex. Man has to deal not only with what is present to him, that is, his immediate environment. He has to deal also with what belonged to the past, and which has yet to happen in the future. This very wide span of time, stretching back to the past and extending forth into the future, has made man's environment very complex. To deal with such complex environments he requires not only those capacities of acting and knowing with which man is born, but lot of other capacities which he has to acquire. Other living beings can manage with the capacities with which they are born. Many of them may not at all have to acquire any new capacities to live in their environment. Some other living beings may have to acquire some new capacities, specially when they are removed from the environment in which they were born. But these acquired capacities are only a few compared to those with which they are born. In case of man, more of his capacities are acquired than inborn, and the processs of acquiring those capacities never comes to an end. This is the reason why man has a very long period of learning to deal with his environment.

Man differs from other forms of life not only because he has to deal with a highly complex environment, and he has continuously to learn newer and newer capacities to do this. In dealing with his environment the activities of his body are much less important for man. There are a great many activities of man of which he is capable that are not bodily. These activities have been called mental to distinguish them from the bodily activities. These are the activities of perceiving, remembering, imagining, thinking, discriminating, desiring, deciding, planning to act, etc., with which every body is familiar because these are the peculiar activities of man. We may get some signs of these activities in other forms of life also, but they are much less developed and much less refined. It is because man possesses these activities in more developed form that man is able to deal not only with the facts and events that are present to him, but also with those that have happened in the past and are likely to happen in the future. The presesnt facts and events have no meaning for him unless he relates them to the past and the future. The past and future with which man deals cover such a wide span of time which compared to his own span of life is but a drop in the ocean.

We have said that man takes much longer time to learn new activities as compared to other forms of life because man's learning is less concerned with bodily activities. Man's learning involves to a much greater extent the mental activities that we described earlier. His perception, his remembering, his imagination, his thinking, his power of discrimination, of making a choice, taking a decision, all these too undergo a course of learning. They too become more and more complex and varied, more and more developed and refined as a result of his personal effort. That is why we talk not only about the growth and development of the bodily organs and their functions, but also about the development of perception, of memory, of imagination, thinking, reasoning, etc.

Besides these activities that are developed in man to enable him to cope with his complex environment, there are certain mental states and processes that arise within him while he is engaged in his bodily and mental activities. He becomes aware of these states and processes, and they also influence his activities. These are the feelings of pleasure and pain, and the emotions of anger, fear, disgust, hatred and love, etc. These also undergo change in the course of man's life. Besides the feelings and emotions, man has also likes and dislikes; he prefers some objects, activities and persons; he is attracted to them. There are other objects, persons and activities from which he is repelled; he dislikes them; he turns away from them. These likes and dislikes, attractions and aversions are described as interest and attitudes. They too are subject to change with the change in man's capacities and his environment.

As we said at the outset, man lives not only in the environment of objects. He also lives in the environment of persons. In fact, it is environment of persons which makes so much demand upon the activities we have called mental. When man acts to the objects of his environment, they do not act to him. The action is one-sided; there is no interaction. But the persons to whom he acts, are as much acting to him as he is acting to them. An interaction is taking place at every moment. Man's mode of acting becomes much more complex for this reason also. While acting to objects, he can anticipate what will be the result of his action. He knows, for example, that if he goes into the open in the cold season without properly covering his body, he would catch cold. But when he is acting to persons, he can much less correctly anticipate the result of his action. When a beggar enters the house of a person, he does not know whether the person will have pity on him or will turn him out of doors.

Psyschology studies the various activities of man, both bodily and mental, that he performs while dealing with the environment of objects and persons. In psychology we try to understand the nature of these different activities,—how one kind of activity differs from another kind of activity. We try to understand how the learning of these activities takes place. We, further, try to understand what the other states and processes are which occur within him while man is engaged in the bodily and mental activities. What is their nature ? How they are to be classified ? How they differ from each other ?

Definition of Psychology

We have seen above that while dealing with his environment, the mental activities of man are more important and much more complex and diverse than his bodily activities. With the development of the knowledge of the world of nature, thinkers became also interested in the world of man's own being. Their attention was directed chiefly to his mental activities. They found man's mental activities to be very different from the natural processes whose knowledge led to the births and growth of the natural sciences. One can directly observe the natural objects, handle, and manipulate them at his will. They are relatively stable and fixed, and do not appear to be acting by themselves. The earlier thinkers, therefore, ascribed the mental activities of man to a power that was supposed to be as intangible, as impalpable, as much hidden from the outer senses, as the mental activities themselves. They called it *soul*, with which, at that time philosophy and religion were very specially concerned. The knowledge these thinkers started gaining about the mental activities was called by them the study of the soul or psychology, Psycho means soul, and logy means systematic knowledge. They called themselves psychologists.

The later psychologists realised that though the mental activities are also intangible, impalpable and unstable, i.e., changing every moment, one can get a direct knowledge of them at least when they are taking place within himself. Every one can know directly whether he is perceiving, remembering, imagining, thinking, deciding, etc., at a certain moment; he can know about his wishes and desires, his feelings and emotions, his likes and dislikes, etc. All these are open to him in his observation of himself. But the soul to which he related them is always beyond his grasp; he cannot have even a glimpse of it. To know and understand the activities of man, it was not felt necessary, therefore, to refer them to the soul which ever remains unknown and unknowable. Psychologists, however, retained the term psychology but came to mean by it not the study of the soul, as it literally means. But even the natural sciences had not developed then to the extent of accepting activity, force, and energy as existing by themselves. They referred them to matter as a substance to which they were supposed to belong. Similarly, the psychologists also related the mental activities, they were studying, to the *mind* as a substance, whose activities or functions they were supposed to constitute. They defined psychology as *the study of the human mind.*

It gradually came to be realised that the mind as a substance was as unknown and unknowable as the soul. Psychologists, therefore, introduced the term 'experience' as a general name for the mental activities and defined psychology as the '*study of experience*'. They selected the term experience for defining psychology, because the term experience is used for whatever a person *has been* aware of, whatever he *is* aware of at the moment, and whatever he *is likely to be* aware of in the future. The term has a personal reference; mental activities too have a personal reference; they are some person's mental activities. Experience was, thus, thought to be the most suitable label that could be attached to the mental activities to make them different from the natural processes studied by the physical sciences.

Still later, some more ambitious psychologists, who sought to use the natural sciences as the model for developing the new science of psychology, objected to the term experience. They maintained that experience is something very personal and, therefore, private, to be used as the proper subject matter for a science of psychology. What science studies is something public, something which every body interested in the study can directly observe and deal with. None can observe the mental activities of another person. These psychologists, therefore, insisted that the subject matter of psychology should consist only of those activities of man that are open to every body's observation. Mental activities being not such, psychology should be confined only to the study of the bodily activities of man. They classified the bodily activities into *explicit* or overt bodily activities, and *implicit* or covert bodily activities. The explicit bodily activities can be observed with the naked eye, i.e., unaided observation. They consist of the movement of the limbs, the fingers, the head, the eyes, etc. The implicit bodily activities need some delicate apparatus for observing them. These activities involve the functioning of the heart, the lungs, the stomach, the movement of blood in the blood vessels and so on. All of these activities are started by the different types of forces and energies which act upon the bodily organs. They called these physical forces *stimuli*, the plural for stimulus, and the explicit or implicit bodily activities they called *responses*. They sought to explain all activities of man in terms of stimulus and response connections, and the learning of all new activities as the formation of new stimulus-response associations. They used the term behaviour as the general name for all bodily activities, both explicit and implicit. They defined psychology as the *Science of behaviour*, and the psychologists who strictly confined themselves to the study of behaviour called themselves behaviourists. These psychologists extended the scope of psychology also to the study of animals. They thought that the bodily activities of man, that is, human behaviour, are a more developed, more evolved, forms of animal behaviour. The understanding of animal behaviour, they accordingly maintained, would lead to a better understanding of human behaviour. The psychological laboratories that were started under the influence of the behaviourists were used to study not only human behaviour. They were concerned also with the study of animal behaviour, specially, with the learning of new skills and activities by rats, cats and monkeys.

It was, however, noted that confining psychology only to the study of the bodily activities of man and animals, would not serve the purpose of understanding how and why these activities do really take place. If psychology is to be a science, it should not only describe behaviour, it should also be able to explain behaviour. A science does not only tell what the facts are with which it is concerned; it also says why they are so; the function of science is both description and explanation. As it is evident, the mental activities are always at the back of the bodily activities of man. In fact, the bodily activities are not only initiated but also controlled and regulated by the mental activities. We first perceive an object, and our bodily activities are directed to it in the light of our preception of it. Before starting the activity, we compare the alternative courses of action open to us; we *fore-see* their consequences. For doing this, we are influenced by the *memory* of our past actions and of their consequences. We *choose* one course of action in preference to another, and take a *decision* to enter upon the chosen activity which we may start at the moment, or postpone it for a future time. The behaviourists tried to explain these mental activities also in terms of bodily activities. For example, they described feelings and emotions as implicit responses of the internal organs of the body, namely, the heart, the lungs, the blood vessels, the glands, etc. Similarly they called thinking as sub-vocal talking. They argued that thought and language always go together and so we can account for the thinking process in terms of the responses of the organs of speech, namely, the throat, the palate, the tongue, etc. While talking loudly they maintained, the responses of the speech organs are explicit; in thinking they are explicit and, therefore, hidden from our view. But the account they gave of feelings, emotions, and the thought process, in terms of bodily movements, was not found to be sufficient to serve the purpose. Moreover, the behaviourists could not succeed in translating all mental activities in terms of the bodily activities.

The mental activities and the bodily activities, experience and behaviour, are so closely related that one cannot be separated from the other. The human organism is a unified whole. We can only artificially separate man's mental activities from his bodily activities, and study them as though they were independent of each other. Hence, we would include under the subject matter of psychology both the bodily and the mental activities of man. We would, therefore, prefer to define psychology as *a systematic study of experience and behaviour*. We would have no objection to defining psychology as *the science of behaviour*, as some psychologists do, who do not at the same time drive out the mental activities from the domain of psychology. We will only enlarge upon the behaviourist's definition by adding to it *as interpreted in terms of experience*.

In fact, we may even accept the definition of psychology as the systematic study of behaviour, without adding any phrase to it. Mental activities, the facts of experience, as we have seen, are very personal. The psychologist does not, generally speaking, study his own behaviour. He collects the facts or data for his study of psychology from other persons who are called '*subjects*' of study. Evidently, the psychologists can not observe the mental activities of his subjects. He can only observe their bodily activities. To collect data about the mental activities of his subjects, he requires them to make a report of their mental activities. The report will be verbal, that is clothed in words. It may be given orally, i.e., uttered by the mouth of the reporter. It would then involve the responses of the organs of speech, which are facts of behaviour. Or, it may be written, which would involve the responses of the hand, the wrist, and the finger, these too are facts of behaviour. Thus, though the report would relate to mental activities, its presentation would involve bodily activities or behaviour. Only, we have not to forget that the report furnishes more an account of the mental activities of the subject than of his explicit or visible, and implicit or invisible behaviour, made visible with the aid of some sensitive apparatus.

Scope of Psychology

It follows from the above discussion regarding the subject matter and definition of psychology that in psychology we study both experience and behaviour. We use the term experience for the activities that can not be directly observed by another person. We have called them mental activities. We use the term behaviour not only in its literal sense as the behaviourist does, that is, only for those activities that can be observed by any person who is interested in studying them. We have called such activities bodily activities, for example, running, striking, grasping, lifting, talking, writing, dancing, playing, salivating perspiring, shedding tears, etc. We are prepared to use term behaviour also for those activities we call experience, because reported in spoken or written words, the psychologist observes them in the same manner as he observes the other bodily behaviour of the persons who report their experience. We, thus, try to understand in psychology how man perceives objects and persons, how he remembers and forgets facts and events, how he imagines objects or persons he has not known before, how he thinks about the qualities he knows objects and persons to possess, how he solves his problems. We further try to understand how man feels pleasure and pain, how he gets into the emotions of anger and fear, how he develops love for some and hatred for other persons. We also try to understand how man solves his problems, how he plans his course of action, how he selects one way of acting and rejects another, how he makes a decision, and how he actually acts to objects and persons. To understand all these activities as manifested in a fully grown up person, we seek to understand how the learning and development of these activities take place. We also try to find out, therefore, what capacities man possesses at the moment of his birth; how and when they unfold themselves, and how they attain there full growth.

As stated above, in psychology we study man's modes of experience and behaviour. But this is not enough. We should also know why man behaves in this or that way in a situation, and why he has this or that kind of experience. We claim psychology to be a science. A science does not only describe the facts with which it is concerned. It also attempts to explain those facts. Psychology too, therefore, both describes as well as explains the activities of man, his experience and behaviour. We may finally define psychology as *a systematic description and explanation of the various facts about man's experience and behaviour.* For this end in view, psychology makes a *systematic* collection of observed facts; the facts are collected, in other words, in accordance with a definite plan and method. Conclusions are drawn from the facts according to the laws of *reasoning*. Only a systematic study of facts according to a reliable and valid method of study, can be called a scientific study. It is its scientific method of study that entitles psychology to be called a science.

Methods of Psychology

Objective Observation and Introspection

Psychology, as we said above, is a systematic description and explanation of man's behaviour. But to describe any fact or event, one should have observed that fact or event. To describe man's behaviour also, we have first to observe man's behaviour. Observation is called, therefore, the method of psychology. By observation of man's activities alone we can know what the various activities of man are, and how one activity is related to another activity. By observation we can, further, discover under what conditions what activities take place. This discovery would alone enable us to explain man's behaviour. Thus, to describe and explain behaviour, psychology uses the method of observation.

But we have seen that the psychologist can not observe all activities of man. He can observe only those activities that can be observed by any other person. For example, when a person is acting to an object, or to another person, you may observe that he is walking towards that object or person, and that in the process of walking, his arms and legs move to and fro. The person who is walking may also observe these movements taking place in him if he gives his attention to them. But in the same movement, several other activities may be going on within that person. These we have earlier called mental activities or facts of experience. The person himself can only observe these facts. No other person can observe them. For example while observing him, you can not know why the person is walking to the object or to the other person. Does he wonder what the object or who the other person is ? Or, does he want to possess the object, or meet the other person ? You can not know what feelings he has for the object or the person, what he desires to do about the object. Only, the person himself will tell you the actual facts, and then you will know them. He alone can observe them, and, thus, directly know about them.

When the psychologist observes the behaviour of another person, the observation is called *objective observation*. When a person is angry, you can objectively observe that his face is red, his eyes are wide open, his lips are moving rapidly, he shouts and roars. By observing his bodily activities, you come to the conclusion that he is angry. When a person is sitting quiet, you may not have much to observe when you look at him. You will know very little about him. But he may be engaged in very complex mental activities. He may be thinking out the plot of a new story that he is proposing to write. He may be calling to his memory the themes of some stories which he read in the past. He may be comparing them with the plot of the new story he is thinking about. He may be feeling discouraged in his attempt to write an original story. When you ask him what he has been doing, he may report all these facts to you. The account that he gives is based upon his observation of his mental activities. The observation that a person can make of his mental activities is called *introspection* or self-observation. The psychologist, while collecting facts or data for his study, is making use of the method of objective observation. He encourages the other person, who is the subject of his study, to observe his thoughts, feelings, desires, etc., and report them faithfully to the psychologist. To be able to do all this the other person has to introspect.

We have called introspection self-observation. But every self-observation is not introspection. Introspection is the observation that a person makes of his mental activities. A person may touch his forehead and find his skin to be hot. He may count his pulse and find its beating to be quick. He may observe his breathing after a foot race and notice it to be very rapid. In all these cases too he is observing himself. But this observation is not introspection; he is observing what other persons too may observe. It is objective observation. The same person may *feel* heaviness in his head; he might *think* that he has fever; he might *worry* that he is going to fall ill. When he observes these thoughts and feelings of his own, his self-observation is introspection. Introspection is self-observation of ones mental states and activities.

Objective observation and introspection were regarded as two separate methods of psychology. It is true that we study in psychology all activities of man in his environment, both bodily and mental. To obtain both kinds of facts, facts about experience and facts about behaviour, use has to be taken of both objective observation and introspection. But the psychologist, while collecting the facts or data for his study, makes use of objective observation only. The *subjects* of his study give him the report of their introspection. They tell him about their feelings, perceptions, recollections, thoughts, desires, decisions, etc., by knowing about them through introspection. The psychologist, however, has to be careful in making use of the introspective report that he obtains from his subjects. Introspection, to be successful, to provide reliable and truthful data, is a difficult task to perform. In order to introspect, the same person has to engage in a mental activity and also to observe the mental activity. He thinks as well observes his thought process. He feels happy or sorry and also observes how he feels. The danger is that introspection, the intention to observe one's mental activity as it is running its course, may cut short the course of the mental activity. A person may be seriously engaged in solving a problem. He may be performing various types of mental activities. The problem may make him think of other similar problems: He may recall how he was able to solve those problems. He may realise that it was beyond his power to solve the problem. He may feel worried about the matter, and so on and so forth. If the same person is also required to observe all these activities minutely so that he is able to report about them faultlessly after the problem-solving process is completed, the problem-solving activity may come to an end as soon as it starts. Observation of the mental activity requires attending to it, which is also another activity of the same person. Both have to be carried on simultaneously. One may interfere with the other. As a result, the person may perform the activity without observing it, or engage in observation without carrying on the activity he seeks to observe. To perform this difficult task, it is suggested that the person concerned should allow his mental activity to complete its course. He should then turn back his attention to it by recalling it. The introspection really becomes retrospection, or reviewing the mental activity immediately as it completes itself. How far this recollection, which the retrospection or reviewing would involve, will be free from error is difficult to answer. The lesson is that while making use of the introspective data, contained in his *subject's* report, the psychologist has to examine them critically in the light of his objective observation of the behaviour of his *subject* while the latter is engaged in the task, say, of solving some problem.

There is also another shortcoming of the introspective data. The information obtained from introspection is limited. For most facts of no less importance for his study, the psychologist has to depend only upon objective observation. The child, the insane person, the animal can not introspect. They can not be expected even to observe their mental activities, what to speak of reporting about them. The psychologist observes their bodily behaviour. He interprets the bodily behaviour. The bodily behaviour throws light on the mental activities accompanying it. A three-year child, for example, who has learned the alphabets, may be asked to repeat them. He repeats some without hesitating, some he repeats after long pauses; some he fails to repeat. We conclude that the child remembers some alphabets well, for some his memory is weak while others he has forgotten. A dog is observed to bark when a stranger enters the house. It does not bark when those who reside there get in. We understand his barking behaviour. The dog has memory for familiar faces; he can recognise them. An insane person is observed to talk in such a manner that his words are unconnected, his sentences are incomplete. We understand that his ideas are confused, his thoughts are unrelated.

As we saw above, the psychologist makes use only of the objective method for collecting the data for his study. He observes the behaviour of persons. He also observes the account those persons give of their perceptions, thoughts, feelings, desires, etc. The account, as we noted above, may be furnished either by talking about these mental activities or by describing them in writing. In both cases the psychologist observes the spoken or written account. The method of study that he uses is, therefore, objective observation. He does not introspect. It will not be incorrect to say that introspection is not the method of psychology, as the psychologist does not use it. As a science, psychology, therefore, uses the method of objective observation alone. Introspection or self-observation is just the process by which the persons whom the psychologist studies become aware of their mental activities. Without introspection they can not describe these activities to the psychologist. We can, thus, conclude that a psychologist may also use, besides the objectively observed facts, the introspective data he obtains from his subjects of study.

Naturalistic Observation and Experiment

We saw that, truly speaking, objective observation alone is the method of psychology. The psychologist observes behaviour of persons. He also observes the description given by those persons of their mental activities, when possible. Such description has been called verbal behaviour, because it is made with the use of words, that is, spoken or written language. The psychologist may observe behaviour under natural conditions. Such method of observation is called naturalistic observation. For example, he may observe that the students who are rewarded by their parents for success in examination study more seriously. He may come to the conclusion that reward for good work increases one's interest in the work. The observation on the basis of which he comes to the conclusion is naturalistic observation. One observes the behaviour of a person when the behaviour is taking place in natural course. Let us take another example. A psychologist may observe the behaviour of a child from the moment of its birth up to, say, the age of 12 years. He keeps a record of the first word the child utters and of the age at which he does this. Similarly, he notes at what age the child uses the next word, at what age he uses the first sentence, at what age he uses a word that stands for an idea, and so on. He observes the language development of the child. The observation is naturalistic. In this way he may observe several children and determine the stages in the development of speech in the average child. He may use this knowledge to judge the language development of a particular child. When the child does not reach the stage of development observed in children of that age, the psychologist judges that this child's language development is slow. He thinks that, perhaps, the child is of less than average intelligence.

There is another kind of observation. This is called experimental observation, or experiment. Here one observes the behaviour of a person not in its natural course. He performs an experiment on the person. In an experiment one brings about such conditions that produce the behaviour that is to be observed. For example, a psychologist wants to observe with the help of an experiment the effect of promised reward on the performance of a task. He collects, say 20 boys and 20 girls, all aged 12 years. He writes their names on separate slips of paper that are of equal size, colour, etc. He puts all the slips in a small box and thoroughly mixes them. He takes out any two slips and writes 1 on the first and 2 on the second. Then he takes out another two slips and writes 3 on one and 4 on the other. In this manner he takes out all of the 40 slips and numbers each one from 1 to 40. He then divides them into two sets, all slips bearing odd numbers—1, 3, 5. . .39, in one set, and all slips bearing even numbers—2, 4, 6...40 in another set. He has thus divided the larger group of 40 boys and girls into two smaller groups of 20 each. If he finds that there are more girls in one group than the other, he makes them equal. Supposing, there are 8 girls in one group and 12 in another. He shifts two girls from the second group to the first and two boys from the first to the second.

The person on whom an experiment is done is called a *subject* (S). The person who does the experiment is the *experimenter* (E). In the above example the method by which the experimenter divides the subjects in two separate groups is called random method. Such selection of subjects for experiment is called random selection. In random selection, each subject has the same chance of being placed in one group as in the other. The example we have taken shows a very simple method of selection. In psychological experiments more complex methods of selection may be used.

To perform the experiment on the effect of reward on the performance of a task, the experimenter prepares a list of, say, 25 words, each word consisting of, say, 8 letters. He writes each word in bold letters on a 2 sq. inch card. He tells each subject that he has to look carefully at the words that are to be shown to him for he has to get them by heart. Ho shows the cards, one by one, to each one of the 20 subjects of the first group. Each card is shown for 2 seconds. After all cards have been shown, each subject is required to write, on a piece of paper, the words that he remembers. The experimenter collects the piece of paper. He again shows the words one after the other. He repeats this for several trials. Every time he collects the slip on which the subject has written the words he was able to reproduce. He stops the experiment, say, after 10 trials. He then examines the result of the experiment. He finds that one or more subjects correctly reproduced the words after 5 trials; a few did so after 6 trials, and so on. One or more subjects could not correctly reproduce all words even at the end of 10 trials.

The experiment is done with the second group also, much in the same manner. But before starting the experiment, the experimenter tells the subjects that he has three prizes which will be awarded to those who get the first, second, and third positions in the experiment. This he did not tell the first group. The first group, therefore, did not work for any reward. The first group is called the *control* group. The second group that is made to work for the reward is called the *experimental* group. It is so called because this experiment is done to find out the effect of reward. On completing the experiment with the second group in the same manner as he did with the first group, the experimenter examines the result of the experiment. He finds that all subjects in this group reproduced all words correctly in the eighth trial. Some reproduced all words even after four trials, and so on. The exprimenter comes to the conclusion that when the subjects were promised a reward for superior performance, their learning was more quick. Reward for good work has an effect on the performance or learning of a task.

The result of an experiment is more reliable. It is not so in the case of naturalistic observation. In an experiment, the experimenter observes his subject's behaviour under the conditions which he himself brings about. He knows all the conditions and he also knows that there are no other conditions. This is not possible in naturalistic observation. When any event takes place in the course of nature we do not know all the conditions under which it has happened. A condition may remain unknown and that condition may account for the happening of the event. We are, therefore, liable to make errors in naturalistic observation. Such errors can be avoided in an experiment. Further, it is possible to repeat an experiment any number of times and find out whether the same result is obtained.

Some experiments in psychology require delicate apparatus. Some of these apparatus record minute changes in behaviour which cannot be easily observed. Others consist of the materials for the task which the subject of the experiment may be required to perform. Still others are so designed as to present the conditions under which the subject is required to act. But many valuable experiments have been done in psychology for which no delicate or expensive apparatus is necessary. The apparatus is not so important for an experiment. The method of experiment is most important. The example that we considered above does not require any special apparatus. Still it is possible to come to a very valuable finding if one carefully follows the method described.

It should not be supposed that in an experiment the subject only performs a task and the experimenter observes his behaviour. An experiment may require the subject also to observe his mental activities while he is performing a task and report them to the experimenter; the subject gives introspective report. In the experiment on the effect of reward, described above, the subjects should also be required to report their mental activities. For example, someone may tell that a certain word reminded him of a very familiar object. He could hold that word in his memory because of its association with that object. Similarly, subjects in the experimental group might tell that all the time they were aware of the reward. They might further tell that for this reason they gave full attention to the task. This knowledge further confirms the experimenter's conclusion that promised reward influences the performance of a task.

Naturalistic observation is sometimes called observation, as experimental observation is called experiment. We thus talk in psychology of the methods of observation and experiment. This does not mean that experiment involves no observation. Experiment also is a method of observation. In an experiment a person is specially made to act under a set of conditions that the experimenter provides. The experimenter *then* observes and records the behaviour of that person. He also sometimes requires the person to introspect and report his mental activities. There are a set of rules and procedures that are to be followed in an experiment to make the experiment a good experiment. These form a part of the so-called experimental method.

Branches of Psychology

During recent times psychology has made very great progress. It is concerned with various forms and aspects of human behaviour taking place under very different conditions and in very different situations. This has led to the division of psychology into several branches. We well describe below some of the important branches of psychology.

Child Psychology

Psychology studies human behaviour. Man's behaviour undergoes constant change from the moment of his birth. To understand man's behaviour we try to understand this process of change in man's behaviour. There is a special branch of psychology that studies how man's behaviour is modified as he grows from a small baby to a fully developed adult, and as he advances further to old age. This branch of psychology is called Developmental Psychology. More important changes in man's behaviour take place, however, when he progresses from childhood to adulthood. Hence, we have Child Psychology which mainly describes and explains the development of a child's behaviour. Child Psychology tells us about the physical and mental development of the child. It tells us what are the early sensory capacities of the child. How do the sensations of light and colour, of hearing of smelling etc.; develop ? How does the child's perception of his environment develop ? How and at what stage in his development the child learns to hold or grasp objects, sit up, and walk ? What is the first sound a child produces ? How his language development takes place ? How does the child express his anger and fear ? How does he comes to be afraid of things of which he was not afraid ? Child psychology enables us to understand the development of thinking in a child. It also tells us in what respects the child's behaviour is different from the adult's behaviour.

Abnormal Psychology

We expect that under similar circumstances man behaves more or less in the same manner. But we find that some human beings, generally, do not behave in the same way as other do. Usually we expect a person to be extremely happy when he comes to know that his son stood first in a university examination. But we may find a person on whom such a news produces no effect. Similarly, we expect a person to be overwhelmed with grief when he knows of the death of his only child. But there may be a person who is not moved by this news. Such persons we very often meet in a mental hospital. They are called abnormal persons. Their behaviour is described as abnormal behaviour. There behaviour is different from what we come across when we observe other persons' behaviour. Who will expect a poor man who is wearing torn clothes to describe himself as the queen of England ? But in the mental hospital you may find an abnormal male who decorates his head with coloured ribbons and walks majestically like a queen. He not only tells that he is a queen; he also believes that he is a queen and the doctors and other attendants of the mental hospital are his courtiers.

We try to study in Abnormal Psychology, or Psychopathology, why the abnormal people behave in a very different manner from the normal. What makes a man abnormal ? What are the types of abnormal behaviour ? What are their causes ? How can the abnormal behaviour be changed into normal behaviour ? How can an abnormal person be made normal ?

Some forms of abnormal behaviour are regarded as mental diseases. In psychopathology, which is another name for abnormal psychology, we try to know what are the different types of mental diseases. A disease has symptoms. The disease is diagnosed by the symptoms it possesses. To diagnose the mental diseases, abnormal psychology tries to find out the symptoms of different types of mental diseases. Several methods have been used for the treatment of mental diseases. Besides medicines, or other physical methods, some psychological methods are also used for the treatment of a mental disease. They are called psychotherapy. The different methods are described in psychopathology and their value in treatment is also discussed.

Social Psychology

While studying human behaviour, we notice that a person acts feels and thinks in one way when he is alone. He acts, feels and thinks in a different way while in the company of others. We may come across a person who is preaching through the newspapers the value of human life. But when a communal or race riot breaks out, the same person is found to arouse the rioters to shoot even women and children of the other race or community. Or you know an experienced physician who believes in the physical causes and cures of diseases. He urges for the advancement of medical research for discovering the causes and remedies of diseases. But you may find, to your utter surprise, the same medical expert consulting an Ojha for doing some tantras for the recovery of his only son who has been ill for some time. In Social Psychology we study such and other similar problems of the social behaviour of man. We study the influence of the society in which a child grows and lives on the formation of his habits and on the development of his ideas and beliefs, his likes and dislikes, his goals and purposes. We study how the public form their opinion regarding important matters. How do rumours spread ? Why and how do a mass of people fight against each other when they know that the result of the fight may be harmful to both ? Why do some people behave as leaders and others as followers ? What are the different types of leaders ? What are the characteristics of a leader ? How people form into groups ? What are the different kinds of groups ? Why and how are people attracted to each other ? Why we like some people and dislike some people ? Social psychology provides answers to these and other similar questions.

Comparative and Animal Psychology

In order to understand human behaviour, we compare human behaviour with the behaviour of other living organisms. We know that man is also an animal like other animals. He too has many similar needs and he too performs many similar activities. Man also requires food, shelter and rest. He also eats, digests and eliminates the waste products. Other animals, specially those that are near to man in the scale of life, also learn many new activities. They also show some signs of such activities as perception and memory. How far is human behaviour similar to the behaviour of other animals ? In what respects does human behaviour differ from the behaviour of other animals ? We can answer these questions only if we make systematic study of animal behaviour. Such studies have been made and reported in Comparative Psychology. Much study has been made of the emotional behaviour and social behaviour of animals, of intelligence and reasoning capacity of animals, and of the ways of learning in animals.

Many facts about learning in man have been discovered from experimental studies of learning in animals. It is easier to do experiments on animals. You can put them under any condition that you like. You can do anything with them that your experiments require you to do. You cannot have the same freedom in experiments with human beings. For example, you can starve a dog for any length of time and observe the effect of starvation on the animal's behaviour. You can inject a drug in its body and produce violent emotions in it. Sometimes you can open the animal's skull to find out what movements arise in its body when you apply electric current to the various parts of its brain.

Physiological Psychology

Psychology is the science of human behaviour. Human behaviour consists of both bodily activities and mental activities. The bodily activities appear in various parts of the human body. The parts of the human body are called organs. They are so called in order to distinguish them from the parts of an object. The organs of the human body form the human organism. These organs have very complex structure. Their functions too are highly complex. The function of each organ is related to the function of other organs and to the total function of the organism. Physiology studies the structure and functions of the organs in relation to each other and also to the functions of the organism as a whole.

In order to understand the bodily activities of man, it is very important to know about the structure and functions of the parts of the human body. Physiological Psychology studies the bodily behaviour of man. It tells us about the structure and functions of the various sense organs that are involved when we see, hear, smell, and taste objects. It gives an account of the structure and functions of the human brain and of its various parts. We know from Physiological Psychology about the structure and functions of the organs which are involved when we move the body and its parts, and when we act to an external object or person. It also tells us about the structure and functions of the organs that are involved in the activities of digestion, breathing, circulation of blood, and so on. All this knowledge enables us to get better understanding of human behaviour.

Applied Psychology

The understanding of human nature that we get in Psychology is also applied to make human life better and more effective in the environment in which man lives. The principles of human behaviour that psychology discovers are used for producing desirable behaviour in man. Those branches of Psychology that apply the facts and principles of human behaviour to the modification of human behaviour come under Applied Psychology. We will describe four important branches of applied psychology.

Clinical Psychology

A person may not know how to act in a given situation. He may remain undecided and perplexed. Another person may act in a particular manner, but he may not get the desired result from his action. He may feel very much disheartened and get worried. A third person may act in a highly unusual manner. His actions create difficulties for other persons who have to deal with him. All such persons are said to be facing a behaviour problem. They are in difficulty. They need help in overcoming the difficulty. Clinical Psychology tells how persons can be helped with their behaviour problems.

The Clinical Psychologist uses several kinds of psychological tests. These enable him to know how intelligent a person is, what he is capable of learning, what his strong likes and dislikes are, what his usual ways of acting to other persons are, how he feels about himself and about others, and so on. The Clinical Psychologist also gathers information about a person by interviewing him, or by interviewing other persons who know about him. He prepares a case history of the person. This enables him to get at the root of the person's problem. He diagnoses the real trouble of the person. The person may be having a feeling about himself, or about another person, that may not be based on facts. He may be striving for a goal that is beyond his capacity to achieve. He may have formed the habit of being influenced more by emotions than reason. In order to help the person, the Clinical Psychologist applies all that he knows about the ways of understanding and modifying human behaviour. He produces such mental conditions in the person that lead him to change his feelings, his attitudes, his ways of looking at things and persons, and even at himself.

Educational Psychology

Children grow to become adults. In the course of their growth, they learn many activities and come to know about new and more facts and ideas. But children are not left to learn all this by themselves. Society creates institutions where the learning of children is controlled and guided. These institutions create conditions which produce more learning and better learning in children. They are the seats of learning—schools, colleges, universities, etc. The process by which learning is produced in these institutions is called education.

To produce effective learning, it is important to know and understand many facts about the learner. One should know the learner's capacity for learning at different stages of his growth. One should know what the learner's needs are so that the learning may be related to those needs. It will then be easier to produce the learning, the learning will have a lasting effect. One should make the learning an interesting affair for the learner. The learning can then be produced without much effort on the part of the learner.

Educational psychology enables us to know what are the characteristics of a good teacher, and what method should be adopted for selection of a successful teacher. It tells us how to judge, from time to time, that those who teach also succeed in producing the learning they intend to produce in their pupils. This has been called teacher assessment. Educational psychology also enables us to know what method of teaching can produce effective learning. Children's differ in their capacity to learn. Some are gifted children, some may be mentally backward children. Educational psychology tells us how to deal with the gifted child, what method of teaching will suit him. Similarly, it also tells us about the best method of teaching the mentally backward child. Then there are some socially deprived children also. Methods of improving their learning capacity are also suggested in educational psychology. Different methods have been used for testing the academic achievement of children. Their merits and demerits are discussed in educational psychology.

Industrial and Business Psychology

Most men have to work in order to earn their living. They may have to work, in large or small factories, on machines for producing goods. They may have to work in business firms and shops that advertise or sell the articles produced. They may have to work in offices that are meant to render service to other persons. Whether it is a factory, a business firm, or an office, in each case, generally, a great variety of jobs have to be performed under a great variety of conditions. No worker can perform all jobs with the same skill or efficiency. Many jobs a particular worker may not be at all able to perform. The few jobs he may be able to perform, he cannot perform equally well. It is necessary to find, therefore, the right man for the right job. It is also important to know the conditions that reduce the efficiency of work, and those that produce improvement in work. For all this one should know how best to select the workers for a job, how to modify the conditions of work, how to prevent accident. Accidents sometimes endanger the life of a worker, or produce some permanent disability in the worker. They cause wastage of the materials used for production of goods and also breakage of machinery.

Industrial psychology tells about the methods of selecting workers who are best fitted for a work. It tells about the ways of maintaining and improving the efficiency of workers, about the ways of reducing fatigue in workers, and preventing accidents. It tells us how to use the facts about human behaviour in advertising and selling goods.

Industrial psychology also deals with the method of maintaining good relationship between the workers and the employer. The workers have to work in large or small groups, and there may be several such groups working at a time. Some workers have to direct other workers what to do and in what manner to do it. Some supervise the work being done by others. Those who direct or supervise form the management. A good relationship between different groups of workers, or between workers and management, is very necessary for the progress of the work. There may be differences or disputes between workers and management. The workers might go on strike. Industrial psychology suggests methods for dealing with all these problems. They are called the problems of industrial relations, i.e., relations between workers and employer, between workers and management, between management and organisations that protect the interest of workers.

Psychology of Crimes

Man lives in the society of other men. In every society there are some rules of conduct according to which every member of the society is expected to behave with every other member. Some of these rules, also called the laws of the land, are meant to protect the security and safety of the property and life of the people. Violation of these rules and laws is called an offense or a crime. It is also called delinquency. Those who violate these rules or laws are called criminals. Their behaviour is described as anti-social behaviour, as it is contrary to approved social behaviour. Examples of anti-social behaviour are theft, assault, murder, which are also punishable by a court of law. It is not only adults who commit a crime. Even younger people are liable to criminal behaviour. They are called juvenile delinquents or youthful offenders.

Psychology of crimes is concerned with the study of anti-social behaviour. The final aim of criminal psychology is the prevention of crimes. For this it is necessary to find the causes of crimes; it is only after knowing the cause of behaviour that one can control behaviour. Different kinds of causes have been suggested, like heredity, feeblemindedness, unsuitable environment. It was believed that criminals come from criminal homes —like father like son But this does not hold for all or even most cases of criminal behaviour. Similarly, all anti-social persons are not feeble-minded; some are highly intelligent. The environmental factor seems to offer the most plausible explanation of anti-social behaviour. Poor homes and broken homes are most likely to go with criminal behaviour. A broken home is one where one parent is dead, the parents have separated, or they are always quarrelling with each other so that there is no peace in the family.

Punishment was thought to be the best method of preventing crimes. For murder, death has had been the common punishment. For less serious offenses, like theft or assault, imprisonment has been the usual punishment. It was supposed that such a punishment has a deterrent effect, that is, the fear of the punishment may prevent those who are inclined to commit a crime from doing so. But now it is being suggested that instead of punishing a criminal, specially the juvenile delinquents, ways and means should be found to change their criminal habits. They should be reformed and corrected so that they too become useful members of the society. This has led to the growth of a branch of psychology of crimes called correctional psychology.

Knowledge of psychology of crimes also helps in the detection of crimes. People who are suspected of having committed a crime may be administered a psychological test. The test response of the person who has actually committed the crime, may be found to be very different from responses of other suspected persons. Then there are some crimes that are committed in a fit of insanity. A crime psychologist may then be consulted to decide as to whether the person who committed a crime is of unsound mind.

Chapter II

THE NERVOUS SYSTEM

Receptor, Effector And Conductor

Man lives in an environment of objects and persons. He sees their shapes and colours. He hears the sound produced by them. He smells the odours of some objects and gets their taste when he puts them in his mouth. He touches objects and finds their surface smooth or rough, hard or soft, feels their warmth and cold, and gets a prick from the pointed ones. All this knowledge of objects and persons is possible to man because he possesses several sense organs. These get impressions from objects and persons. They are also called receptors. The environment of objects and persons influences these receptors. It makes them active; it stimulates them. In the environment there is the sun's light. The light falls on objects. It is reflected or thrown back from the objects and falls upon the eyes of the person who is looking at objects. The person sees the shape and colour of the object. The eyes provide the receptors. The light that is reflected from the object makes the receptors in the eyes active; it stimulates them. The light is the stimulus.

Man has several receptors each of a separate kind. There are receptors for shape and colour in the eyes, for sound in the ears, for taste in the tongue, for smell in the nostrils, for touch, pain, warmth and cold on the skin, and for deep pressure under the skin. Each kind of receptor has some special kind of stimulus to make the receptor active.

Man does not only see, hear, taste, smell and become aware of warmth, cold, pressure and pain. He also acts to objects and persons. Part of the action is performed mainly by arms and legs. Several other actions are performed by those organs of the body that lie inside the body. Man is surrounded by air which he breaths. The activity of breathing is done by a part of man's body that is not to be seen from outside. Similarly, when a food particle is put in the mouth, activities of chewing and swallowing follow. These activities are possible only when the mouth is not dry. The mouth is kept wet by the activity of an organ of the body called the salivary gland. The chewing and swallowing involve the activities of other organs also, namely, the jaws, the tongue, the palate, the throat, etc. Likewise when the food passes into the stomach, various other activities are performed. These are called the activities of digestion. Other parts of the body that are inside the stomach perform these activities. There are several other kinds of activities performed by several other organs inside the body.

The parts of the body by which man's actions to objects and persons are performed are called motor organs or organs of response. Any kind of movement is possible only through them; through them the organism responds to the objects and persons in the environment. They are also called effectors. They make man effective in his environment; they enable him to do something to objects and persons.

Objects and persons in man's environment provide stimulus to his sense organs. He becomes aware of them and of their various qualities. The motor organs, or organs of response, enable man to act to the objects and persons, according to the knowledge he gets of them. To make this possible, there must be some relationship, an integration, between the sense organs and the motor organs, the receptors and the effectors. A person sees a food object. He picks it up and putting it in his mouth, chews and swallows it. The same person sees a nail lying on the floor. He picks it up, but puts it in the drawer. He hears a friend calling him and walks in the direction from which the sound is coming. He sees a policeman approaching him and runs away in a nearby lane. There must be some parts of man's body that connect the receptors with the effectors, the sense organs with the organs of response. These parts of the body form the nervous system. The sense organs receive impressions from objects and persons; they are stimulated and become active. The activities of the sense organs are not limited to them. They put into action the nervous system with which the sense organs are connected. The activity of the nervous system, in its turn, makes the organs of response active. Man responds or acts to the objects and persons that stimulate his sense organs.

The nervous system connects the receptors and the effectors. It is, accordingly, also named the conductor. The activity of the sense organ produces what is called nervous energy or neural impulse. The nervous system conducts or conveys impulse from a particular sense organ to a particular motor organ, or sets of motor organs, which become active and produce action. It is thus possible for man to act in one way to one set of stimuli or object, and to act in a different way to another set of stimuli or object.

Neuron

The entire organism is made of myriads of cells or cell bodies which are tiny organisms. A cell body is the smallest unit of life. The human life starts from a single cell body. It is called the spermatozoa. This single cell multiples itself in the mother's womb. The multiplication of cells produces the human body. Every organ of the body and part of every organ consists of cell bodies. There are muscles cells, bone cells, skin cells, gland cells, receptor cells, etc. The cell of the nervous system is called a neuron. A neuron is a nerve cell with a cell body and nerve fibres as shown in the following figures.

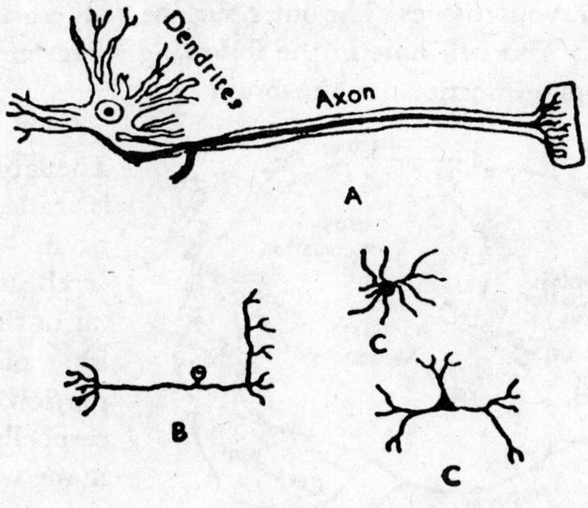

Fig. 1
A. Motor neuron. B. Sensory neuron. C. Connector neuron.

Some nerve cells have two types of nerve fibres dendrites and axons (A). Nervous energy passes from the dendrites to the axons. Neurons are of three types: motor neurons, sensory neurons, and connector neurons. These are shown in Fig.1.

The nervous system has three divisions: (1) the central nervous system (2) the peripheral nervous system and (3) the autonomic nervous system.

Central Nervous System

The central nervous system consists of the spinal cord and the brain. In the middle of the back, there is the spinal bone. It extends from the lowest part of the back to the neck. If you touch the spinal bone from the top to the bottom, you will notice that it consists of small bits or knots set one above the other. Inside the spinal bone there is a semi-solid substance, or nervous tissue. Like the spinal bone, the nervous tissue also extends from the bottom of the back to the lowest part of the skull. It thus forms a thick string or cord, and is, thus, called the spinal cord.

Structure of the Brain

The brain is inside the skull of the head. Like the spinal cord, the brain is also made of semi-solid substance and forms a mass of nervous tissues. The outer surface of the brain is called the cortex. You will note in the following diagram that there are three main portions of the brain:

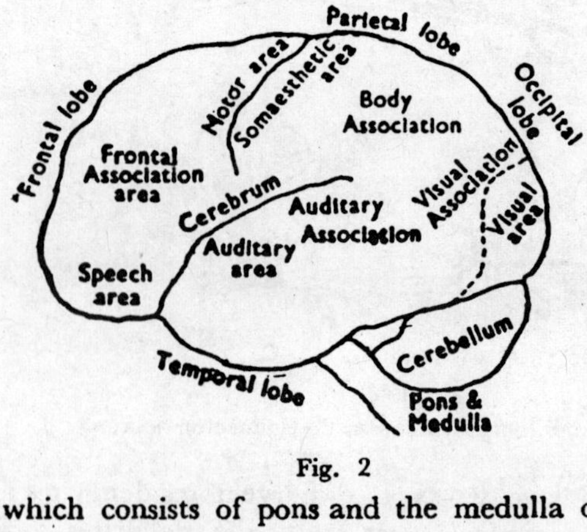

Fig. 2

The largest portion is called the cerebrum. Below the cerebrum and towards the back there is a muchsm aller portion, called the cerebellum. Continuing with the spinal cord and at the back of the cerebellum is the portion which consists of pons and the medulla oblogata.

The surface of the brain, the cerebral cortex, is not all plain or even. It is not like the outer surface of an apple. It has numerous folds or raised portions. There are pits or depressions in between the raised portions. These depressions, or fissures, divide the entire surface into small areas. There is a long depression that divides the entire cortex into two equal halves, right and left. Each half is called a hemisphere. The two hemispheres are identical in shape. Fig. 2 shows the left hemisphere. Each hemisphere is further divided by its fissures into four broad areas. Each area is called a lobe. The division of the cortex just behind the forehead is called the frontal. Above the frontal lobe there is another division called the parietal lobe. A third division lies at the back of the head. It is called the occipital lobe. Behind the temple, the side of the head, is the fourth division. This is called temporal lobe. (Fig. 2).

Peripheral Nervous System

The spinal cord is connected with the receptors or sense organs. It is also connected with the effectors or organs of response. The connections are made by nerves. A nerve is a bundle of nerve fibres. One set of nerves connects the spinal cord with the sense organs. These nerves are called sensory nerves. They are also called in-carrying or afferent nerves. They conduct or carry nervous impulse from the receptors to the spinal cord. Another set of nerves connects the spinal cord with the motor organs. These nerves are called motor nerves. They are also called outgoing or efferent nerves. They carry or conduct the nervous impulse from the spinal cord to the effectors. Fig. 3 shows the sensory nerve that carries impulse from receptro to the spinal cord and the motor nerve that carries the impulse out from the spinal cord to the effector.

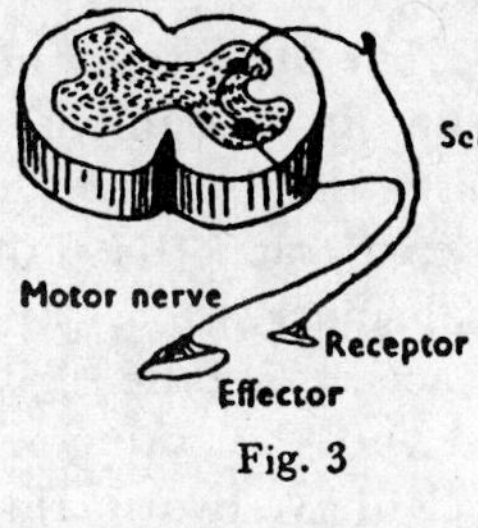

Fig. 3

There are several such sensory and motor nerves at the different levels of the body.

These nerves form the peripheral nervous system. They are so called because they connect the central nervous seytem with the receptors and effectors that are located on the surface of the body.

Muscles and Glands

Before we know more about the nervous system, it will be useful to know something about the effectors. Any motor activity can take place only through the action of the effectors. The effectors are, therefore, the chief movers of the organs of the body. There are two kinds of effectors : (1) muscles and (2) glands.

Every part of the body is provided with muscles. The muscles contract and relax. The contraction and relaxation of the muscles produce movements in the bones, joints and tendons to which muscles are attached. Tendons join the muscles with the bone. When a muscle contracts, the tendon, joint or bone attached to the muscles is pulled. When the same muscle relaxes, the pull is gone. The pull and the removal of the pull produce movement in the bone; the part of the body also moves. Continuous movement is produced when the muscles repeatedly contract and relax. You can bend and then straighten your finger. The bones and joints in a finger are provided with two sets of muscles. These two sets function in a manner opposed to each other. When one contracts, the other relaxes. In bending the fingers one set of muscles contracts, the finger is pulled down; the other set of muscles relaxes to make it possible for the finger to bend. Had the other set also contracted, the finger could not bend. At the next moment when you straighten the finger, the muscles that pulled the finger down relax, the pull is released. The other set of muscles now contracts; the finger is pulled up, it straightens. Such sets of muscles are called antagonists; they function in a manner opposed to each other; when one contracts, the other relaxes. This process is called reciprocal innervation. By this is meant that when one innervates or acts, the other gives way. Every part of the body is provided with the antagonists.

Muscles have two main typer of structure. One type of muscles is called striped or striated muscles; the muscle has stripes on it. The other type is called unstriped or unstriated muscles; the muscle has no stripes on it. It is also called smooth muscles. Fig. 4 shows the two types of muscles.

Striped muscles

Smooth muscles

Fig. 4

The parts of the body with which we act to an external object or person are provided with striped muscles. These parts are the arms, the legs, the trunk of the body, and the neck. The sets of bones supplied in these parts together form what is called the skeleton. The muscles of these parts are, therefore, also called the skeletal muscles. The organs that are inside the body, e.g., the heart, the lungs, the stomach, the blood vessels, etc., are provided with the unstriated or smooth muscles. These internal organs are called visceral organs. Every activity in these organs is produced by the contraction and relaxation of the smooth muscles.

Glands are the other kind of effectors. The action of glands consists in providing a fluid or watery substance. The process by which the substance is produced is called secretion. Some of the glands are quite well known. For example, the tear glands secrete tears that flow from the eye. The sweat glands secrete perspiration. There are several other glands inside the body. The secretion of some of these glands passes through a fixed path. These glands are called duct glands; they have a fixed path or tube for the flow of their secretion. Other glands are provided with no path for their secretions to pass through. They have no duct and are called ductless. The duct glands, like the tear gland, or the sweet gland, are also called glands of external secretion. The ductless glands are called glands of internal secretion or endocrines. Their secretion passes directly into the blood that surrounds them. The entire body is supplied with blood through what are called blood vessels or arteries. These arteries run in every part of the body; blood is flowing through them every moment. The continuous flow of blood through the arteries is called blood stream; the blood is always running like a stream.

The endocrine glands have very important functions. Their secretions influence the growth of the body and the production of some useful substances in the body, increase or decrease the activities of different organs of the body, and so on. Fig. 5 shows the place of some of the important endocrine glands in the human body.

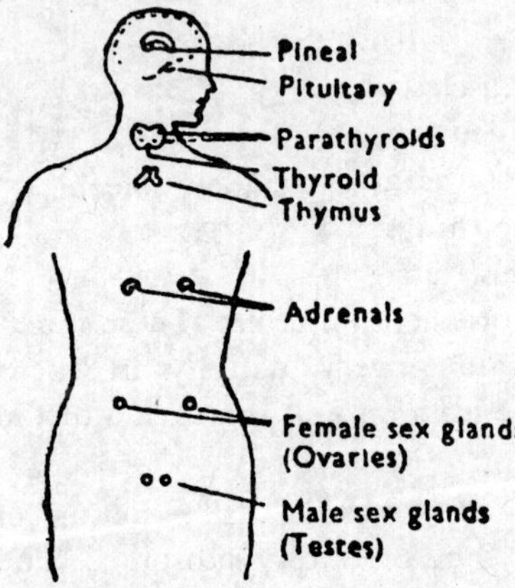

Fig. 5

Spinal Cord

The spinal cord is a string of nervous tissues. It extends from the bottom of the back to the lowest portion of the brain. The different parts or levels of the spinal cord are connected all the way up and down with each other. They are also connected with the brain. When a receptor is stimulated, the nervous impulse travels through the sensory nerve to a certain part of the spinal cord. The impulse may be conducted upward to the brain. It may also be carried outward through the motor nerve to a motor organ. (Fig. 3). A child sees a doll. It extends its hands to grasp the doll. The light reflected from the doll strikes the receptors in the child's eyes. The receptors are stimulated; nervous impulse is produced. The nervous impulse passes along a nerve, called the optic nerve. The optic nerve connects the eyes with the uppermost portion of the spinal cord that continues into the lowest portion of the brain. From this end, the impulse passes along the nerve fibers that go upward. The impulse finally reaches the cerebral cortex, in the region of the occipital lobe. The nervous tissues in the occipital lobe are activated. This results in the seeing of the doll, that is, the awareness of its shape and colour. Besides being conducted upward to the cerebral cortex, the impulse is also carried along a downward path or tract in the spinal cord. The impulse then passes out along the motor nerves to the muscles of the arms and hands. The arms and hands move in extending to the doll and in grasping it.

Autonomic Nervous System

The spinal cord is also connected by nerves with those organs of the body that are specially important for life. These are such organs as the heart, the lungs, the lever, the different parts of the stomach, the blood vessels and other organs inside the body. These organs are not used in man's actions to objects and persons in the environment. They maintain the life and health of the body. They supply energy to the various organs of the body that are used by man in his actions to objects and persons. The heart, the lungs, the stomach and all other organs that are important for the life and health of the body are connected with each other. They are also connected with various levels of the spinal cord. The set of nerves that connect these organs and connect them with the spinal cord together form the autonomic nervous system (Fig. 6).

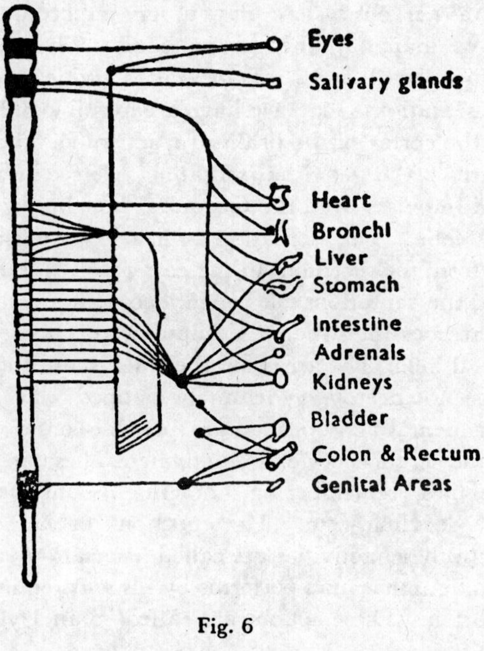

Fig. 6

The autonomic nervous system is the third division of the nervous system. It is called autonomic nervous system because the organs that it connects are not under the control of the brain; they are autonomous. Ordinarily, one cannot, at his will, change the beating of his heart, increase or decrease the flow of blood in the veins, or influence the movements within his stomach. On the other hand, one can at his will raise or lower his arms, move his legs, drop his eye-lids, scratch the back, and so on. These organs are under the control of the brain. The autonomic nervous system is also called the sympathetic nervous system. The organs of the body that the autonomic nervous system serves are also connected with the spinal cord (Fig. 6). The impulses that are created by the actions of these organs are carried to the brain through the spinal cord. That is why we sometimes become aware of these actions. You become aware of the palpitation of your heart, of your breathing when it becomes rapid, of the pain in your stomach, etc.

Functions of the Brain

The central nervous system plays a very important part in the activities of man, both mental and bodily. The brain is specially important for all types of mental activities. The different types of sensations that we have are possible only when some areas of the cortex of the brain are activated. These are called sensory areas. We get visual sensation, we see light and colour, when the impulses from the receptors in the eyes reach the occipital lobe. The sensation of hearing is possible when the impulses from the receptors in the ears reach the temporal lobe. Similarly, the sensations of touch, cold, warmth, pain, and pressure are possible when the impulses reach specific areas in the parietal lobe. The areas for the smell sense and the sense of taste have not been very definitely mapped out.

Other mental activities too are possible only when specific areas in the cerebral cortex are activated. These are the activities of perceiving, remembering, imagining, thinking, desiring, choosing, deciding, etc. The portions of the cerebral cortex involved in these activities are called association areas.

The actions that man performs by his will require the activity of the brain. These actions are called voluntary actions. The voluntary actions are possible when a portion of the cerebral cortex within the frontal lobe is activated. This portion is, therefore, called the motor area. Most learning of new activities or tasks involves voluntary activities. Learning is not possible, therefore, without the activities of the cerebral cortex. For the performance of a learned activity, called a habit, the cerebral cortex is important. When a person has fully learned bicycling, the movement of his legs in the act of pedalling becomes habitual. The moment he rides on the cycle, the movement starts. But the habit may be lost if a portion of the brain is damaged. Fig. 2 also shows the sensory, motor and association areas.

Reflex Action

There is one kind of man's actions for which the brain is not essential. Such actions are called reflex actions. A reflex action results directly from the stimulation of a sense organ. When one applies snuff to his nostrils, this is followed by sneezing. The sneezing is a reflex action. Similarly, when any eatable object is put in the mouth, the mouth becomes watery. This is called salivary reflex. There are receptors on the tongue. The object in the mouth stimulates these receptors. The stimulation of these receptors starts the action of a set of glands in the throat. These are called salivary glands. The action of these glands results in the production of the watery substance which makes the mouth wet. The gland secretes the substance called saliva. Your hand touches a hot dish. The hand is automatically withdrawn. The temperature receptors on the skin are stimulated. The neural impulse that is created is carried along the sensory nerve to the spinal cord. From the spinal cord the impulse is carried out along the motor nerve. It reaches the effectors in the hand. This results in the movement of the hand. The hand is withdrawn. The reflex action is called a withdrawal reflex. Fig. 3, above, also shows the mechanism involved in a reflex action. The mechanism is called a reflex arc.

When the nervous impulse reaches the spinal cord, it may also be carried upward to the brain. When the impulse reaches the cerebral cortex, awareness of the stimulus takes place. You become aware of the warmth of the dish. You get the sensation of heat. When the withdrawal reflex takes place, your hand moves away from the hot dish, you may become aware of the movement also. The movement of an effector produces sensory impluses. We will see in Chap. 3, that the effectors, i.e., muscles, joints, and tendons, also contain some receptors. When the muscle contracts or relaxes, movement is produced. The movement of an effector brings about the stimulation of the receptors contained in the effectors. Sensory impulse is generated. The sensory impulse travels along the sensory nerve and the spinal cord to the sensory area in the cerebral cortex. You become aware of the movement of the effector, i.e., the reflex action.

One does not become aware of all reflex actions. In many cases the sensory impulse from the receptor does not travel to the brain. It reaches the spinal cord and then passes out to the effector. The reflex action is produced, but the person does not become aware of it. Most of the actions that are going on inside the body are reflex. The movement of the heart in pumping out the blood into the veins, the movement of the lungs in breathing air in and out, the circulation of blood through the arteries, the actions of the glands in the body, the activities of digestion, and so on, are all reflex actions. Generally there is no awareness of these reflex actions.

We have said that the brain is not essential for reflex actions. This fact can be illustrated in lower animals. It is possible to remove the brain of a living frog, or to slice off the cerebrum of a living dog. When the entire brain is removed the animal is called 'Spinal' animal. When only the cerebrum is cut off, the animal is called a decerebrate animal. A spinal or decerebrate animal can act only when its receptors are stimulated. For example, a spinal frog may be starving, but it will not perform the voluntary activity of searching for food, or jumping into a tank. But if you put some food object in its mouth, the reflex activities of chewing and swallowing will follow. Or, you place the animal on the surface of water, the reflex activity of swimming will start. The decerebrate dog will not be able to recognise its master or to perform any voluntary activity. Its movements will be produced only when its receptors are stimulated. It will be capable of reflex actions only.

There are many reflex actions that are found from the moment of birth. Each of these reflex actions is a specific response to a specific stimulus. For example, the activity of salivation is a specific response to the specific stimulus of food or any other substance that can dissolve in the mouth. The food stimulus activates the receptors on the tongue and the reflex action of salivation takes place. This happens in animals or in man from early infancy, i.e., salivation as a specific response occurs when the tongue receptors are stimulated. With the process of growth, other stimuli acting on other receptors may also produce the same response. Pavlov, a Russian physiologist, experimented on dogs. He succeeded in producing the salivary reflex in dogs in response to a noise, i.e., a sound stimulus. At first, Pavlov put powdered biscuit in the dog's mouth and also sounded a bell. He then first sounded a bell and after a little while put the biscuit. He went on increasing the time between sounding the bell and putting the biscuit in the animal's mouth. He noticed that the dog's mouth became watery when the bell was sounded. Saliva dripped from the dog's mouth. Originally, the sound stimulus did not produce salivation. With the help of the experiment, the sound could be substituted for the food and produced the activity of salivation. A connection was established between the response and a new stimulus. In other words, a new receptor-effector connection was established. The reflex action could now be produced by the new stimulus. The activity of the salivary gland could now take place on the stimulation of the receptors in the ear. Such reflex action, Pavlov called a 'conditioned reflex'. The new stimulus, he called the 'conditioned stimulus' (CS). The original stimulus was called the 'unconditioned stimulus (US). The response produced by the conditioned stimulus came to be called the 'conditioned response' (CR). The process by which the new connection is formed and established has been called 'conditioning'. In Pavlov's experiment, food was the original or unconditioned stimulus (US) and salivation the unconditioned response (UR). When the conditioned reflex was formed, the sound of the bell became the conditioned stimulus (CS) for the conditioned response (CR) of salivation. The process of conditioning is illustrated in the diagram on p. 40.

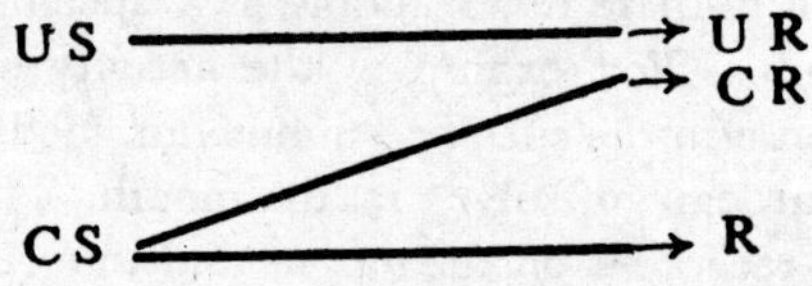

Originally, as a small child, your mouth became watery when you put a piece of tamarind in your mouth. Later, you chewed tamarind several times and heard its name also. Conditioning took place between salivation and the sound 'tamarind'. Your mouth becomes watery when you hear the word tamarind, and even when you see a tamarind, or the written word tamarind. The conditioned stimulus of the sight of tamarind, or the sound or sight of the word tamarind, came to be substituted for the original, unconditioned stimulus of the taste of tamarind. Not only the taste of tamarind, but also the word tamarind, spoken or written, makes your mouth watery; conditioned reflex has been established.

Reflex actions is called involuntary actions. The action is not produced at one's will. Willing and desiring are possible only when the brain is activated. In a pure reflex action the brain plays no part. Hence the action is called involuntary action. In a voluntary action, the impulse is first created in the brain. It then travels down to the spinal cord. From there it passes out along the motor nerve to some part or parts of the hand, the arms, the legs, the trunk of body, the neck, the lips or the tongue. These are the organs generally involved in voluntary actions. We can move them at our will. The activities of lifting, writing, walking, turning the head round about, sideways, back or forth, speaking, etc., are examples of voluntary actions.

A habitual action too, when highly practised, follows very much the way of a reflex action. The sight, touch or sound of an object immediately releases a series of movements. In case of a habit, one may not be aware of a desire or urge for action; or, there may be no exercise of the will. When a child has learned to eat with his hand, once the child is in presence of food an entire series of movements involved in mixing the food, forming the morsal, lifting it to the mouth, opening the mouth, and so on, takes place. The movements follow, generally, in the same order and continue till the food is consumed. An established habit becomes as automatic as a reflex action. Once a habit is formed, it becomes difficult to break it. The will has no influence over it. Sometimes a habitual action is performed against one's will. A patient is advised by his doctor to give up smoking. The patient knows that unless he follows the doctor's advice, his disease cannot be cured. The patient desires to give up smoking. He even decides to do so. But he is forced by the habit to disregard the doctor's advice. He continues smoking and feels helpless in the matter. A very strong will is required to resist the force of habit.

Chapter III

SENSATION

Nature of Sensation

Sensations are the simplest mental activities of man. A sensation is the awareness of a quality of an object that stimulates any sense organ. An object has many qualities. It may be red, blue, green, yellow, or of any other colour. It may be hot or cold. It may have a rough or smooth surface. It may be light or heavy. It may have a good or bad smell. It may taste sweet, sour, or bitter. It may produce a faint or a loud sound. One is said to have a sensation if one becomes aware only of one of the qualities and not of the object as possessing the quality. If you look at the green field and become aware only of the greenness, you have a colour sensation. It will be obvious that an adult person seldom has a sensation in the pure form. He is aware of objects that possess sensory qualities. It is also difficult to view that a newly born infant has pure sensations. Some psychologists thought that the world is a "blooming, buzzing, confusion" to a newly born baby. They thought that objects and persons surrounding him stimulate his sense organs. The stimulation produces sensations. But the child gets bare sensations. He has no awareness of objects and persons. His world is not a world of objects and persons. It is a world of sensations. It is difficult to decide the matter. But psychologists are agreed that adults do not, ordinarily, have bare sensations. For adults bare sensation can occur only under the special situation of the laboratory.

There are as many kinds of sensations as there are sense organs. We have visual sensations of light and colour related to the eyes. We have auditory sensations of noise and tone related to the ears. Similarly we have sensations of taste, smell, touch, pain, temperature, that is, warmth and cold, strain and movement. Each one is related to a special receptor.

We can view the different kinds of sensations also in relation to the different types of stimuli that produce the sensations. For example, visual sensation is produced by rays of light. Auditory sensation is produced by the vibration or back-and-forth movement of the air particles. Sensation of taste or smell is produced by chemical substances, i.e., objects that can dissolve. We will know about the type of stimulus that produces a particular kind of sensation, when we deal with the various sensations.

In order to study sensations we have to study the nature of the stimulus that produces a sensation. We have also to study the sense organs, or receptors, whose stimulation produces a sensation. Finally, we try to study the characteristics of the sensations themselves. Some of these characteristics of sensations have also been called the attributes of sensations.

The Attributes of Sensation

There are some general attributes of sensations. They are found in most sensations. One such attributes is quality. Any sensation may be of this or that quality. For example, a visual sensation may be of one colour or of another colour. The quality of a taste sensation may be sour, sweet, bitter or acid. Same is the case with other sensations.

Another attribute of sensation is intensity. We distinguish a bright colour from a dull colour. We have a loud sound or a mild whisper. We have a strong smell or a weak smell, and so on.

A third attribute of sensations is duration. A light may appear for a moment and then disappear, or it may last longer. A sound may come and go or it may persist.

The fourth attribute of sensations is extensity. There may be a point light, the light of a tiny star in the distant sky, for example. Or, there may be an expansive light, for example, the light reflected from a shiny surface. You get a point sensation of touch, if a hair end touches your skin. You get an extended touch sensation if a coin is placed on your palm.

Of the above four attributes of sensations, quality and intensity have been very much explored. We know a great deal about them. The other two have only been mentioned; some psychologists do not even accept them as the simple attributes of sensations. We will know about the attributes of the different sensations when we discuss each type of sensation in detail.

Psychologists have discovered interesting facts about the relation between the attributes of sensations and the characteristics of the stimulus. A very weak stimulus produces no sensation; it is unnoticeable. A light of very low intensity, for example, is not visible. There are some stars that cannot be seen by the naked eyes. They can be seen only with a powerful telescope. Similarly, when the atmosphere is very calm, the ripples on the surface of the river produce no sound to hear. The stimulus is too weak. But during a storm or when the river is flooded, the current produces a roaring sound. The stimulus becomes strong enough to produce a sensation. There is, thus, a limit of intensity below which a stimulus produces no sensation. There is also a limit at which a change in the quality of a sensation occurs. You will find that below a certain intensity of light, you can see no colour. You see objects, but you do not see their colours. When the intensity of light is increased, you see colours also.

The lowest value of a stimulus that can produce a sensation is called the threshold. You must have seen a threshold at the door of a room. It is of a certain height so that it prevents the entry of water from the floor outside. To cross the threshold, the water must come up to the level of the threshold. It should reach that height. Similarly, the value of a stimulus should reach a certain height in order to produce a sensation. Hence the term stimulus threshold. The German word for stimulus is Reis, and for threshold limen. Reis Limen, thus, means stimulus threshold. RL is used in Psychology as the abbreviation for stimulus threshold. It has been possible to find out the RL for the different sensations. You have RL for light or colour sensation, for noise, or tone sensation, for sensations of touch, pain, warmth or cold. etc.

As we saw above, RL is the least noticeable value of a stimulus. It is the smallest value that can produce a sensation. We can also think of the least noticeable difference between any two values of the same stimulus. Suppose you fill two identical, jars with sugar putting one kilogram or 1000 grams in one jar and one kilogram and 18 grams in the other. Suppose, further that a person who does not know the difference in the actual weight of sugar in the two jars is asked to lift them one after the other several times. He is very likely to judge their weights to be equal. The two jars produce, in other words, the same sensation of weight. The stimuli are not of the same value, but the sensations they produce are the same. The difference between the two stimuli is unnoticeable.

Suppose you add two more grams of sugar to the second jar making its total weight 1020 grams. This is also done without the knowledge of the other person, who is again asked to lift the jars one after the other. You may find that now he judges the second jar as heavier than the first jar. You ask him to repeat the judgement, by lifting the two jars several times, and you find that very often he judges the second as heavier. You notice that addition of another two grams to the weight of the second jar produces difference in the sensations also. You come to the conclusion that addition of twenty grams to a weight of 1000 grams can alone make a difference in the sensation of weight. Below this difference in the weight, there is likely to be no difference in the sensation. Thus twenty grams will be the minimum noticeable difference to a weight of thousand grams. It becomes the limit of the difference to the weight that can produce sensation of different weights. It is, therefore, called the differential threshold or limen, the minimum difference to be noticed as difference. DL is the abbreviation for differential limen. Like RL, DL can also be found for all types of sensations. We have, thus, DL for brightness, for colour, for taste, for smell, for touch and so on.

Psychologists have discovered one interesting fact about DL. The DL for a stimulus value has a constant relation to that stimulus. We saw above that 20 grams was the DL for the lifted weight of 1000 grams. For weight of 500 grams, we expect the DL to be 10 grams, and for a weight of 100 grams the DL is likely to be 2 grams. You will find that $\frac{20}{1000}=\frac{10}{500}=\frac{2}{100}=\frac{1}{50}$. Hence a noticeable difference to a lifted weight is likely to be $\frac{1}{50}$ part of that weight. Knowing a weight, we can estimate the DL for that weight. This is so because of the general law that in order to produce a difference in sensation the increase in the value of a stimulus must have the same ratio to it, or should always be the same part of it. This law has been found to apply to all types of sensation and is supposed to be generally true.

Different methods have been devised to calculate the RL and the DL. These are called psychophysical methods. They are so called because with the help of these methods we can determine the relation between the stimulus and the sensation. The stimulus is physical. It is an energy of the physical world. The sensation is psychological. It is produced within the organism.

The application of the psychophysical methods has shown that the RL or the DL for the different senses is not the same for all persons. One person may see a very dim light which another person may not see. Similarly one may hear a very mild sound which cannot be heard by another person. Or, one may smell an odour which does not exist for another person. Persons differ in their capacity for sensations. One person is more sensitive than another. Similarly one person can make more minute differences in sensations than another person. For example, very slight differences in taste may be marked by one person but missed by another. Similarly, some persons have very keen ears for music. They can appreciate very minute differences in musical tones. Some have strong eyes for colour and can make fine discrimination in the shades of the same colour.

Having known a few facts about sensations in general we pass on to an account of the various kinds of sensations :

Visual Sensation

Much of the information that we possess about the world of objects that surround us comes through the medium of the eyes. Vision is, perhaps, the most valuable sense. Its loss is, therefore, felt to be the greatest. The eye patient whose eyes are bandaged finds himself completely cut off from objects which are still there all about him.

The Stimulus for Vision

The visual stimulus is provided by the sun's light. In the absence of the sun's light, light produced by other sources forms the stimulus for vision, e.g., candle light or electric light. The rays of light are bent as they pass to objects from their source. Each ray forms into waves. The waves may be of different lengths. They are called light waves.

Fig. 7

We see above light waves of different lengths as well as of different heights. The lengths of a wave is the distance between the crests or troughs of two nearing waves. It is measured by very small units of measurement. These are called millimicrons. A micron is one millionth of a meter, or one thousandth of a millimeter. A millimicron is one thousandth of a micron. A millimicron is, thus, one millionth of a millimeter. You must have seen a millimeter in a foot scale. It is a little more than a twentyfifth part of an inch. A millimicron is also expressed as $m\mu$. The light waves which the human eyes can see range in length between 760 $m\mu$ and 390 $m\mu$.

The visual stimuli differ not only in length. They differ also in strength or intensity. The strength of a light wave is expressed by its height or amplitude. The light may be coming from a strong or a weak source. Besides the difference in strength of the light stimulus, there may be a difference also in the complexity of the light stimulus. The stimulus may be pure or unmixed. Or, it may be a mixture of different wave lengths.

When a light falls upon an object, it is thrown back or reflected. The sun's light, as we will see, is a mixture of different wave lengths. But when the light falls upon an object, the object does not reflect all wave lengths. Some wave lengths are absorbed. They are not reflected. Objects that appear to be of the same colour reflect one wave length, and absorb others. This is due to the difference in the physical properties of the surface of different kinds of objects. Thus an object whose surface looks red reflects light waves whose length is near-about 700 millimicrons. It absorbs light waves of other lengths.

The light reflected from an object falls upon the eyes. The receptors in the eyes are stimulated. We get visual sensations. We see light and colour.

Before we know how the sensations of light and colour take place, we should know something about the structure and functions of the human eye.

Structure and Functions of the Eye

The eye balls are set in the hollow or cavity below the

eyebrows. These cavities are called sockets. There are a set of muscles attached to the eye balls. These make the movements of the eyes possible. The front portion of the eye ball is *transparent. This is the cornea.* Behind the cornea is the pupil. The pupil is a circular hole formed by a set of muscles called the iris. The actions of these muscles make the pupil large or small. Light is admitted to the eyes through the pupil. When the light is dim, the iris expands the pupil so that more light can enter the eye. When the light is bright, like day light, the iris contracts the pupil so that less light is admitted. Behind the iris is the lens of the eye. This is another transparent substance. The lens is kept in position by a set of muscles that are attached to it from all sides. These muscles are called ciliary muscles. The lens can change its shape by becoming flat or curved. This is due to the action of the ciliary muscles. When the object which is looked at is far, the ciliary muscles so contract and relax that the lens is flattened and thinned. When the object is near, the ciliary muscles so contract and relax that the lens is curved and thickened. The ciliary muscles thus adjust the eyes for near and far vision.

Between the cornea and the lens, there is a semi-solid substance called acqueous humor. The eye ball is filled with another semi-solid substance. This is called vitreous humor. This substance keeps the eyes in the shape of a ball. The eye ball has three outer coating or thin layers. The outermost layer is called the sclerotic. Next to the sclerotic is another layer called the choroid. The third or innermost layer is called the retina. The following diagram shows the different parts of the eye :

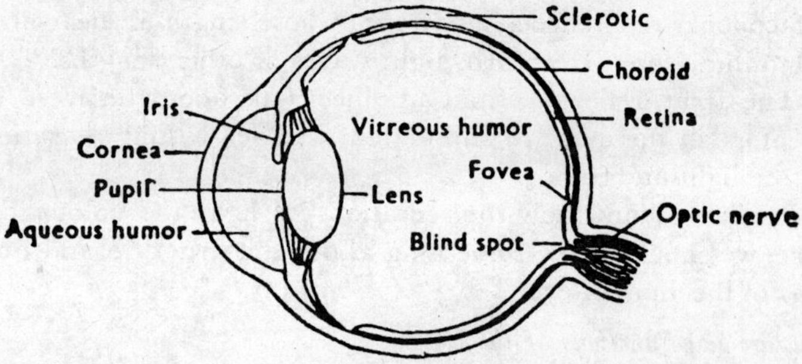

Fig. 8

The retina contains the visual receptors. These are of two types, called rods and cones according to their shape.

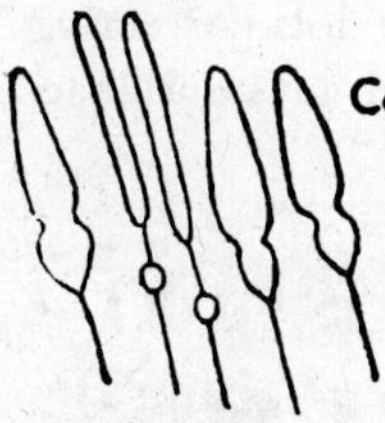

Fig. 9

The rods or cones are very minute cells with long fibers. They are spread over the entire surface of the retina. The fibers of the rods and cones collect at one point and make a bundle of nerve. The bundle of fibers is called optic nerve. The point at which the optic nerve gets out of the retina is called the blind spot. The blind spot contains only nerve fibers. There are no cells in it. Near the blind spot, there is a small portion of the retina which contains only cones. It has no rods. It is called the yellow spot. It is also called the fovea. When you look at something, your head and eyes are turned so that the image of the object falls on this part of the retina. Fig. 8 shows the optic nerve, the blind spot and the fovea. Other parts of the retina contain both rods and cones. There are, however, more cones in the area round about the blind spot and the yellow spot. As we go farther and farther away from this area, the number of rods becomes larger and larger. In the farthest parts of the retina there are only rods and practically no cones. We may divide the retina into the central, the middle, and the outer zones or regions. In the central region there are more cones than rods. In the middle region rods and cones are about equally distributed. In the outer or peripheral zone, there are mostly rods.

The light, that is reflected from an object you look at, enters the eye through the cornea and passes through the acqueous humor, the lens and the vitreous humor. It falls ultimately upon the retina and stimulates the receptors in the retina, namely the rods and cones. When the position of the eyes is such in relation to the object that the light falls upon the yellow spot, the object is said to be in direct vision. In this position the eyes are said to be fixating the object. One gets clearest vision of the object. This is also called foveal or focal vision. If you fixate an object lying on a table in front of you, the object is seen very clearly and distinctly. Other objects on the table are not seen as clearly. If you turn your head and move your eyes in the direction of one of these other objects, this object will be seen very clearly or distinctly. The previous object will be seen indistinctly. Fixate *a* in Fig. 10 below. You will be able to count the dots correctly. You will also see *b* while fixating *a*. But you will not be able to count the number of dots.

Fig. 10

You will get focal vision of *a* and marginal vision of *b*. The image of *a* falls on the yellow spot, in the central region of the retina. The image of *b* falls on the outer region. If you turn from *a* to *b*, *b* gets into focal or clear vision.

When the image of the object falls on the blind spot, the object is not seen. Close your left eye and with your right eye look at the circle in Fig. 11. The star on the right of the circle will also be visible to you. Now hold the book straight in your hand. Keep looking at the circle, with your left eye still closed. You will see also the star. If you gradually bring the book nearer to you, or take it farther from you, at one position the star will disappear. In this position the image of the star falls on blind spot.

Fig. 11

The cones function in bright light. The rods function in dim light. Cones are receptors for colour vision. We see colours of objects only in bright light. In dim light, as after sun set, we may be able to see objects. We cannot see the colours of objects; we distinguish them as different shades of grey. If you reduce the intensity of light in your room, you cannot see the colours of objects lying on the table before you. But when you increase the light you are able to see the colours. In dim light the cones cease to function. The rods alone function in dim light. Whatever is seen is due to the stimulation of the rods. We have seen above that when the image of the object falls on the fovea, we get distinct vision. We see clearly not only the shapes of objects. We also see their colour. The fovea contains only cones. We do not see the colour of those objects whose image falls on parts of the retina further away from the fovea. These parts contain mostly rods and few cones.

The fact that there are two different kinds of receptors in the retina for bright and dim, for colour and colourless vision, was first suggested by Von Kries. This is also called the duplicity theory of vision. The theory has now been established. It means that the receptors for colour vision are different from the receptors for colourless vision.

Hue, Brightness and Saturation

We understood the nature of the stimulus for vision, as well as the structure and functions of the visual receptors. We try to understand now the characteristics of visual sensation. There are three characteristics of visual sensation : hue, brightness and saturation. These characteristics are also related to the characteristics of the visual stimulus.

Hues are the different colours that man can see. We see red, green, blue, yellow and several other colours. The difference in the colours seen is related to the difference in the length of the light wave that falls upon the retina. The longest visible light waves produce the sensation of red. The shortest produce the sensation of violet. Other colours seen are likewise produced by different wave lengths. You must have seen the rainbow. It contains several colours—red, orange, yellow, green, indigo, blue and violet. The colours are arranged in the order of the length of the light waves that produce them. These colours are also called spectral colours. When the light of the sun falls upon the edge of a mirror, we see the spectral colours. The sun's rays contain light of all wave lengths. Hence no colour is seen in the sun's rays when they directly fall upon the eyes. But when sun's light falls upon the edge of a mirror, the light gets broken up or analysed into the several wave lengths that compose the light. These wave lengths are thrown upon different parts of the retina. We see several colours on the mirror's edge. The following Table gives an idea of wave lengths in millimicrons that produce those colours :

430 $m\mu$ Violet	578 $m\mu$ Greenish Yellow
477 $m\mu$ Blue	582 $m\mu$ Yellow
482 $m\mu$ Greenish Blue	610 $m\mu$ Orange
497 $m\mu$ Bluish Green	660 $m\mu$ Yellowish Red
515 $m\mu$ Green	680 $m\mu$ Red

Another attribute of visual sensation is brightness. A red colour seen in clear day light looks brighter than the same colour seen in the light of the lamp. The brightness of the colour is related to the intensity or strength of the light simulus. Strong light produces sensation of a bright colour. Weak light produces sensation of a dull colour. Thus, corresponding to the various intensities of the light stimulus, we have different degrees of brightness of the visual sensation. At one end we have white and at another end black. Between white and black we see different shades of grey. There is, thus, a white-grey black series.

A third attribute of visual sensation is called saturation. You have a deep red or light red. The deep red colour is said to be more saturated than the light red. Similarly a deep green is more saturated than a bluish green. Saturation is, thus, another name for the purity of a colour. A yellowish red is less pure than red. So is a whitish red or pink. The saturation of a colour is related to the degree of complexity of the light stimulus. A homogenous, pure, or unmixed stimulus, produces a saturated hue or colour.

Facts About Visual Sensation

Colour Mixture

In the sun's light all wave lengths are mixed. We can also artificially produce a mixture of wave lengths. This is called colour mixing. We will then see no colour. We will get colourless sensation, the sensation of grey. For mixing colours a circular card board, called a disc, may be used. The disc is divided into seven parts or sectors. Each sector is painted in one of the seven colours. All the seven spectral colours are thus seen on the colour disc, as it is called. The order of the colours on the disc is the same as in the spectral colours. The coloured sectors are of unequal size. As long as the disc is lying before you, you see all the colours on it. To mix the colours, you rotate the disc rapidly by fixing it on a wheel that can be rotated. When the disc is rotating you do not see any colour on it. It becomes colourless. Each sector of the disc is reflecting light wave of the length corresponding to its colour. You see all the colours on the disc when it is not moving. Each colour reflects light wave of the corresponding length, every time when you look at a particular sector of the disc. But when the disc is fast rotating the several wave lengths reflected by the different colours strike the same portion of the retina at about the same time. They become mixed up. You see no colour, but a grey disc. Same thing happens when the sun's light directly stimulates the retina. Then too all wave lengths in the light ray stimulate the same point on the retina. We do not see any colour. Likewise the rotating colour disc is also seen as colourless.

You can produce colourless sensation not only by mixing the spectral colours. If you mix red with bluish green by using a disc painted red and bluish green in a certain proportion, then too you do not see the colours. You get a colourless sensation. Similarly, yellow and blue when mixed by rotating the colour disc produce colourless sensation. These pairs of colours are called complementary colours. Red and bluish green are complementary; yellow and blue are also complementary. When mixed in a certain proportion, each pair produces a colourless sensation.

Some colours do not produce a colourless sensation when mixed. They produce a new shade of colour. When you rotate a red and yellow disc, you see orange. Blue and red mixed in a certain proportion produce violet. Colours whose mixing does not result in colourless sensation are called non-complementary colours. Mixing of non-complementary colours produces a new shade of colour. Most colours can be seen by mixing red, green and blue, one with the other, in different proportions. These colours are, therefore, also called primary colours. Yellow can be produced by mixing wave lengths that produce red and green. Hence yellow is not supposed to be a primary colour.

After-image and Contrast

Look at a small coloured patch, say blue, for about half a minute. Turn your gaze after that to the white surface of the wall. You will see a patch of yellow colour on the wall. Same thing you will find if you fixate any other colour. Fixation of any colour for a while induces its complementary in a colourless background. Blue induces yellow. Yellow induces blue. Red induces bluish green and green induces purple. The induced colour is called an after-image. It is so called because you see a colour in the absence of a colour stimulus and this happens *after* the stimulation of the retina by a colour stimulus. It is called *negative* after-image. The colour that you see is the opposite or complementary of the colour that induces it. You get a negative after-image also for white or black stimulus. Keep looking with one eye closed at the point in the centre of the rectangle in Fig. 12 for about a minute. Then look at a white page. You will see a negative after-image. The white portion of the figure will be seen as black and the black portion white.

Fig. 12

A negative after-image is distinguished from a positive after-image. The latter happens when you look at a colour just for a moment and then turn your gaze to a white surface. You will continue to see a faint patch of the same colour. You see the colour in the absence of the stimulus, because the effect of the stimulation persists for a while after the stimulus is removed. You get a faint sensation of the same colour even when you are not looking at the colour. A positive after-image may not be as easily produced as a negative after-image.

The negative after-image is also called contrast effect. The fixation of a colour induces a contrasting colour. This happens after the colour stimulus is removed. Contrast effect may take place even when the stimulus is present. Place, side by side, two rectangular patches, say, one red and another bluish green. You will find that the red looks more red and the green more green. Any patch of colour tends to induce its complementary colour in its surroundings. If you place non-complementary colours side by side, the contrast effect will appear in a different manner. Say, red patch joins a yellow patch. The red then looks bluish red and the yellow looks greenish yellow. You can mark the difference by looking at similar patches lying at a distance. You will get the contrast effect also in white and black. For this reason, black prints are more distinct on a white page than on a brown page.

Adaptation

When you come out of a closed room in the bright sun, the sun's light looks very bright. Your eyes dazzle. But after a short while your eyes become adapted to the light. It does not look as bright. This is called light adaptation. If you enter a dark room, at first you are not able to see any object in the room. It may be difficult for you to find your way in the room. But gradually you are able to see the objects. Your eyes become dark adapted. You must have experienced this change on entering a picture hall after the film has started. However, even when your eyes have become dark adapted, you do not see the colour of objects around you. We have noted that colours are seen when the cones are stimulated. Cones cannot be stimulated in dim light. In the dark, rods function. With dark adaptation the rods become more sensitive.

Colour Blindness

In bright light you can see colours of objects and distinguish one colour from another colour. But some people cannot see colours even in bright light. They are said to be colour-blind. All objects look to them as white, grey or black. Objects of the same shape and size but of different colours will look to them as alike. The retina of the colour-blind lacks cones. It contains rods only or the cones are diseased and do not function. The colour-blind has difficulty in seeing objects if the light is bright. To shut out the light such persons have to keep their eyes half closed.

Persons that can see no colour are called completely colour-blind. There are others who are partially colour-blind. These are red-green blind. The red-green blind cannot see red and green colours. He confuses them with yellow. His world of colours is reduced to blue and yellow. At the cross road you see signal lights. They are red and green. Red light signals to stop; green light to proceed. Similar signals you find also at the railway station. Motor car drivers, engine drivers, and the signallers have to pass a test of red-green blindness.

Colour blindness can be easily detected. Collect glass beads of different sizes and colours in a small tray. Ask the person who is to be tested to pick up and put the red, green, blue and yellow-beads in four different boxes. If the person is red-green blind you will find him mixing the red, green and yellow beads together.

Partial colour blindness is tested in still another way. Dots of red, green and yellow colour are printed within an area. A set of dots of one colour, say red, makes a figure, say 5. The dots of other colours surround it. A normal person can see the figure. He distinguishes the dots that make the figure from the other dots. A colour-blind cannot see the figure. The red dots are confused with the green and yellow ones. Special tests of this type have been prepared. They are called the Ishihara test of colour blindness.

Colour Zones

Stand in a garden, blooming with flowers of all colours, in spring. Keep looking at one flower from a close distance. You will distinctly see not only the colour but also the different parts of the flower. You will not only be able to name it, if you are familiar with the names of flowers. Perhaps, you will also be able to count its petals. While you are looking at the flower, other flowers and plants surrounding this flower will also be visible to you. But these will not be seen as clearly. You can see the colours of those that closely surround the flower that you are looking at. But you will not be able to see the details of their size and shape. Beyond these flowers also you will see objects but you will not be able to decide what they actually are. Beyond them you see nothing. While you are looking directly at one flower, the total area within which objects are visible to you, some very clearly, some less clearly, and some vaguely, forms, what is called, the field of your vision. Within the total field of vision is a smaller area called the field of colour vision. Within the field of colour vision objects are seen with their colours. Outside this field they are seen without colours.

Like your field of vision there are divisions in the retina also. These are called retinal zones. In the retina you have the central zone. Light waves falling within this area can be seen in their possible colours, red, green, blue and yellow. Beyond the central zone, there is the middle zone. The light falling within this area can be seen only in two colours, namely, yellow and blue. Beyond the middle zone, you have the outer zone. Within this zone all stimuli appear colourless. They produce sensations of white, grey and black only. The retinal colour zones are shown in the following figure :

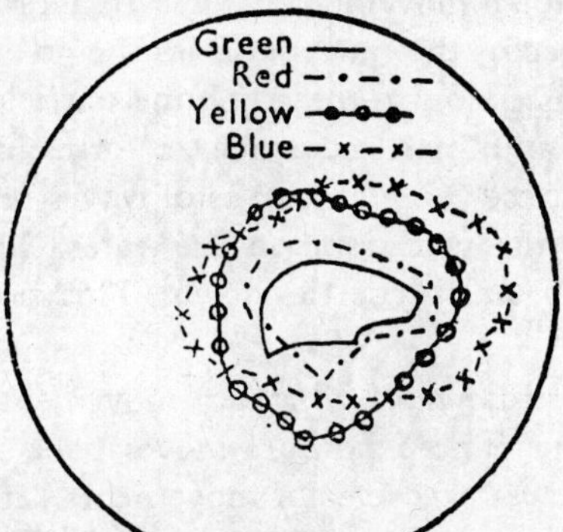

Fig. 13

Auditory Sensation

The sense of vision enables us to adjust to objects. It brings us the knowledge of their characteristics. It also brings us near to the thoughts and experiences of the present and the past generations. These are recorded in the reading materials that are in such a plentiful supply in modern times. The sense of hearing enables us to make adjustment to other persons around us. Man is a social animal. As such he is also described as a talking animal. Social situations involve interaction between persons. Much of the interaction consists of talking and listening. The ideas that move the masses of men are passed on more by the process of talking and listening than writing and reading. A deaf person feels like an outcast. He is lonely even in the midst of a crowd. The sense of hearing is, therefore, of no less importance to man than the sense of vision.

The Stimulus for Hearing

The stimulus for hearing consists of sound waves. Sound waves are produced by the vibration of air particles. Air fills all empty spaces. It contains very minute particles. You sometimes see these particles dancing in the beam of light that enters your room through a hole in the window. Vibration is a back and forth movement. When you strike a steel bar you notice such back and forth movement in it. It vibrates. When any sound is produced, the air particles begin to vibrate. The vibration is passed on to the adjoining particles. As the movement is a back and forth movement, it forms into waves. You must have noticed similar circles of waves on the surface of a pond when you throw a stone on the water. The water moves back and forth, until it settles down. This produces the waves of movement.

You get an instance of vibratory movements in the swings of a pendulum. The pendulum moves back and forth. Every time it completes a cycle of movements. It moves from the middle or resting position to the right, then to the left and back again to the middle. As a wave, the complete cycle takes the following form :

The movement of the pendulum may be slow or quick. The difference can be expressed in terms of the number of cycles of movement in a given time. This is also called frequency of cycles.

Sound waves also differ in the frequency of cycles per second or CPS (cycles per second). The following figure illustrates this difference :

Fig. 14

While *a* has a frequency of 5 cycles, *b* has a frequency of 8 cycles within the same time

You can make an interesting comparison here between sound waves and light waves. Light waves are measured in terms of length. Sound waves are measured in terms of frequency per second. Light waves occur at the same time. Sound waves come one after the other. The visual sense is the primary source for the knowledge of space. The sense of hearing is the primary source for the knowledge of time. Objects related in space exist together. Left and right, above and below, far and near, etc., are the categories of space. Events related in time happen one after the other. Now and then, before and after, are the categories of time. The sense of hearing, however, provides a secondary source of the knowledge of space also. When we hear a sound, we can also localise it. We know from what direction the sound is coming. This enables us to know the position of the object that produces the sound. We know whether it is far or near, to the right or to the left, above or below. Another primary source of the knowledge of space is the sensation of touch.

Besides frequency, sound waves differ in amplitude or height also. This difference depends upon the strength or intensity of the sound stimulus. Difference in amplitude of sound waves of the same frequency is shown in Fig. 14 above. The waves in *d* have higher amplitude than the waves in *c*.

In Fig. 14 we have pure sound waves. Such waves are also called sine waves. All waves in the series are of the same or simple form. Their shape does not change. When you strike a tuning fork, the vibration produces a sine wave. A tuning fork is shown below :

Fig. 15

The sounds that we usually hear are produced by waves that are not pure or simple. They have a variety of forms. They are produced by the mixture of waves of different frequencies. A complex sound wave shows regular changes in its form as in Fig. 16 below.

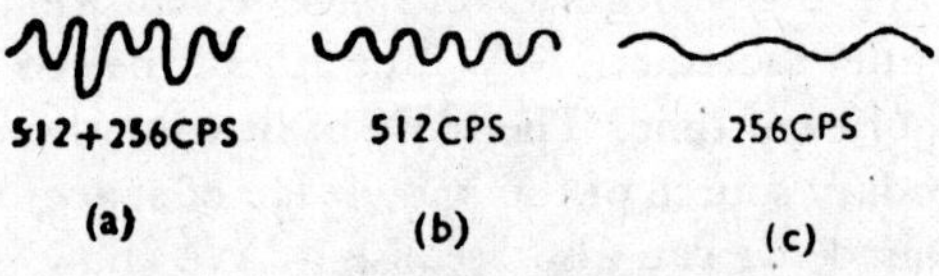

Fig. 16

In the above waves, (a) can be analysed into two sets of simple waves, (b) and (c), that differ in frequency.

The simple or complex waves in the above illustrations have a regular form. Even when there is a change, the change occurs at regular intervals. These are, therefore, called periodic waves. There may be sound waves of irregular form also. They are called aperiodic waves, as illustrated below :

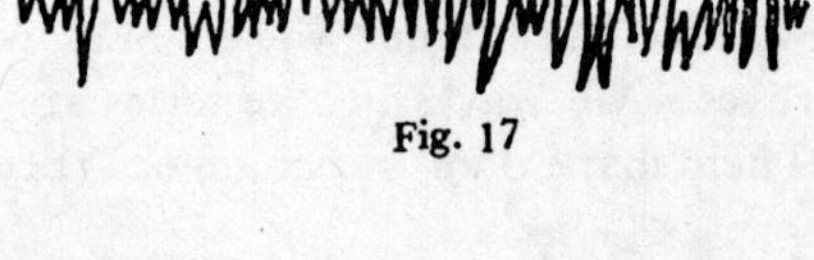

Fig. 17

We saw above that sound waves have frequency and amplitude. They may be pure or mixed, periodic or aperiodic. The various properties of the sound stimulus bear a relation to the attributes of auditory sensation. Periodic waves produce sensations of tone. The sound waves produced by musical instruments are periodic waves. We hear tones when we listen to a music. Aperiodic waves produce sensations of noise, like the rattling of a cart on an uneven surface or the cluttering of a typewriter.

Difference in the frequencies of sound waves is related to the difference in the pitch of the sound sensation. You may sound a tuning fork that is vibrating at the rate of 250 cps and then another vibrating at the rate of 300 cps. The difference in the tones that you hear is a difference in pitch. The human ear can respond to frequencies between 20 to 20,000 cycles per second. Sound waves of low frequency produce low pitch; sound waves of high frequency produce high pitch.

Loudness is related to the other property of sound waves, namely, their amplitude. The greater the amplitude the louder the sound. However, equally intense sound stimuli of lowers frequencies are not as loud as those of higher frequencies. The threshold of intensity of sound stimulus, thus, lowers with the increase in the frequency of the sound wave. The human ear is most sensitive to frequencies between 512 to 2,048 cps. Within this range, sound waves of much lower intensities can produce sensation of hearing.

As we noted above, a tuning fork produces a pure tone. Musical instruments produce complex tones. They can be analysed into sound waves of different frequencies. The tone of the lowest frequency is called the fund amental. The other tones are called overtones. The first overtone has a frequency which is two times the frequency of the fundamental. The second overtone has a frequency which is three times that of the fundamental, and so on.

Different musical instruments differ in the composition of the overtones. They do not emit the same number of overtones. Also the strength of the overtones differs from instrument to instrument. Some instruments magnify a particular overtone and deaden other overtones. The difference in the total sensations produced by the different instruments is due to these differences. The total effect is called timbre. You can find out what instrument is being played from the music that you hear. This is due to the difference in timbre or the total quality of the sound sensation produced. While listening to the radio, you know whether a violin, a flute or a sitar is being played. Each one may be playing the same musical tune, but still there is a difference.

The Structure and Function of the Ear

The human ear is divided into three parts, namely, the outer ear, the middle ear, and the inner ear. The outer ear consists of the flap of the ear. It is also called the pinna. It forms the superficial part of the auditory canal. The flap of the ear does not seem to have any function. The sound waves enter the ear through the auditory canal. They strike at the ear drum or tympanic membrane. The tympanic membrane separates the outer ear from the middle ear. The sound waves set the ear drum into vibration.

The middle ear consists of a chain or three bones, called ossicles. The first bone is the hammer, the second the anvil, and the third the stirrup. They are so called because of their shape. The hammer is attached to the inner side of the ear drum. The vibration of the ear drum produces vibratory movements in the hammer. This leads to similar movements in the anvil and the stirrup. The stirrup is attached to an opening in the inner ear called the oval window. The different parts of the ear are shown in the following figure :

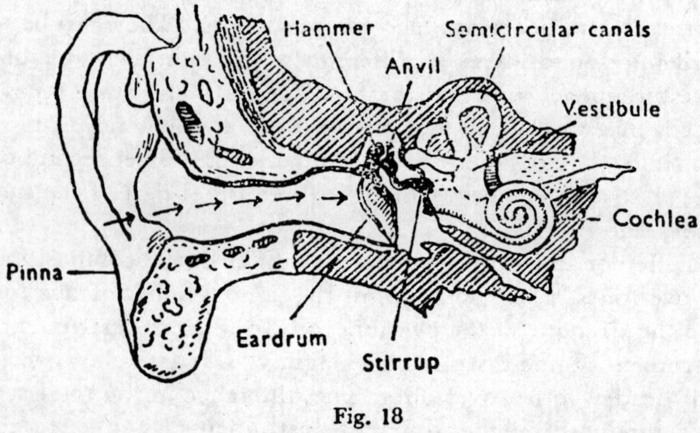

Fig. 18

The inner ear is connected with the middle ear by the oval window and the round window. Both are covered with a very thin membrane. The inner ear contains (1) the semi-circular canals (2) the vestibule and (3) the cochlea. The first two play no part in hearing.

The cochlea contains the receptors for hearing. It is formed into a spiral and looks like a snail. It has three parallel tubes separated by membranes. Each contains a fluid which is called endolymph. One of the membranes is called the basilar membrane. The other is the vestibuler membrane. On the basilar membrane lie the organs of corti. The organs of corti contain hair cells which are the real receptors for hearing.

The vibration of the anvil pushes in and out the oval window. The fluid inside the cochlea is also moved back and forth. These movements produce movement in the basilar membrane and finally in the organs of corti. The auditory receptors are thus stimulated. The nervous impulse passes on through the fibers of the auditory nerve that connect the ear with the sensory centres in the temporal lobe. The neural impulse activates the cortical centres and the sensation of hearing takes place.

Sensation of Taste

The stimulus for the sense of taste is any chemical substance. A solid object in the mouth produces no sensation of taste. You may get a sensation of touch or temperature from such an object. The taste receptors are called taste buds. They are located on the tongue and also in the linings of the cheeks and the throat. The taste buds are stimulated when the chemical substance is dissolved by the saliva in the mouth.

There are four primary taste qualities, namely, sweet, sour, bitter and salt. Most of the other tastes we attribute to objects are combinations of the sense of smell. In the condition of severe cold, one loses the taste of many food articles. Actually we distinguish these articles not by their taste, but by their flavour given by the sense of smell.

It is supposed that there are four kinds of receptors in the mouth, each one related to one primary taste quality. On this account, all parts of the tongue are not equally sensitive to all qualities of taste. The tip of the tongue is most sensitive to sweet, the back of the tongue to bitter, the sides to sour. The entire surface of the tongue is, however, equally sensitive to salt.

Like other simpler senses, the sense of taste is also lost by adaptation. What seems to be very bitter at first becomes less bitter if you continue to eat or drink it. A very salty dish soon becomes quite bearable. The effect of adaptation is also shown in another way. A sweet drink tastes more sweet after taking a pinch of salt.

Sensation of Smell

The stimuli for smell consist of vapours and gases. They are carried high up in the nostrils by air and stimulate the receptors located in the nostrils.

There are six primary smell qualities, namely, spicy, flowery, fruity, resinous, burnt and foul. All other smells are the mixture of these primaries. We sense a greater variety of odours than tastes. In fact it is the smell sense which contributes largely to the fine discrimination of tastes. If the smell sense is blocked, the taste qualities will be limited to a few only, as we stated above.

Like the taste receptors, the smell receptors also get adapted soon. A foul smell loses its foulness after some time. Same thing applies to the other odours also.

The Sensation of Touch

The stimulus for touch is the mechanical deformation of the skin by pushing or pulling. The receptors for touch are located in the skin. In the hairy regions of the skin, the receptors consist of the nerve endings of the so-called hair bulbs. In non-hairy regions, Meisner's corpuscles constitute the receptors.

The entire surface of the skin is not sensitive to touch. There are sensitive spots randomly distributed among insensitive spots. The distribution of touch spots varies for different areas of the body. The number is larger in the extremities of the limbs. The number of touch spots per sq. centimetre is largest on the tip of the tongue and that of the fingers. The number of touch spots is much smaller on the back. The closest distance at which one can discriminate two points stimulated simultaneously on the skin also varies, for the reason, from area to area. The maximum distance in any area at which one can discriminate the two points has been called the 2-point threshold for the area. It has also been called the spatial threshold. It is so called because it gives a measure of the perception of distance between points on different areas of the body. The 2-point threshold is an RL and not a DL value. It is a measure of the least noticeable value of the distance between two points touched in the skin. It is not a measure of the difference between any two values.

The touch qualities have been classified into tickle, contact and natural pressure. Tickle is aroused by weak stimuli, contact by stimuli of intermediate intensity, and pressure by intense stimuli.

Adaptation to the stimulus takes place very rapidly. Continuous application of the stimulus causes the sensation to disappear. When one starts wearing glasses one gets sensation of touch from various parts of the frame that are in contact with the skin. Gradually, the experience disappears. If you are used to wearing a cap, the adaptation of the touch receptors in the head makes you sometimes unaware of actually wearing a cap.

Pain Sensation

Any kind of stimulus that is strong enough to injure the free nerve endings in the skin arouses pain sensation. Pain may be produced, however, in any sense organ when excessive stimulation applied to that sense organ. For example, very strong sound produces pain in the ear. There is no specific stimulus, therefore, for the arousal of pain.

Like touch, the entire surface of the skin is not sensitive to pain. Pain spots are distributed, however, more densely than touch receptors. The more sensitive areas are those at the extremities, near joints, the neck and other places where large nerves and blood vessels come nearest to the surface of the skin. The inner lining of the cheek is insensitive to pain.

The pain qualities are itching, which is connected with weak stimulation, and pricks and clear pains aroused by more intense stimuli.

Continuous application of stimulus of the same intensity soon produces adaptation to pain. A persistent pain is experienced only when the intensity of the stimulus changes at intervals. With constant intensity, the pain sensation will soon disappear. The time of disappearance, however, varies with the nature of the stimulus and with the spot stimulated.

Cold and Warmth

Cold and warmth sensations are also called the temperature senses. The skin surface normally maintains a temperature of 33°C. Any stimulus whose temperature falls between 32.5° and 33.5°C produces no temperature sense. It has a physiologically zero temperature. The physiological zero varies with the part of the body, according to the temperature of that part. Under the tongue, the temperature is 37°C. In the armpit it is about 36.5°C. The temperature of the ear lobes is about 28°C. When you touch your ear lobes, it always feels cool. It so happens because the temperature of the surface of the fingers is 33°C. It is obvious that what really matters for the temperature sense to be aroused is the difference between the body temperature and the temperature of the stimulus.

At the level of the skin, a stimulus whose temperature is above 33.5°C feels warm, while a stimulus whose temperature is below 32.5°C feels cold.

Like the other skin senses, cold and warmth spots are also scattered over the body. A cold spot normally reacts to stimulus whose temperature is below 33°C. A warm spot reacts to a temperature above 33°C. But a cold spot is stimulated also by a temperature above 43°C. The sensation however is one of cold and not warmth, though the stimulus is a high temperature. This has been called paradoxical cold. For this reason, above 43°C temperature, one does not feel warmth. One gets a blend of cold and warmth which is described as heat. The cold spots produce the sensation of cold and the warmth spots produce the sensation of warmth. Heat is aroused by the simultaneous stimulation of cold and warm spots by a temperature above 43°C.

Like the paradoxical cold, there is paradoxical warmth also. This is produced by stimulating a warm spot by a temperature ranging between 25°C and 31°C.

The blood vessels that run to every part of the body provide the temperature receptors. The receptors are the free nerve endings in the smooth muscles of the blood vessels. The smooth muscles react to cold and warm temperature by contraction or relaxation, respectively.

Prolonged stimulation produces adaptation to temperature stimulation. Adaptation to temperature may be demonstrated by raising or lowering the temperature very gradually. No change in the temperature will be reported. Only, when the temperature rises quite high or falls quite low, one experiences the sensation of pain. Adaptation to the temperature stimulus produces an interesting illusion. Place one hand in warm water and another in cold water for some time. Then put both hands in water whose temperature is near to the skin temperature. The water will feel cold to one hand and warm to another hand.

The different sensations we described, namely, of touch, pain and temperature, are also called cutaneous or skin sensations. Below we describe a few other sensations.

Kinesthetic Sensation

We become aware of the movement of our body even when we are looking at something else. When you enter a dark room and move ahead, you know in what direction your legs are moving, how fast or slow they are moving, and what positions they are taking. You know all this because you are getting sensations from the moving body. The sensations are produced by the movement. These sensations are called Kinesthetic sensations or sensations of movement.

The receptors for the kinesthetic sensations are located in the muscles, the joints, and the tendons that attach muscles to the bones. The receptors are called proprioceptors. They are stimulated by the movement of the muscles, joints and tendons. When our muscles, joints and tendons are made to move, the kinesthetic receptors that they contain get stimulated. Sensory impulses arise and reach the sensory centres in the parietal lobe. We get the sensation of movement. The impulses than travel downward through the motor tract to the muscles, joints and tendons and produce movements in them. In this manner a circular chain of movements take place.

Co-ordination of movement also takes place as a result of the kinesthetic impulses that reach the brain and serve as cue for initiating other movements. Thus, is walking, the co-ordination of the alternate forward movements of the two legs is controlled by the kinesthetic sensations produced by the movement of each leg. Kinesthetic sensations provide the cue for all fine co-ordinations of movements. An expert typist can type blind-folded. He does this because each movement of his finger across the keyboard contributes a cue for initiating the next movement. The kinesthetic sensation produced by each movement produces an awareness of the duration of the movement, the position of the movement, the speed of the movement, etc.

The kinesthetic sensations also contribute to our knowledge of weights of lifted objects. The sensation of weight is a mixture of the sensations of strain and effort. In holding a weight there is resistance in the muscles of the part of the body on which the weight is resting against the external pressure exerted by the weight. This produces strain. The sensations of strain and effort are, thus, due to the stimulation of the receptors in the muscles and the tendons.

The qualities of kinesthetic sensation are strain, ache, pressure and tension.

The Static Sense

The body is automatically maintaining its balance. This is possible because of the sensation that we get from the inner ear when the head turns right and left, backward and forward, or moves round about. We saw earlier (Fig. 18) that the inner ear consists of three parts, namely, the cochlea, the vestibule and the semi-circular cannals. The cochlea functions in hearing. The vestibule and the semicircular cannals function in maintaining the balance of the body. They provide the receptors for static sensation.

In the ear there are three semi-circular cannals, resting in three different positions (Fig. 18). Each one contains a fluid. The vestibule in the ear contains hair-like receptors which are bathing in the fluid. When you change your posture, stand up, sit down, or walk, your head moves. Movement is produced in the fluid also. This stimulates the receptors in the vestibules.

Sensory impulses aroused by the stimulation are carried to the cerebellum. Motor impulses arise in the cerebellum. These produce movement of a part of the body by which the balance of the body is restored.

In sea-sickness or air-sickness, the stimulation to the static receptors in the ear becomes excessive. The result is dizziness, vertigo, or nausea. The person loses his sense of balance. He cannot even sit or stand.

Organic Sensations

We have seen earlier that the vital organs in the body are provided with smooth muscles. These form what is called the visceral system (Chap. 2, p. 33). They contain receptors for very complex sensations, called organic sensations. They are related to the general sense of easiness, healthfulness or well-being. Sensations of hunger, nausea, tension in the bladder and the intestine, feeling of suffocation, etc., form the complex of organic sensations.

Chapter IV

ATTENTION

Nature of Attention

At a particular moment one is aware of objects and persons that surround him and stimulate his sense organs. He is also aware of the images of objects or persons that are coming to his mind, of the thoughts and feelings that are arising in him, of some activities that are going on within his body and of the actions that he is performing. But he is not aware of all these very clearly. At one moment he is clearly aware only of this or that object, this or that image, this or that thought or feeling, etc. He becomes clearly aware of it because he attends to it. He does not become clearly aware of the other experiences he is having at the moment, because he does not attend to them. Attention is the name of that condition within a person which enables him to be clearly aware of a certain object or activity. It may be another person's activity or his own mental or bodily activity.

The stimulus object or activity that one attends to stands out against the stimuli or activities to which attention is not given at the moment. Looking at Fig. 19 at one moment you become aware of a black cross and at the next moment of a white cross. At the first moment, the black portion of the diagram holds your attention. The black portion stands out against the white portion. The white portion gets into the background. At the next moment, the white portion stands out, it engages your attention. The black portion gets into the background. At one moment you observe a black figure against a white background. The next moment you observe a white figure against a black background. What

Fig. 19

you attend to is observed as a figure. A figure has some characteristics. These set it apart from the ground against which it stands out. A figure appears to be nearer to the observer than the ground—it stands out; the ground stands back. The figure has clear outlines, which the ground does not have. The figure presents clear details; the ground is vague and without details. Attention may be described as a process by which a part of the total stimulus comes to possess the characteristics of a figure.

Attention may also be described as a process that brings some stimuli into the focus. As a result, those stimuli become distinct and clear. Those that fall out of the focus remain indistinct and unclear. This is just like what happens when you flash a torchlight. The objects that are in the line of the light get into the focus and one notices them very clearly. Objects that lie outside the line of light remain out of the focus. Either we do not observe them at all, or they appear very hazy. We are said to give focal attention to the stimuli that are in the focus of attention and are thus clear and distinct. We are said to give marginal attention to the stimuli that lie outside the focus of attention, and are, therefore, vague and indistinct. We may think of still another case when the stimuli fall neither within focal nor marginal attention. We are said to be inattentive to such stimuli. A pupil in the class room may be giving focal attention to the music that is being played in the street. He may be giving marginal attention to the noise coming from the next room. He may be giving no attention to the teaching in the class. When the class is over, you may ask him about the various happenings. He will be able to give you a vivid description of the music and may even be able to repeat the tune. He will also be able to tell you that he heard some noise in the next room. But he will not be able to describe its nature. He will be quite unable to tell anything about the subject taught in the class room.

Attention may also be further described as a process of adjustment of the organism to the stimulus situation. When one attends to a noise coming from a distance, his auditory receptors become specially prepared to receive the stimulus. You may mark him turning his head in the direction from which the noise is coming. This enables both ears to receive the stimulus more adequately. You must have noticed a horse or some other animal prick its ears when the animal hears a loud distant noise. Similar adjustment of the visual receptors is to be noticed when one looks at an object attentively. Attention is, thus, a condition of preparedness or alertness. When one is attentive, the sense organs become specially prepared to receive the stimulus.

Besides receptor adjustment, there is also effector adjustment in attention. The muscles of the body are specially prepared to act to the object of attention, or to engage in the activity that is in the focus of attention. In the condition of attention, one may notice state of tension in the muscles. You must have observed the N.C.C. parade. Before the officer says "attention", every person in the parade is standing at-ease. The moment the word "attention" is uttered, the postures change and the muscles become stiff and tense. Same thing happens with competitors in a foot-race. The moment the "ready" signal is given, competitors become alert. They take their position. Their posture changes. They bend forward. They become specially attentive to the activity which is to start. They get prepared for it.

Attention also involves mental alertness or preparedness. When you give attention to a task, the mental activities related to the task become specially acute. This increase in mental alertness is noticed in improvement in the performance of the task. When a pupil does not pay full attention while listening to the teacher in the class room, reading through the pages of the text book, or working on problems in mathematics, his understanding of the lesson taught, his learning of text book, or his solution of the problems will be of inferior order. On the other hand, if he listens, reads or works attentively, the results of the listening, reading or working are much better. This difference will be there because attention specially prepares him to exercise his mental activities.

Determinants of Attention

We tried to understand the nature of attention and noticed that the process of attention can be described in various ways. We now seek to understand the factors which produce the condition of attention in a person. These factors are also called the determinants of attention; attention is determined by them. The determinants may be external or objective; they may be internal or subjective. The external determinants are some characteristics of the stimulus to which attention is given. One such characteristic is intensity or strength of the stimulus. A more strong or intense stimulus is more likely to arouse attention than a less strong or weak stimulus. Our attention becomes easily directed to a loud sound, a bright light or a strong smell. A mild whisper, a dim light or a weak smell may pass unnoticed by a person.

Another objective determinant of attention is the size of the stimulus object. A large object in his environment is more likely to catch the attention of a person than a small object. As you look at the sky in the night, your attention will be first directed to the moon though there may be a more shining star also to be seen on the horizon. If an elephant and donkey are before you, the elephant is more likely to catch your attention, unless you are specially interested in donkeys.

Duration of the stimulus also favours attention. A light or sound that appears only for a moment is likely to escape your attention. While a light or sound that persists catches your attention. However, if a light or sound is continuous it is less likely to hold your attention than a light or sound that comes and goes at intervals. If a noise is going on without break it passes out of your attention. But if a noise is produced at intervals, every time it comes your attention is diverted to it.

A moving object catches your attention more quickly than an object that does not move. If you are working in an open field and a snake is lying motionless before you, it might escape your attention. But the moment it starts moving, your attention is aroused by it.

Change and variety strike attention more easily than sameness and absence of change. You may not be attentive to the ticking of the time-piece on your table. But the moment it stops ticking, your attention becomes directed to the change. Similarly an advertisement printed in letters of different colours is more likely to catch attention than the same advertisement printed is one colour. The effect of contrast on attention is greater than the effect of mere difference. An advertisement in white and black, or red and green, is more likely to attract attention than the same advertisement in white and red, or green and yellow. If a very tall and a very short person are walking together you are more likely to notice them than when one person is just a little taller than the other.

The findings about the objective determinants of attention have been used in designing advertisements. When any article is advertised, the advertisement is intended to catch and hold the attention of the buyers of the article. A good advertisement should be able to do this. Size, duration, movement, change, all these characteristics of the stimulus are kept in view while planning an advertisement. A good printed advertisement is made in bold letters, and is given more space in the magazine or newspaper. In large cities they use electric lights for advertisement. The name or shape of the article is flashed at intervals, it comes and goes. Some such advertisements also use movement. One object is shown moving behind another object. All these devices are used to catch the attention of persons so that they become aware of the articles advertised.

The internal or subjective determinants of attention are interests, needs, desires, purposes and goals of the individual. Objects, activities, or tasks one likes both catch and hold his attention. Objects, and activities that fulfil one's desires, or serve some purpose of the individual, are more likely to attract his attention. One may like a particular kind of fruit, or one may be interested in a particular type of game. The fruit or articles used in the game are more likely to catch his attention than other objects that are also there. Similarly, the sight of an object of food is more likely to strike the attention of a hungry man than the attention of a person who had just had a full meal. If a person is out for bird shooting, a bird sitting on the trees is more likely to catch his attention than the fruit borne by the tree. If a person goes out to buy a pair of shoes, his attention will be attracted more by shoe shops than by cloth shops.

Facts About Attention

There are certain facts about attention which one should know in order to understand attention better. If you give your attention to a very mild stimulus like the ticking of a time-piece heard from a distance, or a very dim point of distant light, the ticking or the light may appear to come and go. At one moment it is within your attention. At the next moment it passes out of your attention. This is called fluctuation of attention.

There is another fact about attention, very similar to fluctuation of attention, but really different from it. It is called shift of attention. Earlier you saw a diagram whose figure changes. Here is another similar diagram. If you look at it for some time, you find your attention shifting from one figure to another. You cannot hold this or that figure very long in your attention.

Fig. 20

The child's attention is very shifting. It flits from object to object. It cannot remain fixed on the same object or activity for more than a moment. The child is not able to concentrate his attention on any object. The adult can concentrate his attention. This does not mean that the adult's attention does not shift. The adult's attention shifts from one object to another related object. When you hold the playing cards in your hand and give concentrated attention to the game, your attention shifts from one card to another. It will not shift from the game to the noise coming from the rice mill nearby. In fact when concentrated attention is given to the game, the noise may not be noticed at all. The child is unable to hold any object in his attention for longer than a moment. When the shift of attention is limited to related objects and activities, attention is said to be absorbed or concentrated; unrelated objects or activities fail to catch attention. When unrelated stimuli attract and hold one's attention, attention is said to be distracted. The child's attention is more easily distracted.

The child has to be trained to keep his attention absorbed or concentrated. He has to make special effort in the beginning to do this. When attention requires special effort in order to be fixed on some object or objects, it is called effortful or voluntary attention. Teachers of small children know how difficult it is to train the child to give concentrated attention to anything. The difficulty can be overcome by creating the child's interest in the object or activity. The play method of teaching small children trains the child to give absorbed or concentrated attention because the child is interested in playthings. Coloured beads or glass balls are used to give the child early training in counting and in the use of numbers. Gradually the child learns to give effortless attention to those activities; he develops habit of concentration. Once the child learns to concentrate his attention, his attention does not easily shift to unrelated objects, activities, ideas or images.

With the development of interests in certain types of objects or activities, attention to the objects and activities becomes effortless, spontaneous, and involuntary. If a pupil is interested in working out sums, he can easily concentrate on this activity, without any special effort of attention. His attention would not easily shift to other stimuli that may also be present in his environment, or to unrelated images, ideas or thoughts. They would not easily distract his attention from the task in his hand.

Voluntary or effortful attention is to be noted also in adults. When two persons are talking near you, while you are reading your text book, your attention is distracted from the text book. You experience difficulty in concentrating your attention. You have to make special effort to ignore the distracting conversation. Your attention becomes effortful or voluntary. Sometimes you may have to do something in which you are not interested. You experience great difficulty in concentrating your attention. You can do this only by exerting a good deal of effort. You may be asked to copy pages after pages of figures from one book to another. To make the copy correct, you have to concentrate your attention to the task. You have to make special effort for this. Your attention is effortful or voluntary; you have to exert your will. On the other hand, if you are interested in poems, you can easily concentrate your attention on copying any good poem yon come across. Your attention becomes spontaneous, effortless or involuntary. You have to make no effort to hold the task before your attention. Some stimuli make it difficult for one to concentrate on his task. Loud noise is one such stimulus. It requires very great effort to work in the midst of noises. The worker has to apply more energy and gets easily fatigued. In factories, or even in big cities, noise has accordingly become a problem.

Various devices are used to control the noise. However, one also gets used to noises in due course. They fail to distrtact his attention. This has been called negative adaptation. If you rent a house in a busy street, you some time find it very difficult to concentrate on your studies. But gradually you get adapted to the noise. It does not distract you.

One may get distraction not only from external stimuli. Sometimes a person may be distracted from sources within him. Some ideas spontaneously keep coming to his mind. They distract him; he cannot concentrate on the task in hand. Some students become absent-minded when the class is going on. They start thinking of some matters unrelated to the class work. They cannot concentrate on the class work. Some people develop the habit of becoming absent-minded in the midst of important engagements. This can be overcome by forcing one's attention on the task in hand; one has to exert his will in order to be able to concentrate. In course of time, he will gain the power of concentration.

We often think it is possible to divide one's attention. It is supposed that one can concentrate his attention on more than one unrelated objects or activities at one moment. It appears, for example, that one can listen to a statment as well as write it down while listening. It seems that the activities of listening and writing are performed at the same time and attention is divided between these two activities. Actually what happens is not the division of attention. It is shift of attention. The shift is quite rapid and hence it seems that both activities are receiving full attention at the same moment. At first, everybody experiences difficulty in writing while listening. A pupil who has just started to take notes from his teacher's class room talk finds that both his listening and noting become at times erroneous. He does not listen exactly what is told, or does not write exactly what he listens. When he concentrates his attention on listening, the writing becomes incorrect; when he gives attention to the writing, he misses some important points mentioned by the teacher. The difficulty is there because it is not possible for him to shift his attention rapidly. The same pupil finds his note taking much easier after a few months of practice. The practice makes it possible for him to shift his attention more rapidly. He can then both listen correctly and write correctly. Some pupils take notes by understanding the points made by the teacher. They have learnt to shift their attention rapidly between understanding and writing. Others take notes mechanically, without any or much understanding. They can concentrate their attention only on writing being able to shift their attention back and forth—from understanding to writing and from writing to understanding. A satisfactory notes taking habit should involve both understanding and writing, i.e., shifting attention from the one to the other without a loss in either.

There is one more interesting fact about attention. It has been sought to find out how many objects one can hold in a single act of attention. For example, a few books, paper weights, pencil and pen, ink-pot, a time-piece, and similar other objects, are lying on a table. Suppose you are allowed to look at the table for a single moment and then a curtain is drawn between you and the table. How many objects would come within your attention ? Most likely you would be able to get more than one object within your attention. It is also most likely that you would not be able to get all objects. The number of objects that you would be able to get in a single act of attention will be described as your span of attention. The more the number of objects one can grasp in a single moment of attention, the larger his span of attention. Individuals differ in their span of attention. Experiments have been done on the span of attention for letters or digits. It has been found that most persons can attend to four to five letters in one moment of attention out of a much larger number actually presented to them to look at. For most persons the span of attention for digits has also been found to be about the same. But some persons have been noticed to grasp seven or eight letters or digits in a single moment of attention.

A person's span of attention has influence on his speed of reading. Some people are fast readers, some are slow readers. The fast reader can grasp many more words in one glance than the slow reader. Some readers can get only a word. It is an advantage to be a fast reader. A fast reader can manage to read much more than a slow reader within the same period of time. It is very easy to test the speed of reading. A class of children may be given copies of the same printed passage to read within a fixed period of time. Wide differences will be noted in their speed of reading. While one may be at the end of the passage, another may be only half way through it, though both start at the same time. After the time is over, they may be asked to answer some questions on the content of what they read. This is to see whether a person has just given a glance to the written material or he has also understood what he read. A good reader is one who reads fast with understanding. It is possible to improve one's speed of reading by practice.

CHAPTER V

PERCEPTION

NATURE OF PERCEPTION

When an object or person is before you, you become aware of that object or person. You are said to perceive the object or person. Perception is thus the knowledge of an object or person that is before the perceiver, that is here now. Whatever is before an individual stimulates his sense organs. The light reflected from the book lying on your table strikes your visual receptors. You perceive the book. On hearing a noise coming from the next room, you know that your brother is speaking. You perceive your brother. The speaking produces vibration in the air. The vibration strikes against the drum of the ears. The auditory receptors are stimulated. On touching an object in the dark, you come to know that it is the water pot. You perceive the water pot. The touching of the water pot stimulates your skin receptors.

Stimulation of any sense organ may produce perception. Whatever stimulates your sense organ is thereby before you. You perceive it. It is a common error to suppose that an object is before a person and is perceived only when the object is seen by the person. An object is before a person and is perceived even when it is smelt, when it is tasted, when it is touched, or when its sound is heard. Perception does not involve only seeing. It may invol e hearing, smelling, tasting, touching, etc.

Perception is not possible when no sense organ is stimulated. I meet a person in the street. I perceive him. When I leave him, I no longer perceive him. On returning home, I tell a friend that I met the person. I describe to the friend the features of the person. I have a picture of the person in my mind. But this will not be perception of the person. At the moment I am describing the person, he is not before me. None of my sense organs is being stimulated by him. The picture of the person that I have in my mind is the image of the person. It is possible to have the knowledge of an object or person at a particular moment, without perceiving the object or person at that moment. The knowledge is in terms of the image of the object or person. Perceiving an object or person is, thus, to be distinguished from having an image of the object, or person. When I am having the image, the object or person is not before me. It does not stimulate any of my sense organs. On perceiving an object or person, the object or person must be here now. It should stimulate any of my sense organs. While sitting in your room, you may call up the image of a friend you met last week. But you will not perceive him unless he comes into the room or calls you.

I said above that there can be no perception without stimulation of a sense organ. But perception does not consist of only sense impressions. When you see an object and perceive it as an orange, you get the sensation of colour and shape only. But the orange as you perceive it is not only that. In perceiving it, you know that it has taste, it has a smell, it has a weight, it is eatable, and, perhaps, also that it is good for health. All these, and may be something more, constitute your perception of the object that you call orange. But at the moment you are looking at the object from a distance, you are getting no sensation of its taste, smell, weight, etc. You never get any sensation of its use and its value. The knowledge that you have of these qualities of the orange—its taste, its smell, its weight—consist of your images that you carry in your mind. The images are derived from your past experience of eating the orange and thus getting sensation of its taste and smell. Similarly, in the past you have lifted an orange in your hand and got the sensation of its weight. The knowledge that you have of the use and value of the orange does not consist of images. It consists of what are called ideas. Perception, thus, does not consist only of sensations. It is made up of sensations, images and ideas. But perception is not a mixture of sensations, images and ideas. We do not get sensations first and then come up the images and ideas. All these are experienced at the same moment as forming our perception of the object. They are all given together as a unified whole in a single act of perception.

At the moment I am perceiving an object or person, there may be other objects or persons also before me. These are also stimulating my sense organs. But I do not perceive all of them at the same time. When I look at my table, I may perceive at the moment the ink-pot, though there are several other objects lying before me on the table. They are also stimulating my visual sense organs, as they are within the field of my vision. In addition, my auditory receptors are being stimulated by the noise produced by the working of the flour mill close by, my olfactory receptors are being stimulated by the fragrance of the roses blooming in the near-by garden, and so on. Those other objects too are not perceived at the moment. I perceive the ink-pot. Perception is, therefore, described as a selective process. At a moment only a particular object gets selected for perception. Others are left out. How this selective process takes place is described in what follows.

Perceptual Organisation

At any one moment you are getting a mass of sensory impulses produced by the objects and persons that surround you. They are stimulating several of your sense organs. Out of the mass of sensory impulses, a limited set of impulses is organised as 'one whole'. This 'one whole' or organised set of sensory impulses constitutes the object that you perceive. The remaining sensory processes are not organised as single objects; they are mixed up with each other. Other objects are, therefore, not perceived at the moment. At the next moment, when you perceive one of the other objects, the sensory impulses produced by this object become organised as one whole. The sensory impulses produced by the object you perceived at the previous moment get mixed with the impulses from all other objects that are not perceived. Perception is, thus, described as a process of organisation. Some psychologists prefer the term, 'perceptual organisation' to 'perception'. They do so in order to emphasise the organisational process in perception. The sensory impressions produced by a small set of stimulations are organised as the perceived object. The rest of the total mass of stimulations remains unorganised. The process of perceiving is, thus, the process of perceptual organisation. Out of the total mass of stimuli, a certain part gets selectively organised as perception of an object or person.

Various factors determine the organisation in perception. They explain why out of a total mass of stimuli only a certain part gets organised in perception. Some of these factors are called Gestalt factors. A group of psychologists, called Gestalt psychologists, specially brought these factors into ligl.. Gestalt is a German word which means a pattern or configuration. We have earlier seen that perception consists not only of sensations. Images, ideas and sensations are all unified in perception. They together make one organised whole, the perceived object. What we perceive is the unified pattern or Gestalt. It is not sensations plus images plus ideas. We may analyse a perception as consisting of bits of sensation, bits of image, and bits of ideas. We may do the same thing when we break a word into the letters that compose it. But the moment we do this, the word ceases to be a word. It becomes a combination of letters. The words as we understand it is one whole, a single unit. The letters belong to the word not as its separate parts, but mingled together as one whole. Similarly, our perception too is a unified whole, a single unit of experience.

Gestalt Factors

The Gestalt factors are some characteristics of the stimuli. A set of stimuli are organised as one whole because they possess those characteristics. The following characteristics have been specially noted by the Gestalt psychologists as factors that influence perceptual organisation :

1. *Similarity*. Similar stimuli are more likely to be perceived as one whole than are dissimilar stimuli.

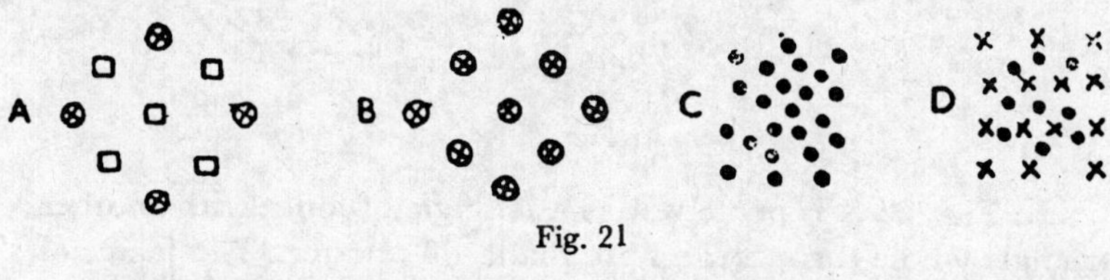

Fig. 21

In figure 21, A and B have the same number and arrangements of parts. But the parts of B are similar. B is perceived as one whole—a square pattern. A contains dissimilar parts. It is perceived as a cross and a square. C and D also have the same number and arrangement of parts. But D has dissimilar parts. You clearly see the letter S in D. C also contains this letter. But it is lost in C. Its parts are similar to the other parts of the sequre which C looks like.

2. *Proximity or nearness.* Among several stimuli those that are near to each other are likely to be perceived as one whole and distinct from others that are distant.

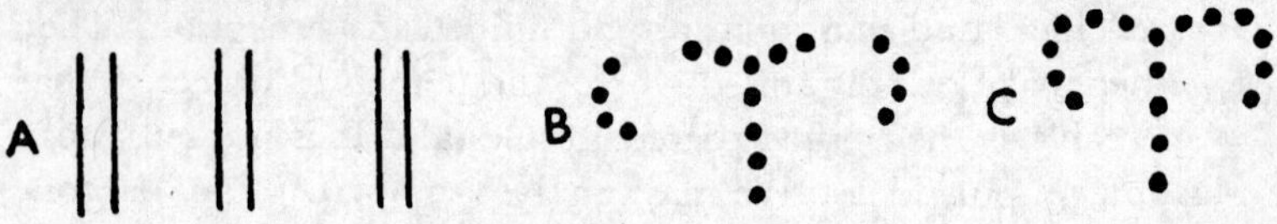

Fig. 22

In Fig. 22 A is perceived as three pairs of vertical lines, and not six vertical lines. Nor do we perceive two pairs of vertical lines in the middle, and a single vertical line on each side. The lines that are close are perceived as a single unit, distinct from the lines that are not so close. Similarly the set of dots in B may be perceived as the letter T in the middle with two arcs on each side. C too has the same number of dots. But the letter T is lost in C. All dots in C are equally close. They are perceived as a single unit. The factor of proximity accounts for the difference in the perception of B and C.

3. *Good figure or symmetry.* Stimuli that form a symmetrical figure or good figure are more likely to be perceived as a single unit.

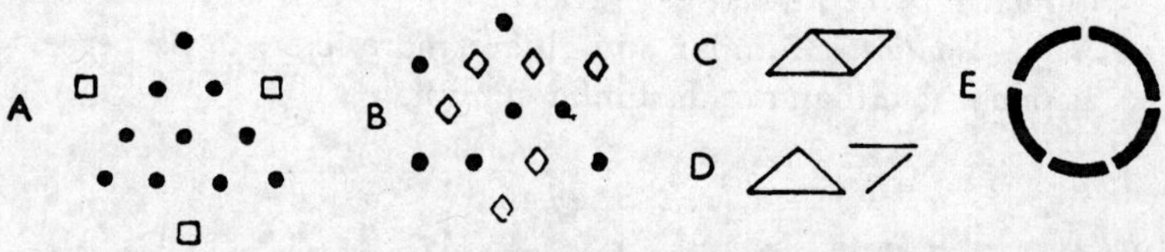

Fig. 23

In Fig. 23 A is perceived as a triangle of dots with another triangle whose three corners are made of squares. The factor of similarity accounts for the perception. But similarity fails to operate in B. The similar parts have no symmetry. They do not form a good figure. B is perceived as one figure in spite of the similarity. It may be perceived as a hexagon. Similarly, C is perceived as two triangles or as a parallelogram. D is perceived as a triangle and two straight lines.

E is more likely to be perceived as a circle than as a set of five separate arcs. The circle is a good figure. If a set of stimuli make a good figure, they are perceived as a single object in spite of a gap in the figure. This is called the principle of closure. In a good figure, the gap is bridged.

4. *Continuation, common direction, or common fate.* Stimuli that have a common direction are organised in perception as a separate object from those stimuli that have a different direction.

Fig. 24

In Fig. 24, we perceive A as one set or dots forming an arc and another set of dots forming a straight line. The dots that are perceived as an arc have a common direction, or common fate. Those forming a straight line have a different direction. In B we perceive two figures, one is super-imposed·upon the other. Each figure has a different continuation. The factor of continuation is also illustrated in C. We do not perceive three figures here. We perceive a square and a circle. The curve line of the circle is perceived as continuing as a curve line; the straight lines of the square are seen as continuing as straight lines. The straight lines make one figure. The curved lines and inside the square also make one figure.

Personal Factors

We noted some characteristics of the stimulus that favour the perception of a group of stimuli as one object. The stimuli sharing a common set of characteristics are likely to be organised as one object in perception. In addition to these, there are some factors within the perceiver that account for the organisation in perception. The past experience of the perceiver is one such factor. When you have already perceived a group of stimuli as one object, you are more likely to perceive it as the same object in future. If a child has been bitten by a dog, he perceives all dogs as dangerous and runs away at their sight. His perceptions of dog become organised in the same way. Another child who has had no such experience has a different perception of dogs. He perceives them as a companion and approaches to play with them.

Fig. 25 is perceived as a sickle by an illiterate farmer. A primary school pupil perceives the same figure as a letter in the Devanagri script. An educated Englishman will perceive the same figure as a hook attached to the lid of a jewel case. The different persons have different perceptions of the same figure becaues of the difference in their past experience.

Fig. 25

Past experience plays a very important part in the perception of persons. A child whose father is very irritable perceives his teachers also as irritable when he first comes near them. He becomes timid before them. If a person has once harmed you, you are likely to perceive him as your enemy. If the same person shows kindness to you, you suspect him. You think that he is just making a show of kindness to cheat you. You get the suspicion because you still perceive him as an enemy and not as a friend. Your present perception of the act of kindness is influenced by your past experience of the harm received from the person.

Besides past experience, there are other internal factors that influence perceptual organisation. The needs and motives of a person are such other factors. If a man is hungry, he is more likely to perceive the food objects in a shop than the dishes on which the objects are lying. The stimulations from the food object are organised as a separate object and perceived. The stimulations from the dish are mixed up with other stimuli. If a person has just had a full meal, he is more likely to perceive objects in the shop other than food objects. Let an ambiguous figure, a figure which does not present any object, be seen by a hungry person just in one glance. Ask him to describe what he saw. He is likely to report a food object, or something connected with a food object. A person who has had a full meal is less likely to see any such object.

Illusion

There is one form of perception that is called illusion. An illusion has all the characteristics of a perception. Like perception, illusion is the knowledge of an object that is before a person, here now. Like perception, therefore, illusion is not possible without the stimulation of a sense organ. Psychologically, there is no difference between illusion and perception.

It is believed that illusion is incorrect perception. In Fig. 26 A a straight line is divided into two parts.

Fig. 26

The part on the left will be perceived as longer than the part on the right. The line is perceived divided into unequal parts. In B the same line is perceived as divided into equal halves. If we actually measure the two portions of line A we will find them to be equal. But they will still be perceived as unequal. Perhaps, you will always perceive them as unequal, while you will always perceive the two divisions of line B as equal. As psychological facts the two perceptions are equally correct. The difference in the perception of the two lines, one perceived as divided into equal halves, the other perceived as divided into unequal halves, is due to the difference in the pattern of stimuli that the two figures present. We do not get the same total stimulations from the two figures. There is no wonder then that we get different perceptions of the two. We cannot call one perception as correct and the other as incorrect. As perceptions, they are both equally determined by the characteristics of the stimuli that produce the perceptions. Geometrically line A is divided into equal halves, like line B. Psychologically, as a fact of perception, the parts of line A are unequal, while those of line B are equal.

In Fig. 27 we perceive A as three staight lines joining each other at one point. They form three obtuse angles; each angle is perceived as greater than a right angle. In B the same lines are present. But they belong to a pattern which has six other lines. B is perceived as a cube or a box with its three sides visible and three sides invisible. The angles formed by the lines that are common in A and B are perceived as right angles in B. We cannot say that the second perception is false perception or incorrect perception. Since the figure is perceived as a cube, the angles formed by the lines are perceived as right angles. The perceptions of the angles are different in the two figures, because the patterns of stimuli of which they are a part are different.

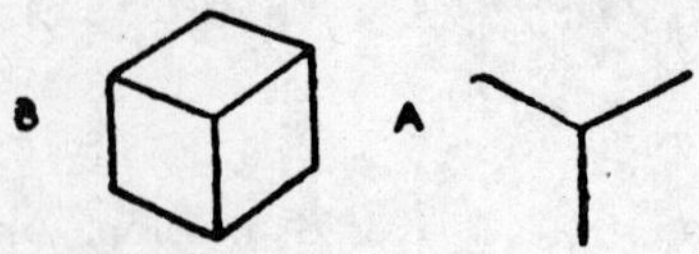

Fig. 27

In the Fig 28, at one moment you perceive an old woman; at the next moment you perceive a young lady. At one moment one set of sensory impressions are organised as one object. At another moment, another set of impressions are organised and perceived as another object. Let us now go back to the illusion of the line which is perceived as divided into unequal parts, while another line is perceived as divided into equal parts. Here too in one case one particular pattern of impressions is produced when the oblique lines are joined to the horizontal line. We perceive the horizontal line as divided into unequal parts. In the other case another pattern of impressions is produced when the vertical lines

Fig. 28

replace the oblique lines. We perceive the horizontal line as divided into equal parts. We cannot call the perception produced by one set of impressions as correct perception and the perception produced by another set of impressions as incorrect perception. This is just as we cannot say that the perception of the old woman is correct while the perception of the young lady is incorrect, or vice versa.

The above illustrations evidently show that what we call an illusion is psychologically the same as perception. The difference is due to this that in one case the perception is based upon one pattern of stimulation, in the other case it depends upon another pattern of stimulation. As psychological processes, illusions and perceptions are the same.

Following are the examples of other similar illusions :

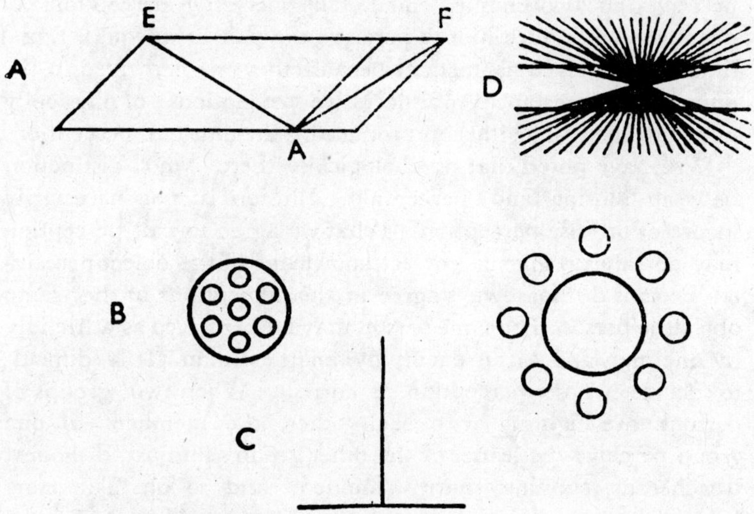

Fig. 29

In (A) line AE perceived as longer than AF, though they are of equal length. In (B) the circle on the right is perceived as larger than the circle on the left. In (C) the vertical line is perceived as longer than the horizontal line on which it stands. In (D) there are two parallel lines, they are not perceived as parallel.

The above illusions are more or less permanent illusions. The perceptions that the above figures produce usually do not undergo any change. There are other illusions which are not permanent. They do not usually occur in our experience. For example, a rope is usually perceived as a rope. But when given under unusual circumstances, like dim light, one may perceive a rope as a snake. The perception will then be called illusion. We may as well call it unusual perception. There are other cases of unusual perceptions which may be the result of unusual conditions within the perceiver. Two equal lines when shown together for comparison are likely to be perceived as equal. The same individual may first be shown different sets of two lines, one set after the other. In each set one line is longer than the other. After say, about ten pairs of such unequal lines have been shown, he is shown a pair of equal lines. He is not likely to perceive the two lines as equal. The successive perceptions of unequal lines induce him to perceive the pair as unequal. Equal lines are perceived as unequal because they are perceived in the unusual circumstances of successive perceptions of physically unequal lines. The illusion produced is an unusual perception.

We have noted that psychologically there is no distinction between illusion and perception. Illusion is not necessarily incorrect or false perception. What we agree to call perception may not always give us correct knowledge of the object perceived. Persons do not always agree in the perceptions of the same object or person. The same person may be perceived as a friendly by one man and as an enemy by another man. It is difficult to decide whose perception is correct. When two groups of persons are fighting with each other, the members of one group perceive the leader of the other group as unjust, dishonest treacherous, cunning, narrow-minded, and so on. The same leader is perceived as just, honest, truthful, considerate, sincere and all that by the members of his own group. An average Indian perceives a rat as a repugnant, harmful and inedible object. An average Japanese perceives the same object as attractive and useful for human consumption.

Our perceptions are determined by our individual needs, purposes, habits and attitudes. These are the internal factors of perceptual organisation, as we described them earlier. Some psychologist has expressed this by saying that "we perceive things not as *they* are but as *we* are". Whatever a person perceives is determined by the pattern of stimulations that he receives from the object as well as by the factors that are within him. The perception of one object may be different from the perception of another similar object because of the difference in the pattern of stimulations aroused at the moment. It will not be psychologically proper to call one perception as correct and the other as incorrect. Similarly, the same pattern of stimulations may produce different perceptions in different persons, because of the difference in the motives, beliefs, habits, and attitudes of those persons. We cannot call the perception of one person as psychologically correct and the perception of another person as incorrect or false. In psychological sense, there is no incorrect perception. The so-called incorrect perceptions, or illusions, may, in some cases, be described as unusual perceptions.

Chapter VI

LEARNING

Verbal and Motor Learning

Man learns to know about objects and persons. He also learns to act to objects and persons. In learning to know, he learns about facts, as a pupil learns history, geography, physics and chemistry. He also learns about ideas, as a pupil learns the definition of a triangle, the meaning of democracy or the concept of 'conditioned reflex'. Many things man comes to know from his own observation of facts and their relationships. But many other things he learns from other persons. Other persons inform him about many things from their own observation or knowledge of facts and ideas. Other persons have also written books which describe facts, ideas and some general principles. What a man learns from other persons or from reading books written by other persons is mostly learned through the medium of words. Words stand for objects, facts, ideas and their relations. They are signs or symbols. There are some symbols which stand only for relations between facts or ideas. These are numbers. Man learns words and numbers; these help him in learning about facts and ideas from other persons and from books. Learning of words and numbers, and of facts and ideas expressed by words and numbers, is called verbal learning. The processes by which verbal learning is done are called memorising and understanding. A pupil learns words of numbers by memorising them. He learns the ideas and relations for which the words and numbers stand by understanding them.

The pupil does not only learn words and their meaning, i.e., what they stand for, so that he can learn what is written in a book or what others teach him. He also learns to use the words in making others understand him. He learns to speak and to write. He learns to use numbers also, to work out sums and to calculate his gains and losses. Such learning is called the learning of verbal skill. Speaking, writing and mathematical work constitute verbal skills.

Learning to write does not involve only learning to use words. Before a child is able to write a word or a sentence, he has to learn to hold a pen between his fingers and move his arms and wrist in the activity of writing. At first the child has no control over these movements. Instead of proceeding from left to right in a straight line, may be, his hand moves up and down and in a zig-zag manner. The movement of the pen in his hand produces no letter or word on the paper. With practice the movement becomes steady and precise. It gets within his control and his pen moves in direction it is required to move. After some time, he learns to write a beautiful hand.

All persons may not learn to write. But all persons learn several activities that requires the movement of the arms, the legs, the fingers, the toes, and of the other parts of the body used in voluntary activities. They learn to eat, to dance, to play various types of games, to use a typewriter, to ride a bicycle, even to fly an aeroplane, and several other activities. In these activities they have to make fine movements and combinations of movements.

Learning of the activities that involve movements of parts of the body is called motor learning. Some such learning may also be called *sensory motor learning* when the movement of the body is made in relation to some sensory impressions. For example, learning to play football or learning to type. The player sees the football and his movements are directed and controlled by the sight of the football. The typist receives sense impressions from the letters on the keyboard of the typewriter. The movements of his fingers are directed and controlled by these impressions. The typist, however, controls his finger movements by the visual sensations from the keyboard only in the beginning, i.e., when he starts to learn typewriting. With practice, the visual impressions cease to have any function. The *kinesthetic sensations* produced by the movements of the fingers are sufficient. The direction of the fingers follows the cues from the kinesthetic receptors. A well-practised typist can type blindfolded when the material to be typed is just dictated by another person. In operating a large machine, the operator makes seveal types of movements like pressing a button, pushing a lever, turning a wheel, etc. He gets the direction for the various movement, i.e., when to make which movement, from several needles that are moving right or left, and several lights of different forms and colours that come and go on a disc or dial that is in front of him. We get an instance of sensory motor learning of a highly complex character in such a case. The learning involves not only a coordination between sensory response, i.e., what is seen or heard, and a motor response, i.e., what is done or manipulated, in order to run the machinery. It requires movements at fixed speeds and, sometimes, in a certain combination and order of time.

Basis of Learning

The above account shows us that learning can be broadly classified into verbal learning and motor learning. Both types of learning involve some common processes, as we will see later. Before we understand how verbal or motor learning takes place, we should know what is the basis of learning. There are a set of conditions without which learning will not be possible. One such condition is the ability to learn. There are children who are not able to read and write. They do not possess the required mental ability. They are called mentally deficient children. We say that they are of poor Intelligence. Intelligence may, thus, be described as the mental ability to learn. Some persons can learn to read and write and also understand words spoken by others, but they cannot learn to understand very complex facts and ideas, or to express them in writing and speech. We say that their intelligence is just average or below average. There are others who can learn to understand and use words signifying complex facts and ideas. They cannot, however, learn to work out other than very easy sums to understand complex mathematical problems. We say that their mathematical ability is poor. Thus, whatever one can learn depends upon his intelligence and other mental abilities. This applies mainly to verbal learning. Motor learning depends upon a person's bodily or motor ability. A person who is dumb cannot learn to speak. A child whose hand persistently shakes cannot learn to write. Another child whose toes and ankles cannot move does not have the ability to learn to dance or to play football.

Learning, as we saw, is not possible without the ability to learn. This applies both to verbal learning and motor learning. The ability to learn also sets the limit to one's learning. Two persons may start together the same learning activity, say, reading, writing, playing a new outdoor game, etc. In course of time the learning of one person may be more perfect than that of the other because the first one was superior also in the ability to learn. The limit of perfection a person can reach as a result of learning depends upon the amount of the ability to learn that the person has. Sometimes we forget this fact and expect learning of a higher order from a person of average or below average ability. We expect something, in this case, which is not possible to achieve.

Besides ability, there is another important basis of learning. Learning is not possible without effort. Unless a child makes effort to speak, he cannot learn to speak. Without making an effort to read and write, no person can learn to read and write. In some cases one may be forced to make the effort. The parent or the teacher forces the child, in the beginning, to read and write. Sometimes the effort may not be forced by outside pressure it may come from within. Hearing his elders using words for objects, the growing baby makes constant effort to learn to use words. Seeing his elder brother riding a tricycle, the youngster also makes persistent effort to learn to ride the tricycle. Aspiring to make good marks in mathematics, a pupil makes all efforts to learn complex mathematical problems and work on difficult sums. Needing more money to spend on the family, a woman makes effort to learn to type. In such cases the effort is not forced by another person. The effort comes from within. The conditions which impell a person to make effort from within are called motives, needs, urges, or drives. They move the person from within to make the effort. Desires, goals, purposes, aspirations are all internal drives or motives. They make a person apply his energy to the learning of most of the activities, skills and knowledges that he comes to learn. When a motive is at work, when a need has arisen, the process is called motivation. Motivation provides a very important basis for learning. No learning is possible without motivation. Even when a person is forced to make effort, he yields to the force because a need or motive is touched. The child is forced by its mother to read on account of the fear of losing mother's love, or for winning mother's affection. The child has a need for mother's love. Teachers often ignore the importance of motivation in learning. They do not try to relate the child's learning to his needs. The result is that they are not able to produce as much or as good learning in the child as they could.

Nature of the Learning Process

Most learning may be described as a modification of behaviour. Before learning to speak a word, the child just bables. When he learns to use words, his babling behaviour is modified. When he learns to use a sentence, his behaviour is further modified. When he tries to write, the movement of his hand becomes modified. When as a person learns to type, this is also modification of behaviour. Before he learned typing his fingers could not move with so much speed and precision.

In verbal learning the modification takes place in the person's existing knowledge of facts and ideas, and in his understanding of facts, ideas and the relations of facts and ideas. Modification occurs also in his skills in expressing facts and ideas, when he learns to use words in speaking and writing.

In motor learning the modification takes place in the number of movements made and the order in which one movement follows another movement. Before a child has learned to open a lock, he makes many movements in fitting and turning the key. These disappear when he learns to place the key in the right position and turn it in the right direction.

Besides reduction in the number of movements, motor learning also involves a modification in speed of performance. A learned activity can be performed in much less time as compared to an unlearned activity. An expert typist will type the same script in perhaps less than one-tenth of the time taken by a person who is learning to type. The reduction in speed of performance applies also to verbal learning. A well-practised reader can read the same page in perhaps less than one-fourth of the time taken by a less practised reader. Similarly, when one has learned a poem thoroughly, he will recite it from memory without a break or halting and in much less time than he would take in reciting a poem that is not well learned.

The performance of a learned activity is without any error or at least it is less erroneous than the performance of an unlearned activity. This is another modification of behaviour that results from learning. When one has practised shooting well, he less often misses his aim in comparison to a person who has started shooting. Verbal learning is also less affected by errors, if the learning is good. If a pupil has mastered the spelling of common words, his writing shows few spelling errors.

We have described learning as a modification of behaviour. But every modification of behaviour is not learning. Modification of behaviour also occurs as a result of the process of growth. This is called maturation. You cannot expect a child to raise his head, sit up, stand, walk or run soon after birth. These changes take place in his behaviour with the growth of his body and increase in the strength of the different parts of the body. They are the results of maturation. They will take place automatically in every healthy child with advance in age. They do not require much special effort on the part of the child. Even if left to himself, the child would be able to perform these activities in course of time. Learning, on the other hand, is a modification of behaviour that takes place under the influence of the environment of objects and persons in which the individual lives. The child is able to produce sounds. With the maturation of the vocal organs in his throat, he may be able to produce more different sounds. But a child will not be able to speak a language without being placed in the environment of persons speaking that language. A child will be able to move his legs and arms freely in different directions as he grows in age. But he will not be able to perform the movements in dancing without special training or without imitating another dancer. The modification of behaviour that results from maturation is natural. It is likely to be produced in whatever environment the child is placed. The modification of behaviour in learning is not natural. It depends upon the environment in which the child is placed. It is quite obvious that very few modifications in behaviour result from maturation. Most modifications of behaviour result from learning. There is another difference also. Maturation produces changes in behaviour in the early life of a person. The effect of maturation on change of behaviour is hardly noticed in the adult. But learning can take place at all stages in the life of a person. Many new activities, both motor and verbal, are learnt when one enters an occupation as an adult. In fact, learning may take place throughout the entire life of an individual.

The modification of behaviour in learning is generally gradual. It does not come about all at once. Hence practice is very important for learning. When you observe a person learning a new motor activity, you will note that the number of movements that he makes in performing the activity gradually decreases. He makes several movements at first. Many of those movements are erroneous movements, they do not contribute to success in the performance of the activity. Later on he makes less and less movements in performing the same activity. Finally, he makes very few movements and all of them are correct movements. They are the movements without which successful performance will not be possible. The time taken in performing the activity also becomes less and less from performance to performance. For example, you may observe a person learning a maze like the one given below, with his eyes closed.

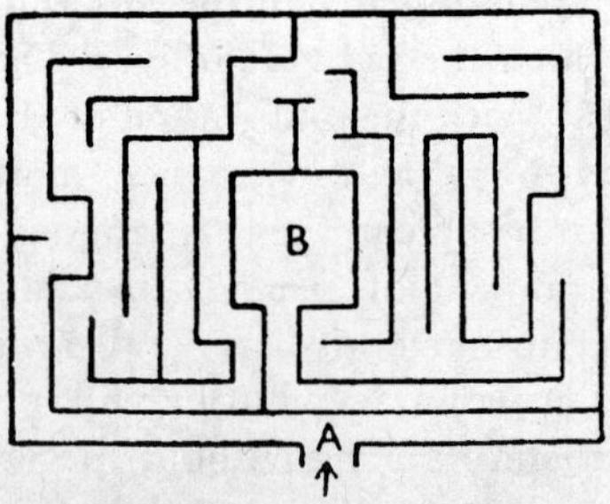

Fig. 30

Suppose this maze is made in a brass plate by cutting out the portions between the parallel lines. Such a maze is called stylus maze. The learner enters his pencil, at point A. He has to trace the correct path with his pencil till he gets in at point B. As you will see, there is only one correct path. All other paths are incorrect. They will not enable the learner to get out of the maze. These incorrect paths are called blind alleys. One gets into a similar real maze when he tries for the first time to find the way to his hotel in some large city like Calcutta, Bombay, or Delhi. While he moves on, he gets numerous crossings. From these crossings run several streets in all directions. If he turns at the right crossing and enters the right lane, he will reach his hotel without making any wrong movement. But if he makes a wrong choice, he just moves about without reaching the hotel which may be quite near. He gets into a blind alley.

When you observe someone learning a maze like Fig. 30, you will note that he makes many wrong movements at first, before he gets out of the maze. The time also taken by him in getting out is considerably long. When he makes several attempts to enter and get out of the maze, you will note the number of wrong movements that he makes decreases from trial to trial. So does the time. Ultimately, after a good number of trials, he learns to avoid all wrong movements, or blind alleys, and follows only the correct path. The total time spent, from the point of entry into the maze to the point of exit from it, also becomes considerably small. In the example of the real maze also after having gone to his hotel a number of times, one seldom makes any error in turning to the right corner and moving into the right street. He will have fully learned the path to his hotel.

Learning Curve

The entire process of learning a maze can be shown by the following figure :

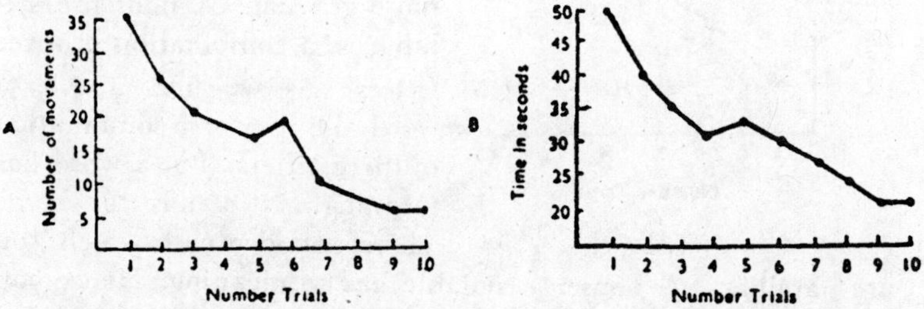

Fig. 31

In the above figures, the horizontal line shows the number of trials, from the left to the right. The vertical line shows the number of movements from 5 to 35 in A and the time in seconds from 20 to 50 in B. In the first trial the learner has made 35 movements and taken 50 seconds. In the last two trials he made only 6 movements and took only 20 seconds. The number of movements made and the time taken from trial to trial are shown by the curved lines in A and B. The lines start at the top left and gradually fall. They finally drop at the right bottom. Such a line is called a curve or graph. Because it shows the process of learning, the graph is called learning curve.

The example of the maze shows us the process of sensory-motor learning. The process of verbal learning is also, generally, as gradual as the process of motor or sensory-motor learning. You may show a person a list of twenty 3-lettered words, like F U R, P A T, M I X, B E G, etc. You show each word of the list for 2 to 4 seconds one after the other. You show the list a number of times and each time after the list is completed, you ask him to recall the words he remembers. At first, he will be able to recall only a few words correctly. In the next trial he is expected to recall more words. In this manner you will note that he would be able to recall more and more words from trial to trial. He will need several trials to recall all words correctly. He will perhaps need a few more trials if you want him to recall the words in the same order as given in the list. His process of learning may be shown by the following curve :

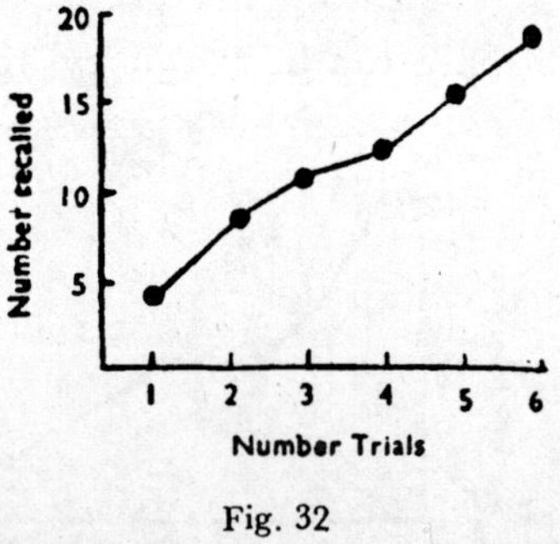

Fig. 32

If instead of learning a list of words, you ask a person to learn a list of nonsense syllables, you will find the learning to be still more gradual. A nonsense syllable is a combination of three letters. As we find above, a word also may be a combination of three letters. But a word has meaning. It stands for some object or idea with which you are familiar. A nonsense syllable has no meaning. Hence you call it nonsense—without sense or meaning. RUN is a word XUR is a nonsense syllable. It has no meaning for you. A word also may become a nonsense syllable for a person who does not know its meaning. The word PUB may be a nonsense syllable for you, if you do not know its meaning. It does not suggest to you any object or idea. There are some syllables that are not a regular word in a particular language, e.g. DAL is not an

English word. But it suggests to you the Hindi word daal (cereal). Similarly NER is not a word. But still it is not a nonsense syllable. It might suggest to a person the North Eastern Railway. If a nonsense syllable suggests anything in your experience, i.e., when it becomes associated with anything that you know, it ceases to be nonsense. It is, therefore, said that nonsense syllables have low or poor association value..

Nonsense syllables have been more often used than words in experiments on verbal learning. As a nonsense syllable has no meaning for the learner, any nonsense syllable will be as difficult for him as any other. Each will require the same amount of effort in learning. For example, you have learned the word RUN long before you learned the word FOG. When the words are given in the same list, it would be easier for you to fix RUN in your memory than FOG. But when you have two nonsense syllables like LEH and BIZ, this may not happen.

Theories of Learning

We noted above that learning is a gradual process. In motor learning there is a gradual elimination of the wrong movements from trial to trial. Finally, only the correct movement remains. The question arises, how the elimination of the wrong movements comes about. Why the same number of movements with which the learner starts is not repeated every time ? We further ask, why after some amount of practice, the right movement is alone made and no wrong movement is made ? How the right movement gets established so that after the learning is complete, whenever the activity is performed only the right movement is made ? The theories of learning attempt to answer these question.

The Trial-and-Error Theory

According to one theory, when a learner is placed in a new situation, he tries all sorts of movements that he can make in the situation. He does not know which one is likely to be the correct movement. Several movements are tried. Most of these are erroneous or incorrect movements. While making all sorts of possible movements, the correct movement is also made; the activity that is required to be performed in the situation comes to be performed. Before a child learns to fit and turn the key in a lock to open it, he makes all possible movements of his hand with the key. He thus goes on trying until accidentally the key fits into the lock and is turned the right way. The lock opens. The correct movement, or the correct response, is made by trial and error process. The theory that emphasises this trial and error process in learning is accordingly called "trial-and-error" theory of learning.

Thorndike, a well-known psychologist, illustrated the theory of trial-and-error by experiments on cats. He placed a hungry cat in a cage. The cage was locked by a latch from inside and could be opened by lifting the latch. A cup of milk was kept outside the cage. The hungry cat made all possible efforts to get out of the cage and drink the milk. It made a series of all possible movements, such as pulling the cage bars, biting and clawing them, pressing the floor, jumping, etc. While the cat was making the various movements, its paw struck against the latch and it was pushed up. The door opened. The cat ran to the cup and drank the milk. Thorndike locked the cat in the cage again and again. Every time the cat was hungry. Thorndike minutely observed and recorded all the responses made by the cat in each trial. Thorndike found that the number of movements the cat was making before it could open the door was gradually decreasing from trial to trial. After a certain number of trials, the cat made no other movements than the correct one. It easily lifted the latch and came out. Thorndike said that the cat had learned to open the cage by trial-and-error process.

It may be asked how did the cat gradually drop the erroneous movements ? Why did it not repeat all movements every time and only accidentally make the correct movement ? How and why after a certain number of trials the cat made only the correct movement ? How the correct movement became established so that in future the cat made only this movement and no other movement when locked in that cage ? Thorndike answered that all this happened because of the Law of Effect. The correct response, the lifting of the latch, produced a satisfying effect for the cat; this response enabled the cat to get out of the cage and drink the milk. The other responses the cat made produced an annoying effect. They prevented the cat from reaching the milk and drinking it. According to the Law of Effect the satisfying effect of a response strengthens the connection between that response and the stimulus that arouses the response; the annoying effect of a response weakens the connection between that response and the stimulus that arouses the response. In the case of the cat the connection between the stimulus of the latch and the response of lifting the latch was strengthened; the connection between the other movements that the animal made in response to the other stimuli within the cage were weakened. These stimuli therefore gradually failed to produce those other movements. As a result, in future the correct response was more likely to be repeated. Thorndike, thus, explained the gradual elimination of the incorrect movements by this Law of Effect. The satisfying effect of the correct response causes its repetition in future, because of the strengthening of the connection between its stimulus and the response. The annoying effect of the incorrect responses reduces the chance of their repetition in future because of the gradual weakening of the connection between these responses and their stimuli.

Thorndike adds to the law of effect also the law of exercise. A more often repeated response becomes established. A less often repeated response dies out. The law of exercise is also called the law of use and disuse. The law of effect, as we saw, explains the repetition of the correct response, and the law of exercise explains the establishment of the correct response. Similarly, the law of effect explains why the incorrect movements are not frequently repeated and the law of disuse explains why the incorrect movements are completely dropped out.

The law of exercise is a well-established principle. The part of the body which is more exercised becomes stronger than the part of the body that is less exercised. Persons who are right-handed use their right hand in doing most things. Their right hand becomes strong and active. A right-handed person will experience great difficulty in performing his day-to-day activity if his right hand is plastered on account of an injury. But if a person is left-handed, as some persons are, the injury to the right hand will cause no special difficulty. In any situation, the more used part of the body is more likely to become strong and active than the less used part of the body. We can, therefore, accept that a response that is frequently repeated is likely to become established in future; a response that is seldom or not frequently repeated, is likely to drop out.

We find that according to the trial-and-error theory, the law of effect and the law of exercise, also called the law of use and disuse, explain why the wrong movements gradually drop out and the right movements get finally fixed and established. The satisfying character of the correct movement accounts for its more frequent repetition. The annoying character of the wrong movements accounts for their less frequent repetition. The more frequent use of the correct movement, its repeated exercise, makes it more and more strongly established. The less frequent use of the wrong movements causes them to become weaker and weaker, and to be, finally, completely dropped out.

It will not be proper, however, to call this theory a *theory* of "trial-and-error". Trial-and-error is a process that can be observed in many activities of learning. Trial-and-error states a fact about the learning process. A theory attempts to explain a fact. The theory actually consists of the law of effect and the law of exercise. Law of exercise, as we noted above, is a common well-known principle. We cannot question it. But the law of effect is not accepted by all psychologists.

As we saw above, Thorndike formulated the law of effect. Thorndike himself observed in some of his experiments on learning that the satisfying effect of the correct response causes the repetition of the response. But the annoying effect of the incorrect response does not always prevent the repetition of the response. Sometimes when a pupil is punished by a teacher for a mistake in spelling, the mistake becomes strongly fixed and the pupil is more likely to repeat it in future. Punishment produces an annoying effect, but still the punished response is repeated just like the rewarded response.

Many other psychologists have tried to find out the effect of reward and punishment on learning. They have also found that punishment is less effective in producing good learning. Punishment does not stop repetition of a wrong action. Reward always has its effect on learning. Psychologists, therefore, do not recommend the use of punishment for correcting the behaviour of children. They generally agree that in order to let the child learn desirable actions reward should alone be used for good action. A wrong action should not be punished. We find, therefore, that the law of effect can only be partially accepted. A satisfying response, an action that is rewarded, is likely to be repeated. Its repetition will gradually establish it. But we cannot answer why and how the wrong response, that has an annoying effect, gets gradually eliminated.

The Conditioning Theory

Another theory of learning is so called the conditioning theory. We have referred to conditioned reflex in the chapter on Nervous System. We have seen how a new stimulus-response connection is established by pairing a new stimulus with another stimulus which could alone originally evoke a certain response. Pavlov used powdered biscuit as the original unconditioned stimulus which produced salivation in his dog. He put the powdered biscuit in the dog's mouth and also rang a bell. Later on, he first rang the bell and a little after that introduced the powdered biscuit. He increased the time interval between the sound stimulus—the bell, and the food stimulus—the biscuit. He noticed that the sound stimulus produced salivation. After a certain number of such paired administrations of the two stimuli, Pavlov presented only the sound stimulus, and every time the sound stimulus produced salivation, that is dripping of saliva from the dog's mouth. Pavlov called the original stimulus, the unconditioned stimulus, UCS, and its response the unconditioned response, UR; he called the new stimulus the conditioned stimulus, CS, and the old response, when attached to the CS, he called conditioned response, CR.

The connection between the CS and CR, the sound stimulus and the salivary response, could be established only when the UCS, the food stimulus, was also subsequently applied. The UCS was, therefore, called the reinforcing stimulus. The CS gained the strength or force from the UCS, which was paired with it, to produce the conditioned response. The paired presentation of the two stimuli could alone establish the new connection.

The conditioned reflex principle, when applied to learning of new responses, came to be called the conditioning theory of learning. We have defined learning as the modification of behaviour resulting from practice. The conditioning of a response to a stimulus which did not orginally evoke that response is also a modification of behaviour. Taking an example of conditioning at the human level, one may find that the same child who used to run to his father's doctor friend would run away from him if the doctor used, subsequently, his syringe to give injection to the child whenever he became sick. The prick of the needle produced fear reaction in the child. The face of the doctor, a frequent visitor in the family, used to attract the child and make him sit in the doctor's lap. But the same face, when paired with the piercing needle, started evoking the response of fear that was originally produced by the needle. A modification took place in the child's behaviour to the doctor.

Since, as we pointed out, the UCS was also called the reinforcing stimulus, the trials in which the UCS was also applied whenever the CS was applied, were called reinforced trials. After a number of reinforced trials the CS could evoke the CR, without being paired with the UCS. To test whether the CS was conditioned to the CR, the CS was alone applied in several other trials. When it was found in these trials that CS evoked the CR, it was thought that conditioning had taken place, and that reinforcement by presenting the UCS was no more necessary. To further test whether the conditioned response once formed would persist with the passage of time, a succession of trials, called non-reinforced trials, was again taken; the CS alone was presented, i.e., without the UCS. It was noticed that the CR became weaker and weaker. In terms of Pavlov's original experiment; the amount of saliva became less and less, and the time between the presentation of the CS and CR, called the latency of the response, also increased. Further non-reinforced trials of the CS, the sound stimulus, failed to evoke the CR, namely, the salivary response. This was called experimental extinction, i.e., the extinguishing or dying out of the stimulus-response connection, as a result of a succession of non-reinforced experimental trials. However, when after an interval of time, CS was again alone presented, the CR was evoked, though the response was weak. This was called spontaneous recovery. But if reinforcement was not done by applying the UCS, even thereafter, then this spontaneous recovery of the CR also could not take place.

The conditioning theory of learning, inspired by the work of Pavlov, was called classical or respondent conditioning. A modified and more plausible form of conditioning theory that could offer a better interpretation of learning was thought out. It was called operant conditioning or instrumental conditioning which was also originally tested on animal subjects. A rat was placed in a box called Skinner's Box after B. F. Skinner, the psychologist who divised it. The box presented a set of different stimuli to the rat, one of them was a lever. The rat was hungry and started responding to the stimuli present in the situation. Accidentally it depressed the lever and a pellet (small ball) of food was dropped from a slot. The rat reached the pellet and consumed the food. Several such trials were taken and the rat finally avoided all other stimuli; it pressed the lever which produced the food pellet. It had learned the connection between the pressing of the lever and the food pellet. The dropping of the food pellet was conditioned to the pressing of the level; it followed the response made by the rat. The conditioning was called operant, because the rat operated upon the stimuli present in the situation; it was actively manipulating the situation. The conditioning was also called instrumental, becanse the lever served as an instrument for obtaining the food object. The food pellet was called the reinforcing or rewarding stimulus, because it strengthened the lever pressing response and weakened the response to the other stimuli present in the situation. These responses were gradually eliminated. We will notice that Thordike also used a similar situation, namely, the cage which his cat manipulated by making all possible kinds of responses, one of which resulted in lifting the latch and opening the door of the cage, so that the cat could reach the cup of milk. The cup of milk was the reinforcing stimulus which strengthened the latch lifting response of the cat. But the principle of reinforcement did not occur to Thorndike and he thought of the law of effect, the satisfying or the dissatisfying effect of the correct response.

The reinforcement that produced the learning was classified into positive and negative ones. The reinforcement was positive if it strengthened the response that could result in the appearance of the rewarding or reinforcing stimulus. It was negative if it prevented the response or led to the avoidance of a punishing stimulus. For example, a rat is placed in a maze having two alternative paths. One path has its floor covered with electric wires and produces electric shock to the rat passing through it. The rat learns, after a number of trials, to avoid, on reaching the choice point, the path producing electric shock. The shock producing electric wire became a negative reinforcer, i.e., a punishing stimulus which followed the rat's entering the shock producing path. A positive reinforcer, thus, is the response produced stimulus which strengthens the response; a negative reinforcer is the response-produced stimulus which weakens and, in the long run, prevents the occurrence of the response.

The operant or instrumental conditioning theory offers to explain the more natural process of learning. Learning is the acquisition of a new response by the learner's own effort. In classical conditioning the animal or human being remains altogether passive; it is the experimenter who presents both the unconditioned and the conditioned stimuli. The response produced cannot be treated as an activity performed by the animal; it is just a passive reaction. In instrumental conditioning, the learning is the result of the learner's own activity. He manipulates the environment in which he is placed. His own manipulation results in the appearance of the rewarding stimulus, the stimulus that can satisfy his personal need of the moment. In classical conditioning the response is evoked; in operant conditioning it is emitted, i.e., it involves the learners own action.

The Insight Theory

Another theory of learning is the so-called Insight Theory. According to this theory, the learner perceives the relationship of a movement, or response, to his goal, or the end result of the activity. He perceives this response as different from those that are not related to the goal. These other responses are left out for this reason.

The insight theory was first suggested by Kohler, a Gestalt psychologist. Kohler did some experiments on a chimpanzee. A banana was placed outside the cage and two sticks were kept in the cage. No one was long enough to reach the banana. The chimpanzee tried to pull the banana by using one of the two sticks. He tried in vain this or that stick. He then started playing with the sticks. Accidentally, the narrow end of one stick got fitted into the hollow of the broad end of another stick. The two sticks were thus joined to form one stick. The monkey tried to reach the banana with the joined sticks and pulled it in. He perceived the two sticks in this new relationship. He got insight. The two sticks and the banana were perceived as one related unit. They formed one unified pattern. In future, he would join two sticks to pull in an object not within the reach of one stick. He, thus, learned to use the two sticks for pulling in the banana. He stopped to use one stick alone for the purpose.

In another experiment, a chimpanzee learned to pile up three boxes, one above the other, and reach a banana hanging from the roof of its cage. Before he learned the trick, the chimpanzee made unsuccessful attempts to reach the banana by jumping from the floor. He, however, came to perceive the relationship of the boxes to one another and to the goal, namely, reaching the banana. In future the monkey used the boxes for the purpose. The boxes, piled on each other, and the hanging banana became the interrelated elements of a whole perception.

The above experiments show how insight or perception of relation between the elements of a situation and the goal plays an important part in learning. But insight cannot account for all the facts about learning. If the insight theory of learning is accepted, once the learner comes to perceive the new relationship between some elements of the situation and his goal, he should never make an error in reaching the goal. He should always make only the correct responses. The erroneous responses should be eliminated all at once. If such were the case learning would not be a gradual process. Once the correct response is made in a single performance of the activity, this response should come to have a new meaning for the learner. This response should alone be repeated by him in future, since this response is alone perceived as related to the goal. But the fact is that learning, in most cases, is a gradual process. The wrong responses are not dropped all at once.

In order to explain the learning process, we must accept the fact that trial-and-error does take place in learning many activities. We must also acknowledge that trial-and-error does not always take place in learning an activity. It is not, therefore, the essential feature of learning, though quite a common fact about the learning process. For example, a person may minutely observe the movements made by another person in performing an activity that the other person has learned. He may understand the relationship that these movements bear to each other, how one movement leads to another movement, and, finally, to the end result. He may then perform the activity in the manner he has observed. He may not make any error. He may practise the activity a number of times and thus learn the activity. This type of learning takes place in what is called supervised training. In supervised training, the learner has less chance of making errors. He gets a demonstration of the activity and is made to understand the significance of the movements required to perform the activity. He gets insight into the interrelation of these movements and of their relation to the goal of the activity. Supervisory training is the most economical and the most effective method of learning any activity.

To avoid the risk of trial-and-error process, a complete direction for using the machine is always supplied with any delicate machine. The direction explains the functions of the parts of the machine, the manner in which the parts are to be operated, and so on. For this purpose, generally a diagram of the machine and of its several parts is also provided. The directions are explained through the diagram. By carefully reading and understanding the directions, with the help of the diagram, one can operate the machine without making any error. By repeating the same operations a number of times, one learns to operate the machine without looking at the direction or the diagram. Such detailed directions are supplied to prevent learning by trial-and-error. In fact, the process of trial-and-error might cause serious damage to the machine in the very first trial.

We must, further, accept that practice is very important for learning. Only by practice, one gets mastery over an activity. Insight and understanding help learning, but practice establishes the learned activity. Practice is not mere repetition. It is intelligent repetition. One should understand the significance of the various movements one has to make in performing the activity, while one is repeating these movements for practice. This is meant by intelligent repetition. The significance of the movements can be understood in relation to the goal of the activity, the end-result that is to be accomplished. An effective learning must be goal-directed learning. It is the goal of the activity that gives special meanings to the movements that lead to the goal. Only when they are viewed in relation to the goal, these movements are perceived as correct movements. But the meaning of a movement, its significance for the goal, is not to be appreciated all at once. At first the meaning is vague. The relationship that the correct movement has to the goal is not definite. Hence the incorrect movements also take place with the correct movement. By repetition the meaning becomes more and more clear. Ultimately, the correct movement is clearly perceived as leading to the goal. It comes to have a feature distinct from the incorrect movement. Hence, learning is, generally, a gradual process.

Importance of Learning

Learning is the most important characteristie of human behaviour. Man is distinguished from other animals by his unlimited capacity for learning. Man can learn very complex activities. Man can also learn a very great variety of activities. Nature has, accordingly, provided man with the longest period for learning. The newly born child starts with a few simple activities. But he acquires in the course of his journey to adulthood a great multitude of very complex patterns of behaviour. What the adult learns gives him the main power to perform his functions and duties as an adult. These are his most important resources for solving the manifold problems that he has to face in life.

A completely learned behaviour becomes a habit. Habits make the matter of adjustment to the conditions of life very simple and easy. Once an activity forms into a habit, it takes place without any effort whenever an appropriate situation arises. A habit can be performed without any attention given to it. Many of our day-to-day activities that are so essential for life are performed habitually. We are not required to make an effort for them, or to apply our thought to them. We do not care for them, they take care of themselves. Once the habit is performed, the habitual action follows spontaneously and smoothly. We are not required to exert our will to perform it. The habit moves us from within. You form a habit of walking in the evening. The habit moves you to do the walking, even if some day you feel attracted by some activity at home. Sometimes one may perform a habitual action even without being conscious of it. If man could not form habits, he could perform very little. Every action would have demanded on his part careful observation, concentrated attention, effort and will. In such a case only a few actions would have exhausted his physical and mental energy.

What we call character is an organisation or habits a person has formed. A man is said to be of good character, because all his actions are habitually directed towards desirable goals and purposes. His habits are good habits. In whatever situation he is placed, his habits would lead him to act in the desirable manner. No greed or temptation would induce him to act otherwise. The more established and firm his habits are, the stronger his character will be. A person is of weak character, if his desirable habits are not well established. He may then fall a victim to temptation. He may then sometimes act contrary to his habits. He has a set of good habits, a set of learned patterns of behaviour. But the learning is not perfect. His good habits, at times, fail to impel him strongly towards desirable goals. A man of bad character has few good habits. Most of his established patterns of behaviour are directed towards undesirable goals. They compel him to act in an undesirable manner.

Formation of desirable habits is essential for the formation of good character. Parents and teachers should give special attention to this matter. If they allow some bad practices in a child with the idea that they may not be as bad for a child, the practice will form by repetition into a habit. It will be difficult then to change the habit at a later stage. Some parents think their child to be clever when the child bluffs other children or adults. They are happy about it because they think that after all the bluffing of a child does not matter; it does nobody any harm. But the child may form a habit of bluffing and become, as an adult, a condemned swaggerer and cheat. Habits are man's great asset. But habits may also become a great liability. Desirable habits are assets and one should try to build up his assets. Bad habits are liabilities. They overpower the individual and drive him into undesirable directions even against his will.

Conditions of Learning

There are certain conditions that influence learning. One such condition is the meaningfulness of what is tried to be learned. A material that is meaningless requires more effort in learning than a material that is meaningful. Words are more easily learned than non-sense syllables. One aspect of meaningfulness is relatedness. Materials that belong together are more easily learned. For example, a paragraph which describes a common theme is more easily learned than a paragraph whose sentences describe unrelated facts. It is, therefore, easier to memorize a written passage by grasping the main idea or fact contained in the passage. The other parts of this passage would hang together around this 'central' point. Learning without the help of meaning is called cramming or rote memory. This is more difficult and more time consuming than learning with understanding. Another important condition of learning is interest. We have earlier talked about the importance of motivation in learning. Motivation varies in degrees. It may be high or low. The higher the motivation, more spontaneous will be the effort made for learning. The learning will be a pleasure. If the motivation is low, one has to force himself to make the effort. The learning will then be an unpleasant task. Motivation is high if one is learning something that one likes. One applies himself without any special effort to an interesting task even when the task is difficult. If, on the other hand, one engages in a task that is uninteresting to him, he has to force himself to perform and learn the task. The task may be quite easy. Being uninteresting, it causes a good deal of strain to the individual. Interest is, therefore, another important condition of learning.

Interest is related to ability. If one has the ability to learn a task, he will develop interest in the task. He will begin to like it. The performance of the task will provide him the experience of success. Experience of success is pleasing to the individual. If the task is beyond the ability of a person, he will develop dislike for it. It makes him meet with failure and disappointment. His learning of the task will be poor. A task that matches with the ability of a person produces interest in him and its learning becomes easier.

One can develop interest in a task by relating the learning to his needs, goals and purposes. A person accepts a job that brings him more wages. In the beginning he may not like the duties he has to perform. Gradually he develops interest in the job. Working on the job, he can live more comfortably by being able to spend more money. A doctor chooses to reside in a remote village with the object of doing public service. At first he may have no liking for the place and for the people living there. But because his stay in the village satisfies his goal of service, gradually he begins to like the rural environment.

Learning is also influenced by such incentives as material reward, praise, or admiration. Children learn their lesson better if they hope to get a reward on accomplishing the learning. Similarly, appreciation by the elders, or praise for good work, results in better learning. Punishment does not influence learning to the same extent as reward does. We noticed this when discussing learning theory. In some cases, punishment has just the reverse effect. Mild expression of disapproval or mild criticism improves learning. But the improvement is less when the disapproval is shown, or the criticism made, in the presence of others. Sense of competition too has a desirable effect on learning. The urge to excel others in a task makes some persons exert more effort in the task. Their learning becomes more efficient.

Methods of Learning

For learning any written material, one may have to read it a number of times. One way of doing this is to learn the material by parts. One may read a sentence, or couple of sentences, a good number of times till they have been fully learned. He may then pass on to another sentence and read and re-read it. In this manner one may complete the entire passage by reading and re-reading it bit by bit. The entire passage is thus divided into parts and each part is learned separately. The other way is to read the entire passage repeatedly till it is fully learned. This is called the *whole* method of learning. The *whole* method is found to be generally better than the *part* method. The *whole* method requires less time and less effort to learn the material.

One may read a passage a number of times, understanding the content as he proceeds. After having given several repetitive readings, he may stop and find that he is able to reproduce what he read. This is called passive reading. On the other hand, after every reading, one may turn his eyes from the passage and try to recite from memory what he has read. In doing so, he strains himself to recite or recapitulate as much as possible. He may then look at the passage and see how much he has been able to recite correctly and where he has made a mistake. He may then give a second reading and follow the same procedure. This is called active learning, or learning by the method of recitation. This active method is to be preferred to the passive method. The active method takes less time and less effort to learn. Within the same time, one can learn much more by the active method than by the passive method. The learning is also better.

If you have to learn something by practising it a number of times, take a short rest after some practice. In this manner, let a set of repetitions be followed every time by a little rest. This method of learning is called distributed learning or spaced learning. You get similar instance of spaced learning when instead of reading without any break, say, for three hours, you take short breaks of, say, 13 minutes, after each hour. If you go on practising until you have learned the task, without taking any rest, or go on reading for three or four hours without any break, the learning will be called massed learning. The distributed learning method has proved to be better than the massed learning method. In some cases, the spaced learning may require less total time than the massed learning. Even when distributed learning takes as much time as massed learning, the rest pauses in distributed learning keep the learner fresh and able to work longer. While studying for long hours, it is useful to take some rest at intervals. One may have a 15 minutes rest after studying for an hour and then start his studies again.

Strength of Learning

A learning is strong when the learned material can be long retained and better remembered. On the other hand, the learning is weak if the material learned is soon forgotten. It is thus possible to think of degrees or strengths of learning. If you do not learn something perfectly, that is, you still make some error in reproducing what you are trying to learn, your learning is weak. It is also called partial learning. For example, you are trying to memorize a list of 15 nonsense syllables. After say, five successive learning trials, you find that you can correctly reproduce 10 syllables from the list. Your learning is partial. Its strength is 66 per cent. You have learned two-thirds of the list. You have not been able to learn the remaining one-third. Supposing, after the seventh trial you are able to reproduce 13 out of the 15 syllables and after one more trial, i.e., eight trials, you are able to reproduce all fifteen correctly. Your learning will then be called simple learning. It may also be called perfect learning since you have been able to reproduce the list completely and there is no imperfection or error. The strength of the learning is 100 per cent. If you continue the learning trials further, say for four other trials, every time perfectly reproducing the whole list, your learning will be called over-learning. The strength of the learning will be 150 per cent. You have given half as many more trials as were needed for simple learning or perfect learning. Perfect learning was achieved in 8 trials. You have given 4 additional trials. The strength of perfect learning being 100 per cent, the strength of the over-learning becomes 50 per cent more than that, or 150 per cent. What is over learned is retained longer and remembered better than what is simply learned. Over-learning, thus, is to be considered as a condition of efficient learning. In studying any book, the student should not be satisfied when he finds that he is able to recapitulate all the essential points. He should give a few more readings. He will have over-learned the book material. His learning will be strong. He will not forget for long what he has learned. To gain a mastery over what you are learning, over-learning often becomes essential.

Transfer of Training

When one learns a task, the learning may influence his performance or learning of another task. For example, having learned Arithmetic in school, the pupil can correctly calculate the change he should get on buying things. The learning of addition and subtraction enables one to learn multiplication and division. The influence of learning one task on the performance or learning of another is called transfer of training. The improvement in the performance of a task that results from the learning is not confined to the task alone. It is transferred or carried over to other tasks as well. Learning of Arithmetic is transferred to the learning of Algebra. Learning of Geometry helps in solving problems in Trigonometry. Similarly, having learned one language, a person can learn another language with greater ease. The test of good training is the amount of transfer that the learning can produce.

We have considered above the ease and facility in performing or learning another after having learned one task. This is called positive transfer or habit facilitation. Sometimes the learning of one task creates difficulty in performing or learning another task. Having learned to pronounce BUT correctly, the child finds it difficult to pronounce PUT correctly. Similarly, having first learned to spell PALE, he experiences difficulty in spelling TAIL correctly. He encounters the difficulty because of what is called negative transfer or habit interference. A child may form the habit of learning his lesson by rote memory, without any understanding. If you subsequently try to train him to learn by understanding, he experiences difficulty. The habit of memorizing without understanding interferes with the formation of the new habit, namely, the habit of learning by understanding.

Chapter VII

REMEMBERING AND FORGETTING

Retention

You do not remember at this moment all that you learned in your school days. Many things you have forgotten. For example, if you are not doing mathematics now as your subject of study, perhaps, you have forgotten much of what you learned in Geometry. But you may not have forgotten all. Certain things you may still remember. What you remember you are said to have retained. What you have forgotten, you have not retained. Retention is the condition in which what we have learned exists before we try to recall it. It is difficult to describe the nature of retention. We may suppose that what is learned leaves its after-effect in memory. This after-effect has been called the memory trace. The after-effect may be some modification in the central nervous system. When we learn something, a change is produced in the central nervous system. This change persists in the form of the memory trace. When we remember what we have learned, the memory trace is revived. What we retain is the memory trace. When we forget what we had learned, it means we do not retain its memory trace. The memory trace has died out. It is no more there.

Recall and Recognition

We can know what we have retained and what we have not retained by trying to reproduce or recall what we once learned or experienced. Recall is, thus, a test of retention. In experiments on remembering and forgetting, one is first made to learn something. After sometime has passed, he is asked to recall what he had learned. If he recalls what he had learned, we say that he has been able to retain all that he had learned. His memory is said to be perfect. If he does not recall all, but only a part, we say that he remembers only that much; the rest he has forgotten. He has not been able to retain it. His memory is said to be imperfect; his retention is called poor.

Recall is a test of retention. But it is quite possible that one may not be able to recall what one had learned, but he may still be retaining it. The retention may be poor; the memory trace may be weak. In such a case, we use another test of retention. If a person cannot recall what he had learned, but he is still retaining it, he should be able to recognise it. Recognition is, thus, another test of retention. You may have learned the English word 'banquet' as standing for a word in your mother tongue. After sometime, the word in your mother tongue is given and you are asked to recall the English word for it. If your retention for the English word is weak, you may not be able to recall it. But if the same word is presented with some other words, you recognise it as standing for the word in your mother tongue. You are able to do so, because you retained the memory of the word. That is why you could recognise the English word as known to you, as standing for the word in your mother tongue. Recognition is, thus, easier than recall. One may be able to recognise what he cannot recall.

When the recall test is given, what is to be recalled is not presented before the person. When the recognition test is given, what was learned, or experienced in the past, is again presented to the individual. He identifies it as having learned it before, or having experienced it in the past. Recall takes place in the absence of what was learned or experienced in the past. Recognition takes place in the presence of what was earlier learned or experienced also in the past. Recognition is the awareness of an object or situation as having been known to the person. If the memory of what was learned or known previously is completely lost, recognition will not be possible. It is possible because the memory trace is still retained. If the memory trace is very weak, if retention is poor, recall may not be possible but recognition may still be possible. Thus if what has been previously learned can neither be recalled, nor can it be identified as having been known when it is again presented to the individual, retention may be supposed to be completely lost.

Relearning

Besides recall and recognition, there is still another test of retention. This is called relearning. One had learned something which he is not able to recall at the moment. He tries to learn it again. It will be found that he would be able to relearn it with less effort and in less time. When he originally learned it, he had to make more effort or devote more time. He is able to relearn it more easily because he had not completely forgotten it. The memory trace was there, but it was not strong enough. So, recall was not possible. But the relearning was easier because the memory trace had not completely died out. For example, you may not have read Geometry for all these years. You try to recall a particular theorem now. You may not succeed. But when you consult the book and try to learn the theorem again, you are able to do it much easily and quickly. Had you completely forgotten the theorem, you might have required as much effort and time to relearn it as you needed when you learned it for the first time. Take another example. A person learns a list of nonsense syllables so that he can correctly reproduce the entire list. Suppose, he needed 10 trials to be able to do this. After a week, you ask him to recall the list. It is quite possible that he is not able to reproduce correctly a single item. His recall is zero. You make him learn the list again. You find that he is able to learn the entire list in 6 trials. This time he has taken 4 trials less. This is possible because he had not completely forgotten what he had learned. But the retention was poor; the memory trace was weak. So, he could not recall a single item correctly. However, he needed less trials; there was a saving of 4 trials, because the memory trace had not completely died out, retention had not completely gone. Had he needed 10 trials also for the relearning, we could conclude that he had completely forgotten what he had learned; that there was no retention. Relearning is, thus, another test of retention. When retention is weak recall may not be possible, but relearning may be possible with less effort or without much practice. There may be a saving in the time and the effort. When there is no saving, when the relearning requires as much effort and time as the first or original learning, one can conclude that there was complete loss of retention.

Curve of Forgetting

Forgetting is due to the loss of what is retained after learning. We have called it the memory trace. But the memory trace is not lost all at once. The loss is gradual. The memory trace becomes weaker and weaker with the passage of time, if no effort is made to revive it in the meantime. Hence, recall is better when the time interval between learning and recall is not long. If it is long, recall is poor. A person learns a list of nonsense syllables so that he is able to correctly reproduce each syllable from memory. You ask him to recall the list after two hours. Perhaps, he will fail to recall one or two syllables only. The person learns another similar list. He is asked to recall it after a day. He will fail to recall many more syllables from this list. In this way he may learn other similar lists and he may be required to recall each one after still longer intervals, one list after a week, another after a fortnight, and still another after a month. You may compare the number of syllables he was able to recall from the different lists. You will notice that with longer interval between the learning and the recall, there is less recall and more forgetting. A curve of forgetting, like the following one, can be plotted to illustrate the relation between amount of forgetting and length of time interval.

We find that time is an important factor in remembering and forgetting. We may frame a general rule, namely, the older an experience the weaker is memory. We will see later that this rule does not hold in all cases. There are also other factors in remembering and forgetting.

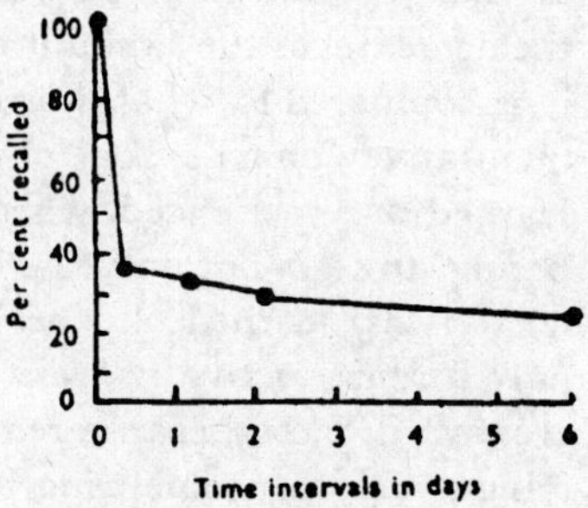

Fig. 33

Constructive Functions of Memory

Forgetting is shown not only by the gradual decrease in the amount of what can be recalled. It may also be shown by a change in the content of what is recalled. One may read a short story several times. He may be then asked to write from memory what he has read. If he has learned the story well, his writing from memory will tally with the contents of the story. All the facts and ideas that are there in the story will be correctly reproduced in his writing. He may be asked to write the story again from memory after an interval of, say, a fortnight. His writing may then be compared with the original story. You may notice that some facts and ideas have been left out, because he has forgotten them. But you may also notice that some facts, ideas, and descriptions of facts, have been modified and added. Thus the recall of the story contains not only a smaller number of the facts and ideas from the original story. It also shows some new facts and ideas substituted for some original facts and ideas. Similar changes in memory take place when you narrate some event before a person and the listener narrates the same event to another person. The narration made by the listener is likely to differ not only in the number of the facts and ideas that the listner fails to recall while narrating the event to the other person. It may differ also in several facts and ideas that the listener might modify or add. He may not modify or add them knowingly. He may, on the other hand, believe that he has correctly narrated all that you told him. Forgetting is, thus, indicated not only by the decrease in the amount or quantity of what is recalled when it is compared to what was learned. It is indicated also by a qualitative change, or change in the content, of what was learned or experienced, when one is trying to recall it. Remembering, thus, is not only the correct recall or reproduction of what was learned or experienced in the past. Memory is not only a reproductive process. Memory is also a constructive or creative process, because remembering is also a process of modifying or adding something new to what was learned or experienced in the past.

The constructive function of memory is very well illustrated in the spread of rumours. As we know, rumours are usually untrue; what a rumour says is not a fact. But a rumour generally starts from a fact; it has a basis in fact. For example, the police might try to disperse an unruly crowd by using force. About a dozen persons from the crowd might receive mild injuries. A person might have been observing what happened and he narrates it to another person who was not present. The listner narrates the event to a third person whom he meets after a little while. He tells the person that quite a large number from the crowd received serious injuries and that the condition of quite a few was serious. This third person meets a fourth person and tells him that over a hundred persons received very serious injuries and some persons died in the hospital. The rumour might spread all over the town, undergoing constant change from mouth to mouth. A representative of some newspaper might report that a serious clash took place in the town between a mob and the police. Many persons were killed and a very large number received serious injuries.

Causes of Forgetting

As we saw above, time is an important factor in forgetting. What is learned or experienced is forgotten with the lapse of time. But besides time, there are also several other causes of forgetting.

We may not be able to recall an experience because of the interference caused by another experience. Generally one does not have a difficulty in recalling the names of places that are well known to him. Suppose you know very well the names of the following places :

Lalpur, Qaisarbagh, Kishunganj, Pachchim Darwaja, Bania Pokhar.

You can easily recall the name of each one when you are required to do so. Suppose, besides Lalpur, you well know the names of the following places also: Lalbagh, Lalgunj, Laldarwaza, Lalpokhar.

While talking to a friend you like to tell him something about Lalpur. But you may find difficulty in recalling the name of the place. You seem to have forgotten it, but you feel sure that you remember it quite well. Or you may incorrectly recall the name of one of the above places and know that your memory is not correct. The failure to recall the correct name is due to a confusion between the names. At a later time you may be able to recall the correct name. Sometimes, therefore, we may retain the memory of an object or event, but still cannot correctly recall it. At the time of recall, more than one memory trace may be revived and, thus, create confusion. A person may then fail to recall what he intends to recall. Hence some forgetting may be due to the fact that what we learn or experience at one time interferes with what we have learned or experienced previously. Similarly, sometimes what we have learned previously interferes with the memory of what we learn afterwards.

The loss of memory produced by interference may be illustrated also in another way. Suppose, you play table-tennis for an hour after memorizing a list of nonsense syllables. You then try to recall the list. On another day you memorize another list of nonsense syllables and sleep for an hour. When you are awake, you try to recall the list. On a third day, you memorize still another list of nonsense syllables. After that, you memorize a fresh list for an hour and then try to recall the previous list. When you compare the number of syllables you were able to recall correctly on the three days, you are very likely to find that you have recalled correctly the largest number on the day you slept after the learning. The next in order of number correctly recalled will be on the day you played table-tennis. The smallest number of correct recall will be on the third day. When you went to sleep, you had no experience that could interfere with the memory of what you had learned. On the other hand, when you learned another list after learning a similar list, the interference was the maximum. The memories of the two lists became mixed up with each other and so there were more errors in recall. There was less interference when you played table-tennis, because the activity you performed was very different from the memorizing of nonsense syllables.

We find from the above examples that similar experiences when they follow each other produce more interference than dissimilar experiences. Our new experiences are, generally, not very different from the old ones. Forgetting is, therefore, produced not only by the length of the time that passes after what we learn or experience. It is produced also by the other experiences that fill up the time.

Feelings and emotions also influence what we remember or forget. A happy event is generally remembered. One is likely to forget his unpleasant experiences. But one is more likely to forget what is neither pleasant nor unpleasant. We observe and do so many things that produce no feelings in us. Generally we do not remember them. One may meet a person in the street whom he often meets and may talk to him. After sometime he may forget about the meeting or what he talked about. But if one meets a person after a very long time and feels happy at the reunion, he is likely to remember the meeting. Similarly, if one meets a person in the street and that person starts a quarrel with him, then too he is very likely to remember the meeting. A person may try to recall the experiences of his childhood. He will notice that most of his recalled experiences will be either those that he had enjoyed or those that caused him pain and suffering.

Emotions influence remembering in still another manner. If you are emotionally disturbed, your memory begins to fail. A pupil may be very much afraid of a teacher. When in the presence of that teacher, the pupil may not be able to recall what he remembered quite well. The fear of the teacher blocks his memory. A pupil may perfectly memorize a poem for reciting it in a school function. But when he stands up for the recitation, his memory fails. He becomes nervous to find the audience looking at him. He becomes emotionally disturbed. Similarly, some students have a fear of examinations. They become nervous in the examination and forget even those things that they had learned quite well.

A several emotional shock may sometimes cause one to forget all things about his past life. A person may be involved in a serious accident and may remain unconscious for sometime without being physically hurt. When he returns to consciousness, he may forget all about the accident. Sometimes he may forget his own name, his home, and his relations. In such cases, the memory is not actually lost. The memory becomes unconscious. It cannot be revived; if the memory is revived, it will again produce mental shock and create emotional disturbance. The forgetting in such cases serves a purpose of the individual. It prevents the recurrence of the shock. For this reason, some psychologists call forgetting an active process. (Certain experiences are forgotten not because they fade out in course of time, or other memories interfere with their recall. They are forgotten because their revival would cause mental shock to the person. It would make him emotionally upset). He would be prevented from giving his attention to his normal duties. In an emotional condition one cannot act in the manner he should in order to achieve his purposes. He cannot make adequate adjustment to the situations of his day-to-day life. We will understand this point better when we discuss emotions in a later chapter.

The active nature of forgetting is illustrated also in some cases of temporary forgetting. You may get invitation to dinner from a person whom you really do not like. Outwardly you pretend to like him and, therefore, you decide to go for the dinner. You forget the date of the dinner and so find a good excuse for not attending. The forgetting may surprise you because you are reminded of the date after the dinner is over. The forgetting has fulfilled your real wish, namely, not to go for the dinner. It has served a purpose for you. Sometimes while visiting a friend whose company you value very much, you wish to prolong your stay with him. But you have to decide to leave in order to attend to some important work. You forget to take your umbrella with you. You return to him after finishing the work, or again visit him in the evening, in order to pick up your umbrella. The forgetting makes it possible for you to visit him again.

Our personal needs also determine what we remember and what we forget. A student needs to succeed in examination. He reads the text-books and learns the facts and ideas stated and described in the text-books. He remembers them and answers in the examination the questions set on them. But soon after the examination he forgets most of what he learned. He does not need to remember them any more. Another student reads his text-books to learn new facts and ideas. His reading and learning serve the need for knowledge. He also takes the examination, like the first student. But he is likely to remember many things that he read even long after the examination. A doctor needs to remember the name of medicines. He has to prescribe them to his patients. Tell him the name of a new medicine and also of a new place. After sometime, test his memory for the two names. He will be able to recall the name of the medicine, but it is quite likely that he will forget the name of the place.

Interests also determine remembering and forgetting. Interests are related to needs. Generally, one is interested in objects, persons, and activities that satisfy his needs. He is indifferent to those matters that are not connected with his needs. A doctor needs to earn in order to pay for his living and for his family. He also needs to be known as a good doctor. Besides these, some doctors develop the need to help other by curing their illness and reducing their suffering. For all this it is necessary that a doctor should know the names and effects of medicines. He, naturally, develops interest in knowing about medicines. His interest causes him to remember about them. A social worker is interested in names of persons and places. His need to serve people living under different conditions and in different places produces his interest in all matters connected with the need. He may have better memory for names of persons and places. His memory for the names of medicines will be poor.

To remember anything well, one should develop interest in it. To have a good memory for all types of things is a very rare exception. Generally, one has a good memory for those kinds of things in which he is strongly interested. If a student has interest in history, his memory for dates and events is likely to be good. On the other hand, if he reads history without much interest in the subject, his memory for dates and events will be poor. In order to improve one's memory for any subject matter, it is necessary to develop interest in the subject. A good teacher creates interest in the subject that he teaches. His students are better able to remember what he teaches. A poor teacher cannot create interest. His students soon forget what he teaches.

Forgetting may also be caused by injury to the brain. As we mentioned earlier, when you learn something, the learning produces a modification in the central nervous system. This modification we called 'memory trace'. In the chapter on Nervous

System, we talked about the association area of the cerebral cortex. The modifications take place in this area of the cortex. When this area of the brain, or even a part of it, is damaged, the memory trace is lost. A brain injury, therefore, may produce considerable loss of memory.

Chapter VIII

IMAGINATION

Nature of Imagination

One perceives objects or persons that are before him and are, thus, stimulating his sense organs. He becomes aware of them as real objects or persons. One recalls the memory of objects or persons that are not before him, that he is not perceiving now and here. When one recalls the memory of objects or persons, experienced in the past, then too he becomes aware of them. But he does not become aware of them as real objects in the same sense as he becomes aware of a real object or a real person when he perceives the object or person. You may perceive a horse standing before you. After the horse has left, someone may ask you whether it was a horse or a donkey. You take help of your memory and tell that it was a horse. At the moment you are telling this the horse is not before you. You are not perceiving it. What you have is an image of the horse which is different from your image of a donkey. What you are aware of is the image of the horse and not the real horse stimulating your sense organs.

What we remember we become aware of as images that stand for our past experiences. We may also become aware of another type of images. These do not stand for our past experiences. You ask a person to think of a horse that has wings, or of a fish that has a woman's face. Quite possibly he will have the image of a winged horse, or of the mermaid. He may also be able to describe his image. The image may be quite clear and distinct. But the image does not stand for an object that he had actually perceived. He has perceived a horse; he has perceived the wings of a flying bird. But he never perceived a real horse with real wings attached to its body. The image of the winged horse is, therefore, different from the image of the horse, and the image of the wings. The latter are called *memory images*. They stand for our past experiences. The image of a winged horse or that of a mermaid is *not a memory image.* It does not stand for past experience. You have never been aware of it as a real object. When you are aware of images that do not stand for past perceptions, you are said to *be imagining*. The process of having such images is called *imagination.*

In imagination also you may have memory images. But the memory images are placed in a new relationship. The separate images stand for objects or persons actually perceived. But they are combined in a manner that can never be noticed in per ception. Imagination is, thus, creative. It makes us aware of objects, persons, activities or situations that were never perceived by us by creating their images. When one writes a novel or a story, his imagination is at work. The characters that are presented are not real. They have never been perceived by anybody. If you visit a new country and write about the people of that country, the account that you give is the work of your memory. But suppose you write about the people that live in the moon. Your account will be the work of your imagination. Art, poetry, drama, and novel are the creations of imagination.

Fig. 34

Look at B in Fig. 34. If I ask you what you perceive, you will say that you see a bat's drawing. Now look at A. When I ask you to describe what you perceive, you will say that you do not perceive any definite object. The first figure is the picture of a real object that you might have perceived several times before. The second figure does not stand for any real object that you have perceived earlier. I ask you, does the figure suggest anything to you ? You may answer that it suggests the picture of a bat, a butterfly, a duck, a mosquito, a flying devil, etc. You say all this from your imagination. You are not actually perceiving the objects that you report. The figure does not correspond to your actual perception of those objects. You are imagining the objects. Your actual perception of the figure will be that of an ink-blot that has been smeared over the surface of the page. Similar ink-blots have been used in tests of imagination. They tell us what types of imagination a person can have. They tell us as to what extent his imaginations tally with those of other persons. They also tell us how fertile one's imagination may be. The same ink-blot may produce more imaginations in one person as compared to another person. The ink-blots have been used also as measures of an individual's personality. They enable us to know about a person's needs and purposes, his attitudes and feelings, his thoughts and beliefs, his hopes and fears. We will discuss them in detail in the Chapter on Personality.

HALLUCINATION

Generally when you imagine some object, you know that the object is imaginary : it is not real : it cannot be perceived. If anybody imagines an object and believes that it is real, that he is perceiving it, he will be taken to be an abnormal person. Such an awareness of a real object when there is no real object to be perceived is called hallucination. An insane person may perceive a robber approaching him with a dagger in hand. In reality there may be no other person present. The insane person imagines the other person. But his imagination becomes a perception for him. He gets a hallucination. If you observe him minutely you will notice in him all signs of a real sense of danger and fear. Similar signs may be observed in a normal person only when a robber actually stands in front of him with a real dagger in hand. The normal person is perceiving. The insane who perceives a robber when there is no robber is not actually perceiving; he is imagining. But his imagination becomes for him a perception. He cannot find the difference between the two. His imagination is then called hallucination. Hallucination is, thus, imagination taken as perception.

A normal person also gets hallucination when he is dreaming. In dreams we perceive objects and persons with our eyes shut and ears closed. Actually we have imaginations, but in the dream we take them as perceptions. One may dream that he is lying in a dense forest and a demon is sitting on his chest. Actually he may be sleeping safely in his bed and in a closed room. He may even start crying and struggling to free himself from the possession of the demon. Another person sleeping in a bed nearby may be awakened by the cry and observe his room mate frantically moving his arms and legs. The dreamer is behaving as though he is actually perceiving a demon sitting on his chest. Such frightful dreams are called nightmares. In all other types of dreams also the dreamer perceives what he is actually just imagining; all dream consist of hallucinations.

Every person dreams. Every person perceives in dreams objects, persons, and activities that do not exist at the moment; they are only imagined. But dreams occur when he is sleeping. An insane person *perceives* imagined objects or persons while he is awake. He cannot distinguish between imagination and perception. He cannot separate what is fact, or real, from what is not fact, unreal, or bare imagination. He perceives danger when there is no real danger and fails to perceive danger when there is a real danger. He perceives an enemy with a dagger in hand when there is no one to be perceived. He may perceive a real enemy pointing a dagger at him as a friend offering a bunch of flowers. His perceptions are hallucinations or illusions. He has a perception when there is nothing to perceive, or his perception of what is there is different from what one would normally perceive. We have seen that in illusion there is something for a person to perceive, but the perception is unusual or abnormal (p. 90). Ordinarily, nobody perceives a dagger as a bunch of flowers. In hallucination there is nothing to perceive, but still one perceives something. Like hallucination, illusions also are common in insane persons. The perceptions of an insane person may be quite unusual, very different from the perceptions of normal or sane persons. His perceptions are illusory.

VALUE OF IMAGINATION

The plays of children are also the work of imagination. In

his play one child may imagine himself as the father and another child, his play mate, as the son. He may then behave with the other child as his father behaves with himself. A stick may be imagined as a horse and the child its rider. He may use his imagined object in a variety of imagined activities that he performs with it. He may imagine himself as flying in the air, fighting and winning a battle, shooting wild animals, and what not.

Imagination serves a purpose for the child. The child is unable to fulfil many of his desires and wishes. He does not possess the power or strength to do so. His body is immature. His abilities and skills are undeveloped. His experience and knowledge of objects and persons and of their ways of acting are limited. The child is at the same time dominated by the urge to become an adult, to do what adults do and to possess what adults possess. The child's urges cannot be satisfied in reality. His desires and wishes have to remain unfulfilled in the world of real objects. The child's imagination provides opportunities for their fulfilment. A child desires to fly in the air. He cannot do so. In his play he imagines himself as flying in an air-ship. This gives him a pleasure which is sometimes as great as the pleasure derived from actual flight in an aeroplane. Imagined objects and imagined activities are the sources of most of the pleasures and satisfactions that a child gets. This is why a child is more interested in play than in any serious activity. In the education of children, the play method has been found useful for the same reason. We referred to this earlier on (p. 75). For a similar reason children's books are different from the books of adults. Children like fairy tales and animal stories more than the descriptions of facts and ideas. A wisdom coming from the mouth of an animal has more effect on the child than the good counsels showered by sages and philosophers.

Adults too sometimes obtain satisfactions of their desires and wishes by indulging in imaginative activities. Such activities are called day-dreaming or phantasy formation. A poor man may dream of becoming rich and imagine himself as living a life of pomp and luxury. But the dream affords him only momentary pleasure. He returns to the reality of his situation and realises that what he was dreaming about was just the creation of his own fancy.

Chapter IX

THINKING

Nature of Thinking

Man has needs and wants. These move him from within and direct him toward a goal. He acts to achieve the goal. When the goal is achieved, the want is removed and the need is satisfied. We will know more about the needs and wants of man in a later chapter.

A need may arise in a situation in which its goal can be achieved. The activities that fulfil the need will take place immediately. You feel thirsty. The need for water has arisen. You drink a glass of water. The need is satisfied. If water is not near by, you go to the place where you expect to get it and remove your thirst. Most of our needs we satisfy in this simple manner. We have learned fixed patterns of activities to satisfy our needs. These patterns are repeated whenever the related needs arise.

A need, however, may arise in a situation where a fixed pattern of behaviour cannot satisfy it. In such a case one has to find a new way to satisfy the need. When a need arises but it cannot be satisfied, one is said to face a problem. As long as one does not find a way to satisfy the need, the problem remains unsolved. When the way is found, the problem is solved and it disappears.

A person is working in a job to satisfy his need for money. By earning money, he is also able to satisfy several of his very important wants. Suppose that he loses the job. His needs cannot be satisfied in the usual way, i.e., by working on the job. He has to find another way. As long as he has not succeeded in securing a new job, he is facing a problem. He tries the methods of solving the problem that he learned previously. He looks into the "Wanted" column of the newspaper. He makes an application when he finds the advertisement of a job suiting his qualifications. Supposing he does not get a response from any quarter; the methods he has learned for securing a job do not succeed. His problem remains unsolved. He has to find a new method. He *thinks* of other possibilities of finding a job, or of other possible ways of earning money. May be he does a lot of *thinking* but does not come to an appropriate solution of his problem. May be he is able to *think out* a solution and starts working on it.

It follows from what we said above that one starts thinking when one faces a problem. We saw that a problem arises when the usual pattern of behaviour fails to satisfy a need because of a changed situation. It also arises when a new want has to be removed. A growing child creates a new want in the young parents for the child's education. Thinking enables one to find out a solution of this problem. It has, therefore, been described as a problem-solving behaviour.

Every problem-solving behaviour is not thinking. When you try to solve a problem by merely doing something in the situation, you are not thinking. Your behaviour in such a case is an overt behaviour. It is objectively observable by any other person who happens to be there. We have described, in the chapter on Learning, the process of learning a maze or puzzle box. The maze, or the puzzle box presents a problem. The animal has to learn to escape from the maze or puzzle box. As long as it has not learned to do so, it makes several responses many of which cannot solve the problem. The animal's responses can, however, be observed. A blindfolded person can make similar responses in a stylus maze (p. 98) and ultimately escape from the maze. He solves the problem by overt behaviour, i.e., by making observable movements of the hand, and the fingers. Such problem solving behaviour is not thinking.

Thinking is an implicit problem-solving behaviour. When one is thinking his overt activity is suspended. There is little to be observed by another person. When one is deeply thinking, he may appear, for some time, to be idle and inactive. But he is not really idle. He is engaged in thinking as the thinking results in the solution of the problem. But the thinking process that produces the solution is not observable. The thinking activity is an implicit activity. It is an activity that proceeds 'inside' the person. Its objective observation is not possible. You must have observed a team of two chess players. You might have seen that every time before a move is made, the player becomes completely inactive. He is thinking. The move that he makes follows the thinking. Every move made by one person creates a problem for the other person. The other person solves the problem by thinking and then makes his move.

We described thinking as an implicit problem-solving behaviour. In explicit problem-solving behaviour we can observe and thus know what it does consist of. In describing the behaviour of his cat in the puzzle box, Thorndike has given the details of all kinds of movements made by the animal. It is not easy to describe an implicit problem-solving behaviour, as it cannot be directly observed. It has, therefore, been very difficult to answer the question : what thinking consists of? Psychologists have, however, investigated the thinking process by obtaining introspective reports from their subjects while they were engaged in solving some problem. Psychologists have also used some very delicate apparatus that can record implicit responses of the muscles. As a result of these investigations they have been able to discover the nature of the thinking process.

The answer to the question : what thinking activity consists of has been given. Thinking is a symbolic activity. It consists of a sequence of symbolic processes. A symbol stands for something other than itself. A very common example of symbol is the name of a person. The name is either a spoken or a written word. It *is not* the person, as a person is not a word. But it *stands* for the person. When the name is uttered you do not take it just as a sound, which may be high or low. It reminds you of the person and of his qualities. All words are symbols. They represent objects, persons, situations, and activities. The spoken or written word 'pen' stands for the external object pen. It is a symbol. It is also a symbol for an internal process. When I say pen, I produce a sound. The sound represents my thought of the pen, which is an internal process. You do not take it just as a sound. And you do not take it just as a symbol for the pen lying outside. You take it also as a symbol for my thought of the pen. My thought of the pen, which is symbolised by the word 'pen' when I utter the word, symbolises the object pen. The word 'pen' stands for my thought of the pen, and my thought of the pen represents the object pen and what I propose to do with the pen. The object 'pen' is thus symbolised by the word 'pen' printed or spoken as well as by the internal process of my thought of the pen.

Thinking is an implicit problem-solving behaviour. The implicit behaviour consists of symbolic processes. When you solve a problem by thinking, the overt activity of solving the problem is represented by the thinking process. The overt activity is suspended. The thinking process becomes a substitute for the overt activity. You must have tried a mechanical puzzle. When such a problem is presented to you, you may try to solve it by one of two ways. You manipulate the parts of the puzzle in diverse ways till, accidentally, you get at the solution. The process is called motor trial-error process. The solution comes about in a manner that we learned earlier about the behaviour of Thorndike's cat in a puzzle box. The other mode of solving the problem is looking at the different parts of the puzzle and thinking over the possible ways of manipulating the parts. Here also you are trying the various possibilities. But you are not doing so by actual manipulation. You are mentally manipulating, not the parts of the puzzle, but the symbols for those parts. Thinking has, thus, also been described as a symbolic trial-and-error process. Several symbolic trial-and-error processes occur one after the other in thinking, until you come to a process that represents the correct solution of the problem. You then apply this symbolic process in action and actually solve the puzzle. Thinking is, thus, a sequence of symbolic processes, as we have stated above.

The nature of thinking as a symbolic trial-and-error process is illustrated in solving the following match-stick problem :

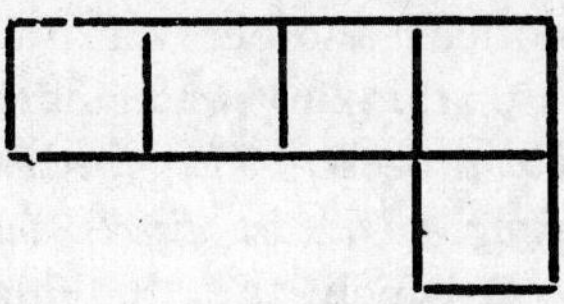

In this figure there are five squares made of sixteen match sticks. The task is to make four similar squares out of the five by changing the position of three sides. Only one stick should be used for each side.

Role of Images in Thinking

The Thinking Process

We have said that thinking is a symbolic process. The question arises : What is the nature of this symbolic process ? In what form do the symbols exist in thinking ? Different answers have been given to this question. The first answer is that images are used in thinking as symbols. We have understood the nature of images in Chapter VIII. The image stands for previous perception. You perceive a cat when the cat is before you. You get its image when it is gone. The image represents your perception of the object. It symbolises the perceived object. We have seen that when we solve a problem by overt activity we manipulate the objects given in the situation. It is said that when we solve a problem by thinking, we manipulate images of objects. *The manipulation is mental manipulation because images are not objects. They are symbols for objects; they stand for objects. Psychologists tried to examine whether images are essential for thinking, or thinking, can be possible without images.* To do this they suggested some mental problems to their subjects and asked them to report on the mental processes involved in solving the problem. It was noticed that some problems were solved without any image to be reported by the subject. Suppose you are asked to measure exactly 10 seers of milk when you have 3 vessels, the first measuring 4 seers of milk, the second 11 seers, and the third 8 seers. You may be able to solve the problem but you may do so without calling up the image of the vessels, the milk, or of the milk being poured into a vessel. Sometimes, a solution comes without anything to be reported. It seems that the person is not aware of the process involved in solving the problem.

The psychologists came to the conclusion that images are not essential for thinking, though sometimes images may form part of the thinking process. They noticed another very important fact about thinking. The process of thinking was guided and controlled. Thinking is a directed process. *The direction comes from what is called set in thinking. The set directs the course of thinking.* It determines the way in which the thinking proceeds. Give two numbers to a person. He will not know what to do with them. But if you also tell him what to do with the numbers, his thinking with the numbers gets a direction. If he is asked to add, the thinking proceeds in one way. If he has to multiply or divide, the process of thinking becomes different. The task you give him determines the course of his thinking. The person is set in the direction in which his thinking flows. When one mentally multiplies any two numbers he may or may not have the image of the numbers; he has no image for the process of multiplying the numbers. He knows however that he has to multiply and not to add or to divide. Without this his thinking will not proceed in the right direction and he will not reach the solution of the problem. It thus appears that (1) images are not essential for thinking, and (2) thinking involves some processes that cannot be represented by an image. These are called sets in thinking. They make thinking a directed process.

Implicit Response

Some psychologists suggest that the symbolic processes in thinking are implicit mascular responses. When we solve a problem by manipulating objects, the bodily activity is explicit. It can be easily observed and described. But when we solve a problem by thinking the bodily activity is so fine and so minute that it cannot be observed with the naked eye. It can, however, be discovered by using some special device.

Any kind of muscular activity produces electric current which can be recorded. If the activity is implicit, it cannot be observed. But the current that the activity releases can be recorded. The existence of the activity can, thus, be proved. A psychologist recorded the electric current released in the muscles when his subject lifted a weight. The strength of the current differed with the amount of the weight lifted. The same subject was then asked to imagine that he was lifting a weight. Similar electric currents were recorded by the device used, though there was no explicit movement of the hand. There was no such current when the subject was not imagining that he lifted a weight. The strength of the current also differed with the amount of the imagined weight. The action current, as it is called, indicated the existence of implicit movement of the muscles.

Another psychologist recorded the action current produced from time to time even when the subject was sleeping and there was no explicit movement of the eyes. He awakened the subject whenever the electric current was noticed and the subject reported that he was dreaming. The current was strong in active dreams, i.e., when he dreamt that he was actively engaged in doing something. The current was weak in passive dreams. Dreaming is an internal activity which is very similar to thinking. It is also, like thinking, a symbolic activity. The action currents accompanying a dream prove that the symbolic process in dream consists of implicit muscular responses. Psychologists thus came to hold that implicit responses of the muscles form part of the thinking process.

Thought and Language

Some psychologists came to the conclusion that thinking involves implicit responses of the muscles of the throat and the larynx. The larynx is the speech organ. Vocal sounds are produced by the activities of the larynx. Talking involves explicit responses of the throat and the larynx. These responses become implicit in thinking. They represent the process of thinking. Thinking was, thus, described as sub-vocal talking or submerged speech. According to these psychologists, thought and language are identical processes. Thinking is language behaviour involving implicit responses of the organs of speech. The evidence in support of this view, however, is not very convincing. Psychologists, therefore, generally do not accept the view that thinking is implicit language behaviour.

There is no doubt a close relation between thought and language. Much of the thinking is done through the medium of spoken or written language. The child originally thinks aloud. He speaks out his thoughts to himself, and talks even when there is no one to listen. But there is no evidence to prove a perfect relation between thought and language. Every thought activity does not seem to be represented by verbal behaviour. The existence of implicit verbal responses can be proved. But the existence of such implicit responses accompanying all thought activities cannot be proved.

CONCEPT

We have seen that the symbolic processes in thinking consist of images and implicit muscular responses. Thinking, however, makes use of another type of symbols. These symbols stand not for particular objects, like images. They stand for classes of objects. They are called concepts. Concepts are verbal responses to the common properties of objects. You can have the image of a particular dog. But you have concept of the class dog. When you think of dog as a faithful animal, you do not refer to any particular dog. You refer to the quality of dogness which all dogs possess.

In forming a concept, you separate one or more qualities found in similar objects from the qualities in which the objects differ. These other qualities are ignored. The common qualities form the concept. The concept becomes sign or symbol for these common qualities. The process of separating one characteristic from other characteristics is called abstraction. The formation of a concept, thus, involves the process of abstraction. When you form the concept of a triangle, you consider the quality of being bounded by three sides alone which all triangles have. You disregard the size, the shape, the colour, and other qualities in which triangles differ. You abstract the quality of triangularity.

It has been found that the lower animals can also learn to respond to the common properties of objects. In an experiment two boxes were used. One contained food; the other produced shock. The box containing food had a triangle drawn on its door. The other box had a circle. After a number of practice trials, the rats used in the experiment learned to enter the box bearing the triangle and avoid the box bearing the circle. Such learning has been called discrimination learning. The size of the triangle and the position of the boxes were then changed. Even then the rat selected the box with the triangle. Same thing happened when a change was produced in the colour of the two geometrical figures. The rat had learned to abstract the form or shape of the figure and responded to the form in the same manner in spite of the change in the size, colour, or relative position of the figure. Learning to respond in the same manner to similar stimuli has been called stimulus generalisation.

The rats in the experiment responded alike to the stimuli that had the same general form or shape.

In the formation of verbal concepts also, generalisation is involved. When we abstract the common properties of observed objects and give them a name, we expect the concept to signify the same properties also in future. We ascribe the quality of faithfulness to all dogs, once we form the concept of dogs as a faithful animal. Concepts, thus, involve both abstraction and generalisation. The common properties of observed objects are abstracted and given a name. The name is then used to apply to the entire class of such objects.

We conclude that thinking is a sequence of symbolic processes. It involves a set which gives the thinking process a direction. The course of thinking is governed by the need to solve the problem which starts thinking. Thinking has been called symbolic trial-and-error process. But the trial-and-error process is not blind. The awareness of the problem or task in thinking guides the trial-and-error process. The symbolic process in thinking may consist of images, implicit, muscular responses, or concepts. All the three are involved in thinking.

Chapter X

FEELING AND EMOTION

Feeling, Interest, Value and Attitude

Meeting a friend after a long time produces pleasure in you. The news of the illness of that friend makes you unhappy. You enjoy the sight of the rising sun. You are sad when you miss the train at the station. All these conditions arising in you are feelings. Some are pleasant feelings. Some are unpleasant feelings. Most of your experiences and activities produce feelings —pleasure or unpleasure—in you. There are also some experiences or activities that produce neither pleasure nor unpleasure. If you meet a person every day, the meeting may not produce pleasure or unpleasure in you. Similarly, when you perform a routine activity like tying the shoelace, or cycling your way to college, the activity generally does not produce any pleasure or unpleasure. In such cases your feeling is described as neutral. A neutral feeling is equivalent to no feeling.

When a feeling is very mild, we do not become aware of it. When you get your meal at the appointed hour, you experience a very mild pleasure while you are eating. But if you are hungry and the food is not ready, you get a feeling of unpleasantness. The feeling may become intense if you have to wait long for the food. When the food is served, you enjoy the food. The pleasant feeling in eating becomes strong. Feelings, thus, differ in intensity.

Our likes and dislikes are closely related to feelings. Generally, objects and activities that produce pleasant feelings are liked by a person. Objects and activities that produce unpleasant feelings are disliked by him. Our likes and dislikes constitute our interests. Liking is positive interest. Disliking is negative interest. What one likes, attracts him—he is interested in it. It produces pleasant feelings in him. What one dislikes repels him —he is bored and annoyed by it. It produces unpleasant feelings in him. If one neither likes nor dislikes an object or activity, he is disinterested in it. His feelings about it are neutral.

When the liking for an object, person, or activity becomes very strong, we are said to value that object, person or activity. The physical or material value of an object is different from its psychological value. Recitation of his poem before a group of eager listeners has a psychological value for a poet. It may have no material or physical value for him. It brings him no tangible reward. Working in the pit has a material value for a miner. It brings him money. It may have no psychological value for him. He may decide to change his occupation, after he has saved some money. The other occupation may have psychological value for him. He has a liking for the work and for the situation in which the work is to be performed. Sometimes the psychological value may become more powerful than the physical value. Mahatma Gandhi suffered physical hardships because independence of the country had a very strong psychological value for him. A scientist often endangers his personal safety and life, because the satisfaction of making a discovery has a strong psychological value for him.

The psychological value of an object is closely related to the feelings produced by the object. If an object always produces pleasant feelings in a person, the object comes to have a value for him. Success in any task has value for a person because success produces agreeable feelings. We dislike failure, on the other hand; it has a negative value for us because it produces unpleasant feelings. Value too, like interest and feeling, may be positive or negative. Similarly, like feelings both interests and values may be neutral. The objects or activities that one neither likes nor dislikes have a neutral value for him. He is indifferent to them. The independence of another country has a neutral value for most of us. But the independence of our own country has a strong positive value for us.

We become inclined toward what we value. We tend to reject what has a negative value for us. Sometimes the inclination or rejection becomes a permanent condition within us. It influences our behaviour. Such a condition is called attitude. One person values religion. He is inclined towards religious beliefs and practices. Another person may develop a negative value for religion. He has a disinclination for religious beliefs and practices. We say that the first person has a favourable attitude toward religion. The second person has an unfavourable attitude toward religion. One may have favourable or unfavourable attitude towards objects or issues like religion, casteism, communism and so on. One may have such attitudes also towards persons or groups like Chinese, one's employer, a political leader, etc. His attitudes will influence his opinion about the person or group. They may also influence his action in respect to the person or group. You have a favourable attitude towards a particular person. You will be found ready to help him, to form good opinion about him and to welcome his company. You have an unfavourable attitude towards another person. You are likely to form bad opinion about him, to leave him in difficulty, and to avoid his company. Attitude has, accordingly been described as a permanent state of readiness, or preparedness to perceive, feel, think and act in a particular manner, to be inclined towards or reject, to be attracted or repelled by an object, issue, or person.

Emotion

Nature of Emotions

When one becomes angry, or he is afraid, he has the emotion of anger or fear. When a comic film makes you burst into laughter, you have the emotion of delight. When the mother clings her baby to her chest, she has the emotion of love. When you are angry, or when you are afraid, you get an unpleasant feeling. When you are delighted or you express your love and affection, you get a pleasant feeling. Emotion, thus, has also an element of feeling in it. But emotion is not only feeling. It is more complex. It includes also a set of widespread bodily activities, besides feeling. When you are angry, you do not only have an unpleasant feeling. Striking changes are also produced in your normal activities. Your heart begins to beat rapidly. Your breathing gets tense. Your voice becomes loud and shrill. Your face turns red. A widespread activity overtakes your entire organism. Changes in your normal activities arise also when you are afraid, delighted, or sad. Emotion, thus, is a disturbed state of the organism accompanied by an unpleasant or pleasant feeling.

Just like feelings, emotion also may be more intense or less intense. In more intense emotions, the disturbances in the normal activities of the organism are more widespread and explicit. They can be easily observed by others. In less intense emotions, the disturbances do not spread over the entire organism and they are not very explicit. They may remain unnoticed by others. A highly intense emotion of anger is called rage. If a person is in a fit of rage, all persons that are there know of this fact. The bodily changes that arise in him are easily noticeable. A mild or less intense emotion of anger may be described as displeasure. The marks of displeasure may not be very visible. Similarly, an intense emotion of fear produces visible changes all over the body and is described as a state of terror. Fear, on the other hand, may also be indicated by a mild paleness of the face and expression of uneasiness, which may not be very visible.

When a person is in a state of emotion, his mental activities are also disturbed. If you are angry, it is difficult for you to concentrate your attention on any activity. You may not be able to get clear perception of an object or a situation. You may fail to recall what you have known quite well. Your memory does not function well. You fail to understand what you read. You cannot think properly. Emotion may, thus, create difficulties in man's day-to-day activities and adjustment. Some people more easily get into a state of emotion than others. If anything happens that they do not like, it makes them angry. We call them men of quick temper. There are others who are very timid. They get easily frightened. Some people become overjoyed when some things happen as they like. They are highly excitable. For these persons emotion sometimes becomes a great handicap. It makes it difficult for them to perform their duties satisfactorily, or adjust with other persons normally.

The child is very highly emotional. He gets into a fit of rage, or in a state of fright much too easily. The bodily activities that accompany his emotions are very widespread and quite explicit. He screams, cries, throws himself on the ground, bites, sneers, trembles, turns pale, all too visibly. But as the child grows, he gets more and more control over his emotions; the bodily expressions of the emotions are, generally, more suppressed. He is not as readily disturbed by ordinary happenings. He does not easily get into fits of excitement, fear or anger. He maintains emotional stability. An adult, generally, has full control over his emotions. He is emotionally stable and does not get easily disturbed by the changes in his surroundings. If a grown-up person does not have full control over his emotions, we call him emotionally immature. In emotional situations, he behaves like a child, in spite of being an adult. An emotionally immature adult moans and cries when in the face of danger. He bites, sneers and spits at the person who does not carry out his wishes. He jumps and dances in delight whenever he succeeds in a task. These are extreme forms of emotional immaturity. Ordinarily, when an adult person does not behave as adults do in an emotional situation, he lacks emotional maturity.

The bodily expressions of emotions have great value in the life of lower animals. Lower animals are capable of complex bodily activities. Their mental activities are few and simple. When an animal is attacked by another animal, it gets into a state of anger. If the enemy is stronger, the animal repulses in a state of fear and runs away for safety. The anger or fear prepares the animal to meet the danger it is facing. In the state of anger, the animal whets its teeth, bends its body, its hairs stand, its breathing is slowed, its eyes bulge. All these prepare the animal better to attack and defend itself against the enemy. The all-round disturbed bodily activities of the animal help it to meet the situation of danger. The special value of emotions in the life of animals was specially recognised by some psychologists. This led them to suggest what they called the emergency theory of emotions. Emotions prepare the organism to meet an unusual situation, the emergency situation. The bodily activities of the animal are intensified, they get more strength when the animal is in a state of emotion.

The emergency theory of emotions does not apply to the emotions that man gets. Man meets his emergency situations, generally, not by strong bodily activities, but by strong mental activities. When a situation is unusual, in order to meet it successfully, man should be able to perceive and understand it fully and in all its details. He should also be able to think systematically about the possible ways of meeting the situation. All his mental activities should function at a high level. But emotions interfere with the mental activities as we noted earlier (p. 147). Man should, therefore, exercise maximum control over his emotions when he has to meet an unusual situation. The emergency theory of emotion was perhaps true of the cave man, when man was living in a primitive state. In the primitive state, man's mental activities were simple and less valuable than his bodily strength. The growth of civilization has brought greater and greater development of the mental activities of man. A civilised adult is capable of very highly complex mental activities. These are expressed in the highly intricate inventions modern man has made. They have enabled him to conquer the forces of nature. Uncontrolled expression of emotions is the greatest weakness that a man may have in civilised society. Control over emotions is the mark of civilisation and culture. Education has, therefore, also been described as a training in control of emotions. It is education that makes a person civilised and cultured.

Theories of Emotions

There are some theories about the origins of emotions. When one becomes angry, or afraid, there is something which makes him angry or afraid. There is some object, person or situation that he perceives or of which he is reminded. It stimulates his sense organs. The impulses that arise in the sense organs reach the cerebral cortex. He becomes aware of the object, person or situation. A boy is sitting in the field. Suddenly a snake starts moving nearby. He perceives the snake; he becomes aware of it. We generally believe that the moment he perceives the snake, he experiences fear, i.e., he gets afraid, and the fear produces some bodily responses in him. He runs away from the place and looks afraid. Thus, perception of the object produces the emotional experience of fear and the emotional experience in its turn produces the bodily responses of fear. This way of explaining emotions is called the common sense view of emotions.

Psychologists do not accept the common sense view of emotions. They have their own theories. According to one theory, the perception of the snake is not immediately followed by the fear of the snake. The perception first produces the activity of jumping or running, together with some other activities inside the body like more rapid blood circulation, quick breathing, etc. These activities stimulate the receptors that lie inside the body—*the kinesthetic receptors and the organic receptors*. Influences from these receptors reach the brain and produce a mass of *kinesthetic and organic sensations* (pp. 68-69). This mass of sensations constitutes our experience of fear. The state of fear, anger, or other emotions that a person experiences is, according to this theory, *a confused mass of sensations produced by the disturbed activities of the organism*. This theory has been called the James-Lange theory of emotions after the name of the psychologist, William James, and the physiologist, G. G. Lange, who independently suggested this theory, We find that according to this theory, the perception of the object is followed by the disturbed bodily activities and the bodily activities are followed by the confused sensations of which a person becomes aware as a state of fear or anger. James has said 'we do not run because we are afraid; we are afraid because we run'. Or, 'we do not strike because we are angry; we are angry because we strike'.

There is another theory of emotions called the Cannon-Bard theory. According to this theory, the perception of the object is followed by the disturbed bodily activities as well as the emotional experience. Both occur at the same time and the one does not produce the other. A person is abused by another person. He hears the abuse which means an insult to him. He gets into anger and assaults the other person or abuses him in return. The anger consists of the disturbed state of his entire organism as well as of his experience of the state of anger. Both the disturbed bodily activities and the conscious experience of anger take place at the same time. Thus, according to this theory the experience of anger is not the product of the disturbed activities. The conscious experience is not a confused mass of sensations, as James and Lange thought. What happens is that the perception of the object produces impulses in the cerebral cortex which are carried to a portion of the mid brain. This portion of the mid brain is called thalamus. From the thalamus, part of the impulse reaches the effectors in the body, i.e., the muscles and the glands. Another part returns from the thalamus to the cerebral cortex and results in the emotional experience. The impulses that reach the effectors produce the disturbed bodily changes. The emotional experience, the feeling of anger or fear that one reports, results from the action of the thalamus that sends the impulses to the cortex. This theory is, therefore, also called the thalamic theory of emotions. The bodily changes and the emotional experience take place simultaneously. One does not follow, or produce, the other.

Psychologists have found sufficient evidence to reject the common sense theory. But it is difficult to decide whether the Jame-Lange theory or the Cannon-Bard theory is the more correct theory. More evidence has been found, however, to support the Cannon-Bard theory. It has also been ascertained now that the thalamus in the mid brain plays an important part in the experience of emotions. If this part of the brain is damaged or separated from the cortex, the person becomes deprived of intense emotional experiences. The thalamus is thus found to be the seat of the emotions.

Kinds of Emotions

There are several kinds of emotions, such as the emotions of anger, fear, joy, sorrow, disgust, anxiety, worry, pride, shame, love, jealousy, etc. When a person is angry, he knows that he is angry and that he is not afraid or delighted. Similarly, when he is afraid, he knows that he is afraid. Thus, as conscious experience one emotion is distinct from another emotion. But this is not true of the bodily activities that accompany the emotional experience. The bodily activities of one kind of emotion may not be altogether different from the bodily activities of another kind of emotion. For example, blood circulation and breathing may be disturbed in both anger and fear. Some bodily changes may be observed also in extreme delight. Not only the internal bodily changes, but also the external expressions of the emotions may not be altogether dissimilar. Sometimes it is difficult to know from the expression of the face or the bodily posture of a person whether the person is in a state of anger, fear or grief. It seems, therefore. that it is not possible to classify emotions on the basis of the bodily changes that accompany them. Several devices have been found for observing and recording the very minute bodily changes that are produced in emotions. Measures have been developed of heart beat, respiration, blood circulation, blood pressure, composition of the blood, electric resistance of the skin and so on. Very delicate and sensitive instruments are used for the purpose. But the results show that there are no quite distinct patterns of bodily changes going with distinct types of emotional experiences. An emotion is, therefore, a highly complex behaviour which consists of a confused mass of disturbed bodily activities and a peculiar conscious experience.

The emotions of anger and fear are among the most noted emotions. The conscious experience of each is different from the other. When you are angry you know that you are angry and not afraid. When you are afraid, you know that you are afraid and not angry. Some bodily changes are similar in both emotions, others are different. For example, the face becomes generally white in fear and red in anger; while breathing may be rapid or suspended in both. However, the causes of the two emotions are quite different. Fear is caused in children by a sudden loud noise and lack of support. A sudden loud noise causes fear in adults too. Many adults tremble with fear at the sound of a loud thunder. Generally, when a sudden noise is unfamiliar, it produces fear in adults. In adults apprehension of danger is the main cause of fear. A sense of danger is a threat to one's security and life. A condition of insecurity also, therefore, produces fear. If the sense of insecurity becomes persistent, it causes a type of fear called anxiety. Anxiety is a state of fear arising from an anticipated danger about which one is not able to do anything. For example, a fond mother may have anxiety about the health of her only child, or about his safe return from school along the busy street.

The emotion of anger is caused when there is some obstruction in one's movement or activity. When you want to do a thing, and something or somebody stands in your way, you become angry. You want to unlock a room, You try a bunch of keys, but no one fits into the lock. You throw the bunch of keys in anger. You desire a thing to be done in one way, but it is done in a different way; this produces anger in you. You need to maintain your self-respect and social prestige. Somebody does something to insult you. You become angry with him. It is not only the obstruction in your activity, but also the obstruction to your desires and needs, that produces anger in you.

When you are angry with a person, you become inclined to attack him; you show aggressive behaviour. The attack may be verbal also. You abuse him, call bad names to him, slander him and so on. Sometimes if you cannot successfully attack the person who produced anger in you, you express your anger on a substitute. A wife when angry with her husband, who is too strong for her, ventilates her anger on her child. A subordinate in office when insulted by his boss may give expression to his anger on returning to his family. Psychologists call this displaced aggression. Instead of being directed to the real sources of the anger, the anger gets directed to some other objects or person. If you are offended by the content of a letter, you sometimes tear the letter to pieces and trample it under your feet.

Fear differs from anger in the behaviour that it produces. When you are afraid you run away from the source of fear. Anger produces attack, fear produces escape. Anger produces a positive response. Fear produces a negative response. Fear may sometimes produce complete inactivity also. In a state of terror one may not be able to move. His limbs may become paralysed. Sometimes he may lose consciousness also.

Often, one cannot escape from the fearful situation by running away from it. The fear haunts his mind. Sometimes the running away is not possible. The situation cannot be avoided. A person has done some wrong and thinks that the guilt will be discovered; he fears the punishment that will follow. He cannot overcome the fear. The only way to escape the fear is to forget the situation in which the fear was produced. Sometimes a persistent fear may produce mental disorder. The person loses contact with his environment. He becomes unmindful of his surroundings. He runs away from the world of reality to the world of imagination and treats it as reality. A person who is mentally ill takes shelter from the fear, anxieties and worries of his real world into a world of make-belief. His world is one in which he believes things to be as he wishes them to be. He lives in an imaginary world.

Chapter XI

MOTIVATION

Nature of Motives

Man lives in an environment of objects and persons. Objects and persons influence him in various ways. Much of man's behaviour can be explained as a result of their influence. But each person has his own needs, wants and desires. Some of these needs and wants he shares with other persons. Some of these wants and desires are peculiar to him. Some needs man shares also with the lower organisms. Man's wants, needs, and desires also determine the way each one behaves. To understand and explain a man's behaviour we have to take into account his needs, wants and desires. These are different from the forces of the environment that influence man. They reside within the individual. They move him from within. A general name has been given to the needs, wants and desires of man. They are called motives.

Motives are internal sources of man's behaviour. Man's thinking, feeling, and actions are determined not only by the environment in which man lives. They are determined also by his motives. A hungry man enters a hotel to buy food. He pays for it and leaves the place. The hotel-keeper supplies the food, receives payment and stays in. The two persons behave in different ways in very much the same environment, because their motives are different. One needs to buy food. The other needs to sell food. Man is influenced by his outer environment. He is also influenced by his own motives. Both types of influences act and interact on him. To explain his behaviour we have to take account of both.

Motives are so called because they move a person from within. As we shall see, some of these motives exist from the beginning of the life of an individual. Other motives are acquired in the course of one's life and development. Whether present from the moment of birth or acquired later, motives form a part of the individual's personality.

Different motives become active at different times and in different situations. Each motive, when active, moves the person to behave in a particular way. When a motive becomes active, the organism is said to be motivated. Motivation is, thus, a process of arousal of motive. At one moment a person is motivated by hunger. At the next moment, he is motivated by thirst. At another moment he may be motivated by love or by aggression.

A motive is aroused when there is a condition of want or lack within the organism. When a person is hungry, there is want or lack of food. When he is thirsty, there is want or lack of moisture. When he is in a strange or lonely place, and he seeks friendship, there is want or lack of company. The want has to be removed. If it is not removed, in some cases, the security, or health of the organism is endangered. In other cases, a state of dissatisfaction, or discomfort, is produced. The existence of the want, therefore, sets the organism into a state of action; the organism is driven to remove the want. It becomes directed to a course of action that can satisfy the want. The course of action that can remove the want is called goal.

A motivated behaviour is directed to a goal. The behaviour persists without interruption or continuously. It may, in some cases, be interrupted and again resumed. When the hunger motive is aroused, reaching and eating food is the goal to which the activity of the person is directed. Similarly, drinking water or a substitute for water becomes the goal of one's activity when the thirst motive is aroused. Or, when a person is motivated by the need for recognition, several of his activities aim at winning for him social position and social respect. The food, water, or position that attracts an individual when he is under the influence of the hunger, thirst, or recognition need, has been called incentive. Incentive is, thus, the object or situation to which a motivated behaviour is directed.

We find that the terms need, drive, goal, incentive all express different aspects of motivated behaviour. We may describe motivation as a state of the organism which involves the existence of a need that moves or drives the organism from within and directs its activities to a goal that can bring about the satisfaction of the need. In addition to these, there is another term which is used when we talk about motivation. When a motive is aroused and the organism is driven to a goal, a condition is produced within the organism called tension. This condition may be compared to the state in which one finds the string of a bow when the string is pulled, or the spring of a watch when winding is applied to the watch. The string of the bow, or the spring, gets into a state of tension. Similar becomes the condition of the organism when a motive is aroused. The state of tension continues as long as the goal is not reached. The tension increases if the goal is obstructed. If food is placed before a hungry child, but the child is prevented from eating, the state of tension will be visible. When the goal is achieved, the motive is satisfied, the tension is reduced. The behaviour aroused by the need or want reaches its end.

Needs, drives, or motives cannot be directly observed. We know about them indirectly. When we experience within us the tension producing a state of discomfort or dissatisfaction, we think that a strong motive has been aroused. We know about them also when other persons report about their wants, desires, striving, and goals. We have to accept the existence of motives when we find that it is not possible to explain the behaviour of a person if we take into consideration the factors in his environment only.

Classification of Motives

Biogenic and Sociogenic

Motives have been broadly classified as physiological and psychological. The physiological motives are also called biological or biogenic motives. The psychological motives are called social or sociogenic motives.

The biological or physiological motives are hunger, thirst, the need for air, activity, rest, and the sex motive. They are so called because they are related to the satisfaction of a physiological want of the organism. They are called biological, because life is not possible without their satisfaction. Sex, however, is an exception. Life is possible without the satisfaction of the sex motive. But the sex motive also is a biological motive because it satisfies a great biological want, namely, reproduction of organisms. The birth of a new organism depends upon the satisfaction of the sex motive. Without sex activity no organism can multiply itself.

Let us first consider the hunger motive. The body needs fat, protein, carbohydrate, vitamins, and a few minerals like iron, salt, etc. These substances are supplied to the body in the food that we take. They are used in building the cells of the body and also in the activities performed by the body. When used up, they are eliminated from the body as waste products. The stool and the urine contain these waste products. Elimination of waste products from the body is also one of the physiological needs of the organism. The body needs fresh supply of these substances to make up the deficiency. The hunger motive serves this need. When food is taken, the want of the body is satisfied for the time being. The hunger motive is a biological motive because the substances the body gets through food are essential not only for the activities of the body, they are necessary for the health and even life of the body. No hunger-strike can last for an indefinite period. Some diseases produce a complete loss of appetite for food. The patients suffering from such a disease cannot survive long.

The thirst motive also serves a physiological or biological need. The body needs moisture. The water we drink supplies the moisture. The moisture contained in the body is, however, eliminated from the body. Perspiration and urination drain out the moisture from the body. The lack of moisture has to be removed. The thirst motive serves the purpose. The motive is satisfied by drinking water or any other liquid. Like food, water is also essential for the health and life of the organism. When a person suffers from diarrhoea, he gets frequent loose stools. The moisture the body needs is more quickly eliminated from the body than supplied by drinking water. The condition that results is called dehydration, which means deficiency of moisture in the body.

The need for air is another physiological or biological motive. The body needs oxygen which the air contains. Oxygen burns. The blood contains sugar supplied by food and stored in the lever. The air we breathe in supplies oxygen to the blood. The blood carries both blood-sugar and oxygen to the muscles.

The oxygen burns the sugar. The burning of the sugar produces energy to be used by the muscles. Oxygen, like blood-sugar, is thus essential for the activities of the body. The breathing activity satisfies the body's need for oxygen. At high altitudes, the air does not contain sufficient oxygen. The oxygen need of the body is obstructed. Artificial supply of oxygen becomes, therefore, necessary for the need to be served. Same thing happens with divers when they plunge deep into the sea or ocean. The condition produced by the deficiency or loss of oxygen is called asphyxia. Such condition causes death, if nothing is done to remedy it.

Activity and rest or sleep are also physiological needs. If a part of the body is made completely inactive for some time, the cell bodies that compose that part die out without being replaced. Persons whose arm or leg is put under plaster for long cannot move the arm or leg when the plaster is removed. The inactivity of the arm or leg makes it weak and sometimes completely motionless and useless. One cannot imagine a stronger punishment to a person than completely arresting his activities for long. This obstructs the activity need of the person. The need-tension created causes him great discomfort. You cannot confine a healthy person to bed, unless he is asleep, without causing him great annoyance. The activity need is very strong in children. The need takes its own course, if not directed into desirable channels by the elders.

The need for sleep is the counterpart of the need for activity. The organism is using up its energy in the activities of the waking life. The cell bodies need time for the recovery of the used up energy. Sleep provides the opportunity. A sound sleep makes one feel fresh and full of energy on awakening. Sleep is essential for health. A state of continuous sleeplessness exhausts the body. The person is likely to become, not only physically sick, also mentally ill without sleep. Insomnia or continuous sleeplessness produces mental disorder.

Sex is a very strong physiological motive. There is sex glands which secrete sex hormones. We have earlier learned about gland secretion and hormone (p. 33). The sex hormone accumulates and arouses the sex motive in animals. The accumulated secretion is discharged by the sexual activity. In lower animals, the sex activity appears at regular intervals. In man, the sex motive is not only a physiological need. It has become an important psychological and social motive. Ideas and feelings play a more important part in arousing the sex motive than do the physiological conditions produced by secretion of the sex glands.

The sex motive, unlike the other physiological motives, undergoes a long process of natural growth and development for its satisfaction. A great psychologist, Sigmund Freud, the founder of psychoanalysis, has noted several stages in the development of the sex motive from the moment of birth to the attainment of puberty. This long processs of development is influenced not only by the long process of growth of those parts of the body that are used in adult sex activity. It is also influenced by the social and psychological factors that govern the development of the total personality. Freud calls the development of sex as psychosexual development.

The above motives are also called primary motives, as distinguished from the psychological or social motives. These are called derived motives. The primary motives are universal motives; they are found in all organisms, human or non-human, in one form or the other. They are essential for the health and life of the organism. They serve the basic physiological needs of the organism. They are inborn or innate. They are not acquired, like the social motives. The social motives are acquried like other forms of learned behaviour. They are called derived because they are acquired in the course of satisfaction of the physiological needs.

Though the primary motives are not acquired and arise from the physiological or tissue needs of the organism, the mode of their satisfaction is very much acquired in the case of man. The hunger motive is satisfied in different manners among different cultures. We develop our likes and dislikes for food under the types of social environment that influence us. Besides the object of food, the mode of eating also is acquired by the child as a result of the social influence. The average Indian eats without the help of knife and fork. The average Englishman cannot do without them. The same thing applies to the other primary motives. The sex motives will be a typical example. Different and divergent customs and practices are associated with the satisfaction of the sex need in different cultures. In some society a man's sexual relation is restricted to one woman; in another society a person can have more than one wife. In some societies, sexual relation outside marriage is permissible. In some cultures a single wife is shared by all brothers.

The psychological and social needs of man are innumerable. Strong habits, powerful emotions, values of objects, persons and situations, ideologies, etc., influence man's behaviour from within in verymuch the same manner as the physiological needs do. They direct and control his behaviour just like the primary motives. Sometimes they become stronger than the physiological needs. A person goes on hunger-strike to achieve a social or political purpose. Below are given some of the very common social needs of man.

The need for belongingness is a social need and is also called the affiliation need. Every individual is influenced by the need to seek the company of other persons. Every person wants to have some friends to give and receive love and affection. Isolation from society, separation from his kith and kin, produces a great want within an individual. He feels unhappy and sometimes extremely miserable if the want is not removed.

Closely related to the affiliation need is the need for dependence upon other persons. This need is very strong in the child. In the adult the need for dependence is counterbalanced by the need for independence. As the child grows, he becomes less and less dependent upon other persons and more and more dependent upon himself. But human life is such that no one can exist in a state of complete independence from others. Man is a social animal. As such, he builds up ties with other persons, not only of companionship, but also of mutual dependence. What we call society is a group of inter-dependent individuals. One gets a feeling of social insecurity if he finds no one to depend upon. This makes him feel very unhappy.

Married life does not only satisfy the sex need of an individual. By providing a permanent companion, it also serves the affiliation need. Above all, it fulfils the need for mutual dependence of the partners in marriage. Each one, however, also seeks to realise his independence as an adult. A healthy balance between independence and dependence makes for a happy married life. If, on the other hand, each one is dominated by the urge to realise his independence, and seeks to satisfy the need for dependence elsewhere, the result is a conflict. Married life then becomes a tale of mutual unhappiness and suffering.

The need for recognition and status is another important social need. Every person is influenced by the urge to possess a status in his society. He earnestly desires his worth and value to be recognised. In every society we find persons occupying high or low position. Those who are in a low position are striving to get to a higher position. They may do so even if the higher position does not bring any material gain like money or physical comfort. People prefer an office job to the work of a technician bccause the former has higher status value. A person desires to possess telephone, own a car, or maintain a good garden not only because of the advantages he gets from them. They add to his status and thus have a value for him. They satisfy his status or prestige need.

The power need is still another important social motive. Every person tries to have some power so that he can influence other persons. Some persons desire power to be able to satisfy their primary needs. But in other cases, power may attract a person as a goal by itself. He may not use his power to satisfy his physiological needs, but still it has a great value for him. The activities of most political leaders are governed by the power motive. They receive special satisfaction in being able to bestow favour or inflict harm on other persons. The 'boss' in office is also influenced by a great need for power. His behaviour to his subordinates reflects this need. He is more interested in seeing that his subordinates carry out his orders than finding how efficiently each one performs his duties.

Measurement of the Strength of Motives

Psychologists have found several methods for measuring the strength of the physiological motives in ainmals. In one such method they use what has been called the *activity wheel.* A rat or a cat is placed in a weeel-like cage; any movement made by the animal produces movement in the cage also. The faster the movement of the animal in the cage, the quicker the rotation of the activity wheel. Hungry or thirsty rats are placed inside the activity wheel. They are kept hungry or thirsty for different periods of time. The more hungry or the more thirsty rats move much faster than the less hungry or thirsty. The wheel also moves at greater or lesser speed. A device is used to record each rotation of the wheel automatically. It is found that the greater the hunger or thirst of the animal, larger is the number of rotations. In this manner the number of rotations within a fixed time limit becomes a measure of the strength of a need.

Another method used for measuring strength of a need has been called the obstruction method. In this method a box is used which has two compartments. A narrow passage connects the two compartments. The animal enters the box in one compartment and as it crosses the passage leading to the other compartment, the door of this other compartment automatically opens. The other compartment contains food or a cup of water visible from the first compartment. Wire net is spread over the floor of the passage and electric current is passed through it. When the animal moves along the passage, it receives electric shock. The animal cannot reach its goal without getting the electric shock. To arouse the hunger or thirst need, the animal is deprived of food or water. In a state of mild hunger, or mild thirst, the animal will not cross the obstruction. When the need is strong, the animal will cross the obstruction in spite of the shock. The strength of the sex motive has also been measured in this manner by keeping a male rat in the second compartment as the incentive for a female rat placed in the first compartment. When in heat, i.e., when the sex need arises in the animal, the rat would pass the obstruction and reach the male rat. The animal is prepared to undergo the shock if the need is strong. In human life also we find that if a motive is very strong, the person may be prepared to undergo hardships and sufferings in order to achieve the goal that satisfies the motive. The strength of social, religious and scientific purposes ideologies can be measured by the amount of difficulties, pain and suffering a person accepts and undergoes, when moved by the purpose or ideology. There are numerous examples showing that no obstacle can prevent a person from struggling for his goal if he is strongly moved from within by some noble cause.

The learning method is still another method used for measuring the strength of a motive. We have seen earlier that without motivation learning is not possible. It is also found that the rate of learning is related to the strength of motivation; the stronger the motivation, the quicker the learning. A strong motive releases more energy in the organism to be used for reaching the goal than does a weak motive. When there is strong motivation to learn a task, strong effort will be made for the learning. The result will be quicker learning. Experiments have been done on hungry or thirsty rats placed in a maze. It has been found that the more hungry or thirsty rats learn the maze. i.e., the correct path to the food or water placed outside the maze, more quickly than less hungry or less thirsty rats.

Frustration of Motive

Motivated behaviour is goal-directed behaviour. The behaviour ceases when the goal is achieved; the motive is allayed. Sometimes the achievement of the goal is delayed. This increases the tension. The tension is reduced, however, when the goal is realised. But often the goal may not be achieved. This is called frustration of motive. Frustration is thus a state produced by the failure to achieve the satisfaction of a motive. It is a reaction to the blocking of goal-directed behaviour.

There are different causes of frustration of a motive. We mention below some general situations in which a motive is frustrated.

1. An obstruction in the environment of a person may prevent him to achieve his motive. A child's need for play is frustrated if his toys are locked in the almirah while he is playing with them, or they are visible through the glass panes but he cannot get them. The locked door of the almirah becomes an obstacle. It obstructs the achievement of his play motive. The motive is frustrated. If a person is starved for want of food in his environment, the hunger need is obstructed by the circumstance in which he is placed. The need is frustrated. Prisoners of war experience frustration of several of

their primary and derived needs, like hunger, sex activity, status, friendliness, etc. The condition of imprisonment in which they find themselves prevents them from achieving the goals towards which these motives are directed.

2. A motive is also frustrated if the goal towards which it is directed is not attainable by the person. The goal is beyond his capacity to reach it. The obstacle to the satisfaction of the motive is not in the environment; he lacks the power to attain it. A student of poor academic ability is frustrated if his ambition is to score high marks in the examination. Every student aspires to achieve success in his school work. He develops an academic achievement motive. But as we have noted earlier, a person's achievement is limited by his ability to achieve. If a person aspires to achieve a degree of success which is not possible for him to achieve, his achievement motive is frustrated. There may be frustration of the sex motive if a poor man desires to marry a girl from a very rich family. The goal that he has set for himself is unattainable for him.

3. Conflict of motives also produces frustration of a motive. A conflict of motives arises when two or more motives are aroused at the same time, but both cannot be satisfied at the moment. The conflict of motives may take different forms.

(i) A person of high status may be approached for subscription to a charity fund. He may experience a conflict between his status motive and his desire to increase his bank balance. If he makes handsome contribution to the fund, his desire to hoard money will be frustrated. If he refuses to contribute, he will lose his prestige; his status motive will be frustrated. Similar conflict of motives may be produced in a female rat left in the middle of a path at one end of which is a male rat and at the other end a piece of cheese. If the sex motive and the hunger motive are equally strong at the moment, the rat will not be able to satisfy anyone. The rat may sit idle.

Such conflict of motives may be resolved by allowing one motive to achieve its goal at one time; the goal of the other motive is achieved at a later time. The person of high status may pay to the charity fund and then cut down some other expenses to save for the bank deposit. An average person is attracted by worldly comforts which can generally be attained by living not a very honest life. He is also attracted by the promised heaven in after-life as a reward for good actions. He satisfies both motives by living a comfortable life and also observing the rites and practices of the religion to which he belongs. He resolves his conflict without experiencing frustration. However, sometimes the sheer strength of one motive overpowers the other motive. If the conflict is repeatedly solved by allowing the first motive every time the conflict arises, the second motive gradually loses all strength. It ceases to influence the person. It is conquered by the person. Great men who have lived a life of sacrifice and suffering had conquered their worldly motives. They were not moved by those motives. When this happens the motive that always wins becomes a part of the person's ideology. It becomes a dominant motive in his life, to which other motives are subordinated. It becomes his strongest value, the source of the greatest satisfaction and happiness to him.

(ii) A conflict of motives also arises when a person has to choose one of two courses of action both of which are equally undesirable. An honest businessman may be required to choose between giving bribe to a corrupt official or suffering delay in the execution of his work. If he gives bribe his conscience pricks him. If he refuses to give bribe, his achievement motive is frustrated. The person has to choose between two evils. Such conflict may be resolved by choosing what seems to the person to be the lesser evil. A child is inclined by the play motive to avoid going to school. He is incliened by the affiliation motive to avoid his parents' displeasure. His choice is influenced by the stronger of the two motives. The strength of the motive determines for him what is less undesirable. If the need for parents' love is stronger, going to school will be a lesser evil for him. If the need for play is stronger, parents' displesure will be the lesser evil. If he finds that he can cut school without causing his parents' displeasure, or that he can ignore parents' momentary displeasure because it does not bring him any loss, in future the temptation to play in school time produce no conflict in him.

Such conflicts may also be resolved by 'getting out of the field'. The honest businessman may find it difficult to compromise with his conscience or to suffer loss in business. He may decide to give up business and join a salaried job. The conflict may also be resolved by escaping into a world of imagination. The child may choose to go to school but instead of attending to the real situation of the class room, he may take to day dreaming. He slips into an unreal world where he is free to play whatever game and in whosoever's company he desires. You will find that a real resolution of the conflict in this case, as in the previous one (i), will be possible by changing the child's values. When the child is able to value his school work more, he gets more interested in the activities of the school; the conflict would not arise in him. He will be fond of going to school. He will experience a conflict when he is prevented from going to school. When he becomes sick, for example, he will be in conflict whether he should stay at home or go to school. Such conflict arises in the situation which is described below :

A person may be both attracted and repelled by the same goal. A young man wants to marry to satisfy the sex motive; he also wants to postpone marriage to avoid the responsibilities of married life. A boy may like his father and be inclined to depend upon him as it makes him feel secure. He may at the same time dislike his father because of the father's interference in his activities. This obstructs his need for freedom and self-responsibility. The boy may, thus, experience conflict of motives in regard to his father. 'A small child is attracted by the glow of fire, but is also repelled by the burn which it may cause. In order to learn to accept some unpleasing object or situation in preference to a pleasing object or situation, one has to resolve this type of conflict. Much of what is called practical wisdom depends upon this capacity, the capacity to bear some loss in order to secure a greater gain. As the common proverb goes, there is no gain without pain. To secure the gain one has to endure the pain. The greater the capacity to endure pain and suffering that a person has the higher and nobler will be his achievements.

We have reviewed the three general types of situations in which mental conflicts arise. In every case some motive is frustrated; the satisfaction of the motive is prevented or denied. In the first situation, a person has to accept the frustration of one motive in order that he can satisfy the other motive. In the second situation he has to tolerate one of the evils. The child has to face the frustration of his need for parental love or the need for play. In the third situation a person has to bear the hardship of a job in order to get the reward for a job 'done well'. A child has to swallow a bitter pill or to suffer the prick of injection in order to secure his health and well-being. In every case a motive has to be frustrated. The resolution of a conflict, therefore, requires the frustration of a motive. The more one is able to stand the frustration of a motive, the greater is his capacity to resolve his conflicts. The ability to stand frustration has been called frustration tolerance. All persons do not have the same power to tolerate frustration.

Effects of Frustration

Those who lack the power to tolerate frustration react to it in diverse ways. Some of these may be described as non-adaptive modes of resolving conflict; they do not produce adjustment to the situation in which the conflict arises. They have been called defence mechanisms. The person saves himself from the undesirable consequences of the frustration that he has no power to tolerate; he defends himself against them. If he does not do this he gets into a state of anxiety which is a very common effect of the frustration of a motive. Anxiety is painful even when it is mild. When the anxiety becomes intense and perpetual, the individual finds himself unable to do anything. Some people suffer from such intense and perpetual state of anxiety. They are in a state of great distress. They feel as miserable as a person who is the victim of a physical disease.

We had described anxiety earlier (p. 151). Anxiety is a vague fear over which a person has no control. It involves a feeling of insecurity, a sense of danger and of utter helplessness. The anxious person sometimes does not know why he is anxious. He may be unconscious of the conflict of his motives. He may be unaware also of the frustration of his motives. But he is clearly of a state of unhappiness and restlessness which he cannot easily explain. The feeling of helplessness intensifies the state of anxiety and makes him feel more unhappy.

We have noted earlier some of the bodily disturbances that accompany an intense emotion. The anxious person also suffers from these bodily disturbances. He may get palpitation of the heart. His blood pressure may rise. His digestion may be affected. He may lose appetite for food. A prolonged state of anxiety may cause bodily illness because of disturbances of the functions of the body. Many stomach diseases may be produced by anxiety. It is now accepted by medical men that serious diseases of the body may arise from severe anxiety to which the patient has been subjected. They call such diseases psychosomatic; soma means body. The diseases have a mixed character; their causes are psychological but the symptoms are physical. Anxiety is the chief psychological cause of such diseases. High or low blood pressure, diseases of the stomach, heart trouble, breathing difficulties as in asthma, diabetes, and several other kinds of illness are described as psychosomatic. Their main cause may be psychological, i.e., the state of anxiety from which the patient suffers.

Aggression is another equally strong effect of frustration. We have already described aggression while dealing with the emotion of anger. We have seen that a person becomes angry and shows aggressive behaviour when he meets an obstacle in his on-going activity. The obstruction of a motivated behaviour is frustration. Frustration, therefore, produces aggression or aggression is an effect of frustration. Aggression sometimes may bring about the satisfaction of the blocked motive and may prevent further frustration. By becoming aggressive the individual may be able to remove the obstacle; he can attack more strongly. In such a case the aggression adds to the strength of the motive by releasing more energy. But generally aggressive behaviour produces counter-aggression. The person is opposed more strongly and may have to face defeat and further humiliation. This produces stronger frustration. If the person cannot tolerate frustration, he suffers from anxiety. There is, thus, a strong relationship between aggression and anxiety. Frustration produces aggression and if the aggression fails to remove the cause of frustration, the failure produces anxiety. The individual is overtaken by the fear of the loss and suffering that might follow his defeat.

Aggression may result in anxiety in still another way. A person may satisfy a motive through aggressive behaviour. For example, an older child who is prevented from taking a toy possessed by a younger child may forcibly snatch the toy and thus satisfy his motive. Or he may express his aggression by abusing his neighbour who intervenes and restores the toy to the possession of the younger child. But if he values parental love, the aggressive behaviour shown produces a fear of loss of parental love or the fear of parents' punishment. His parents may come to know what happened and he will have to face the consequences. He gets into a state of anxiety. Aggressive behaviour seldom brings a gain to the individual in social situations. Civilisation and culture put stronger restrictions on the expressions of anger and aggression than on the expressions of fear and timidity. The latter may expose a person only to ridicule and shame. The former may bring him even physical punishment. Aggressive behaviour, therefore, exposes a person to a greater threat and produces a stronger feeling of anxiety.

Defence Mechanisms

We saw above that frustration produces anxiety or aggression. Unsuccessful aggression, and in several cases even successful aggression, may result in greater anxiety. Anxiety affects both the physical and the mental health of a person. Freedom from worries and anxieties promotes physical and mental health. To protect himself from the effects of frustration, a person reacts to frustration by using one or other defence mechanisms. It should not be thought that he uses a defence deliberately or even consciously. The defence mechanisms are nature's protections to the frustrated person. Frustration of motives is quite common. Toleration of frustration is not so common. We noted earlier that this is a quality observed in very exceptional cases. To tolerate frustration is, therefore, not natural. Most persons will be condemned, therefore, to a life of a perpetual misery if nature does not provide them a protection. The continuous worries and anxieties produced by frustrations would ruin their physical and mental health. Their very existence will be threatened. Nature has, therefore, endowed man with the capacity to defend himself against the consequences of frustration automatically. He has to make no conscious effort for this. The defence mechanisms are brought into play at the unconscious level. Sigmund Freud, the founder of psychoanalysis, has shown how the unconscious functions without the individual's knowledge. It was he who first suggested these defence mechanisms. He was a physician and treated cases of mental illness. He discovered these mechanisms at work in his patients. It was later discovered that these mechanisms are also to be found in persons who do not suffer from a mental illness. They may be described as a part of the normal functions of the unconscious of every person.

The defence mechanisms are reactions to frustration. As we have seen, failure to resolve a conflict of motives is one of the main causes of frustration. The main function of the defence mechanisms is to resolve conflict of motives. They protect the organism against the effects of the prolongation of the conflict. They may, therefore, be called as modes of resolving conflict. A common feature of these modes of resolving conflict is to obliterate the consciousness of one of the conflicting motives. The growing son may be inclined both to like and dislike his father. He likes his father because he provides him a sense of security. He dislikes his father because he interferes with his freedom of action. He has a mixed attitude towards his father. Such a mixed attitude has been called *ambivalence*. The son has an ambivalent attitude, a mixture of acceptance and rejection, of like and dislike, towards his father. Generally the son remains unaware of his dislike and, therefore, experiences no conflict. The dislike for the father is said to be repressed. It passes into the unconscious. It may influence the son's behaviour towards the father. Motivated by his repressed dislike for the father, the son may act against a certain wish of his father. But he would not know that he thus acted because of his dislike for the father.

He would explain his action in other ways. In fact he is not aware of having acted because of dislike. Let us take another example. The sex motive may lead a girl to seek the company of boys. Her moral sense on the other hand requires her to shun the company of boys. The conflict is resolved by the repression of the sex urge. She becomes unaware of the attraction she has for boys.

Repression is a very common mode of resolving conflicts. It will not be proper, however, to call repression a defence mechanism. As we will see, repression is a common element in most defence mechanisms. We will describe the important ones below :

1. *Projection.* The girl who has repressed her attraction for boys and is still attracted by boys defends herself by believing that the boys are attracted by her. They seek her company; only she is not discourteous enough to turn them away. The son who carries an unconscious hostility to his father may believe that his father dislikes him, and unduly creates difficulties in his way. Both the girl and the son attribute their own unconscious motives to another person. They thus protect themselves against the feelings of guilt and anxiety to which they will be exposed by accepting those motives as their own. They see nothing bad about themselves and thus save their conscience. This defence mechanism has been called projection. The person projects or throws out his own undesirable impulses on to another person.

Projection is a very common mechanism. Few persons are ready to accept their own faults. They would rather explain it to be the result of another person's actions. Where one should blame himself, one is more likely to blame others. Projection is illustrated not only in blaming others. It is also reflected in the tendency to find faults with others. It is a common habit to attribute dishonesty, immorality, or similar vices, to other persons without any evidence to prove the allegation. The person who brings the charge is most often subject to the vices himself. He defends himself by attributing his failings to others. Sometimes, he justifies his failings, when his attention is drawn to them, by attributing them to persons holding positions of great responsibility and power.

2. *Reaction Formation.* Another form of self-defensive reaction is found in the person who shows undue and exaggerated friendliness, courtesy, or respect to another person. His outward behaviour may be just a cover to conceal his repressed jealousy, dislike, or contempt for the person. A student may show excessive love and kindness to a rival who ousted him from the top position in the college examination. Actually, he may be hiding aggressive impulses towards the rival. His excessive concern for the rival prevents him from becoming aware of the aggressive feelings. It also prevents him from behaving in a manner not in keeping with his concept of himself as a 'good person'. His outward behaviour protects him against the feelings of guilt and shame. The defence mechanism is called reaction formation. The excessive warmth and sincerity are reactions against the repressed hostility and ill-will aroused by the defeat suffered at the hands of the rival. Sometimes, a person who is outwardly very rigid about religious forms and practices may be hiding in his unconscious a strong temptation for all that is prohibited by religion and morality. Such a person may spring a surprise when in his off moments he falls a prey to the temptation. His outward behaviour is a reaction formation to protect him from the biting feelings of guilt and anxiety.

3. *Regression.* As a protection from the anxiety produced by frustration, a person may turn away from the world of facts and persons. He builds up a world of his own, carved out of his own imagination. He fulfils his frustrated motives in this unreal world. In Chapter VIII we have described the child's world of imagination and seen that he satisfies many of his needs, wants and desires in this world. Adults, too, land in the world of imagination when dreaming. The dream may occur also in the day time. We call them day-dreams. The day-dreams have one main function. They reduce the anxiety produced by a frustrated motive. A rejected candidate may overcome his feelings of dejection and worry by dreaming of having achieved one day sufficient political power to dismiss the members of the selection committee. When the adult person reacts to frustration by satisfying his motives in the world of imagination, he reverts

to a mode of satisfying motives that worked when he was just a child. As an adult he has learnt to seek for a more realistic satisfaction of his needs and wants. But failing to secure satisfaction in the world of reality, he regresses to his long-forsaken world of imagination and fantasy. This defence mechanism is, therefore, called regression.

Sometimes an adult person allays his anxiety not only by satisfying his frustrated motives in an unreal world, like a small child. Often, when in a state of distress caused by the frustration of his motive, he may also outwardly behave like a child. He may cry like a baby and show the same craving for attention and care as displayed by a child. He runs away from the adult situation and acts in a way characteristic of a child.

Few persons escape from reality and permanently regress to the child's ways of satisfying frustrated motives. Most persons react to frustration in this manner under very special circumstances and only for the time being. A few persons, however, may for all times escape from the frustrations of life by permanently landing in a world of imagination and fantasy. Illusion, hallucinations, delusions or unfounded beliefs constitute the elements of their world. We call them mentally sick persons. Abnormal psychology is concerned with understanding and dealing with such mentally ill persons.

4. *Rationalisation.* Quite a common reaction to frustration is to lose sight of the real motive for an action and explain the action with the help of a substitute motive. The real motive is repressed, because it produces feelings of guilt or failure. Many acts of charity a person does are really meant to achieve publicity. The motive is not to help those in distress, but to become known as charitable and kindly, or to show off one's wealth. But a person is not ready to accept the real motive for his action; he thinks, instead, that his real motive is sympathy and kindness. The same person will, however, be very much concerned to find his name printed in the list of donors. For this reason, those who collect donations for a charitable purpose take special care to print or publish the names of the donors. They find this device a very good incentive for other persons to come forward with their donations. The defence mechanism that is at work in such situations has been called rationalisation.

It is human nature to find a reason for every action. Man is by nature intolerant of ambiguity, as he is intolerant of frustration. Since man cannot tolerate ambiguity, he tries to explain every event and achieve satisfaction by doing so. Everyone knows, without an element of doubt, that nothing is more certain than death. Still, even when a pretty old person dies, we become curious to know how the death took place. We do not just accept the fact as the inevitable end of human life. When man fails to explain an event in terms of observable natural causes, he explains it by imagining supernatural forces and agents. The need to rationalise every event, to find a reason for everything that happens, also leads us to rationalise a motive for the action whose real motive we are not prepared to accept. Rationalisation serves as a face-saving device. We sometimes reduce the frustration of failure by consoling ourselves that it was not worth while to succeed. The feeling of failure produces anxiety. The person 'saves his face' by minimising the failure. The fox that cannot reach the grapes hanging from a high wall satisfies herself with the idea that the 'grapes are sour'. A careless student takes the sting out of his failure by emphasising the ineptness of college graduates. His rationalisation provides a good defence from the anxiety. of failure. Rationalisation takes another form when failure to secure a more attractive goal leads a person to accept a less attractive goal. He is, thus, able to dispose of the anxiety produced by failure. Unlike the 'grapes are sour', the 'lemons are sweet' serves to save his face.

5. *Compensation.* A child may feel frustrated on account of a bodily disability or deformity. Sometimes, he overcomes the frustration by developing exceptional mental talent. A bad-looking girl may become a highly attractive singer. A boy with a crippled body may grow to be a famous scientist. Such ways of reacting to frustration are called compensation. The anxiety produced in the girl for her failure to attract others by her looks is removed when she is able to attract them by her voice. Similarly, the boy's failure to dominate by his bodily strength is compensated by his ability to excel others in mental power.

Compensation may be regarded as an adaptive mode of reaction to frustration of motives when a person compensates for his real defect in one area by intensely striving to develop strength in another area. The secret of success, in most cases, lies in ascertaining one's strengths and weaknesses. The weaknesses are accepted and the strengths are further developed by choosing a course of action where one's strengths are likely to produce fruitful results and the weaknesses cause no hindrance.

Sometimes a person may become conscious of a defect which is not real. A fairly intelligent child may come to believe that he is dull. Some parents are over-critical of the achivement of their children. They set for the child very high standard of success and are dissatisfied when the child does not come up exactly to the level they demand. They always underrate whatever success the child actually achieves. The child too gradually learns to underrate his achievements. He comes to believe that his abilities are too poor, that he cannot make any worthwhile achievement. He develops a feeling of inferiority. Such a child builds up a concept ofhimself, that is, of his abilities and powers, which does not conform to the reality. Such a child gets a strong feeling of failure and frustration, for which he may use a compensatory device as a defence. He may bully younger children, those who are weaker than he, and thus secure evidence of his superior power. He may compensate for the feeling of rejection produced within his family by using undesirable devices of catching attention outside his family. He may even feel happy at 'getting a name' for being naughty, mischievous and disobedient. There is a common proverb : 'Even if I get a bad name, I get a name all the same'. The child may take to speaking lie, stealing, and other forms of dishonesty. He steals money to impress upon his companions that he gets enough money from his parents who are very well off. This gives him a false sense of pride before others. He is able to show off his superiority over them. He may also take to bragging and lapsing into undeserved self-admiration.

Another person may adopt another compensatory device. He reacts to the feeling of rejection and inferiority by running away from reality. He develops fantastic notions about his superior abilities and powers. He may come to believe himself to be the only wise man in a world of fools, to be the most illustrious person and, therefore, the object of everybody's jealousy and hatred. He compensates for his inferiority by developing what has been called a superiority complex. Sometimes, the compensation takes an extreme form. The person lives in a world of delusion, in a world of unfounded beliefs and ideas. He becomes a serious mental case.

Chapter XII

PERSONALITY

The Nature and Traits of Personality

Every man perceives remembers, imagines, thinks, feels, desires, decides and acts to objects and persons. Every man has needs and motives which influence his perceptions, memories, imagination, feelings, desires, decisions and actions. Many of these needs and motives every man shares with every other man. Several of the goals and purposes also to which his needs and motives are directed man shares with other men. Some he shares with persons all over the world and some with persons belonging to his own culture and society. But in spite of all this sameness, no two persons behave, think, feel and act in identically the same manner even when placed in the same situation.

Give a hundred-rupee note to each one of two students reading in the same class in a college, both belonging to the upper middle class family, and both residing in the same locality of the town. Let them have perfect freedom to use the money as they like. After the lapse of some time, ask them how they spent the money. You may find that one of them deposited the money in the local bank, while the other spent it all on inviting friends, visting the picture house, and buying some odd things. You will explain the difference in the behaviour of the two persons by calling the one economical and the other extravagant. You will also expect that the first one will, generally, save rather than spend whenever he can save; the second one will generally spend rather than save even when he does not need to spend. You expect this difference in their behaviour because you presume that their personality characteristics are different. The difference will not be limited to the way they use money. It will be reflected also in the difference in their perception of money, in their thoughts and feelings about money, in their desires, hopes and fears related to money.

You may be interested in observing these students while they act in several other situations. You may notice them to differ not only in respect of one being economical and the other extravagant. They may differ also in numerous other characteristics. One may be found to be inhibited, reserve and shy. The other may be assertive, forward and sociable. One may be found to be giving lead in social situations, getting others do what he would like them to do; the other occupies the position of the rank and file, always taking lead from others. One remains calm and self-composed even in very difficult situations. The other becomes anxious and disturbed in the face of minor troubles. If you probe further, you may find differences also in their wants and motives, abilities and aptitudes, habits, interests, attitudes and values, and in their ideas of the self, of other persons and of the world. Instead of listing the vast multitudes of characteristics in which the two persons differ, you make a short description. You say that their *personality* is different.

We conclude from the above that the description of a man's personality is not a simple affair. Such is the case because personality itself is very complex. It consists of manifold and diverse elements. The elements of personality are called the traits of personality. It is the traits of a person which make one person's behaviour different from that of another. Shyness and sociability are different traits of personality because they imply that a person who is shy will feel uncomfortable in the midst of strangers. A person who is sociable would not feel uneasy among strangers; he will be happy and will make friendly contacts with them.

The traits of personality cannot be directly observed. But when you observe a person to display a similar behaviour on meeting a variety of situations you are led to believe that he has a set of enduring characteristics or traits. His traits make him behave in consistent manner though the situations may be very diverse His traits also make his behaviour different from other persons because others possess a set of different traits. If you find a person showing very dissimilar patterns of behaviour in similar situations, you have every reason to conclude that the behaviour does not manifest a trait of personality. If you come across a person who makes as often correct as incorrect statement of facts, you cannot qualify him with the trait of truthfulness. Nor will you be justified in describing him as untruthful person. Observed consistency of behaviour in related situations is the basis for the inference of traits of personality.

We can think of various characteristics of personality, all the characteristics that a person may have. Some of these make one person different from, and some make him similar to, another person. These may also include the physical characteristics. A person may be tall, short, or of average built. It may not be proper, however, to use the term trait for the physical characteristics, though, as we will see, they influence the formation of traits. It is better to reserve *the term for those characteristics of a person that are not directly observable.* Physical characteristics are directly observable. We get our first-hand impression of the person from his physical characteristics. These along with other aspects of his objectively observable behaviour help us in understanding his traits. They do not constitute his traits. *Traits, as we said above, are inferred from the observed consistency of behaviour.*

Every characteristic that can be inferred from the observed consistency of behaviour of persons is a trait. But every characteristic which we call a trait may not be the trait of a particular person. We may use the term in a general and abstract sense as standing for personality characteristics. We may use it in a concrete or specific sense when we talk about the traits of particular persons. In this sense, persons differ in their traits. *A trait that exists in one person may be absent in another person. A person may be shy in some situations where he could be sociable and sociable in some situations where he could be shy. We can describe him neither as a sociable nor as a shy person.* He has no related trait as there is no observable consistency in his behaviour. Individuals differ all the way between sociability and shyness, depending upon the observable consistency or inconsistency of their behaviour in related situations. Those who fall midway show maximum inconsistency. They cannot be described as either shy or sociable. We will find this principle involved in the measurement of personality traits. *A characteristic can, therefore, be the trait of a person only when it can make him distinct from most other persons.* We can thus imagine a vast multitude of personality characteristics, but can think only of a few traits of a person, those that make him unique and different.

We saw above that a person may have several personality traits. Each one accounts for the consistency of his behaviour in a variety of related situations. Should we think that the personality of an individual is the sum total of his traits ? The answer will be in the negative. *Personality is the organisation of the traits of an individual. The traits are interrelated. The personality of an individual is a unified whole of his traits. The organisation of the traits is dynamic. Each trait influences every other trait and together they give a distinctive character to the behaviour of the person. One may discover similar traits in two individuals, but still one may not find them behaving in identical manner in the same situations.* What accounts for the difference in such a case is not the possession of the traits of personality, but the organisation of the traits—the pattern of interrelation between the traits.

It follows from the above that each individual's personality is unique and different from every other individual's personality. Just like the finger marks which are never identical in two persons though they are made of similar lines and curves, each individual's personality is unique. *This uniqueness is the result of difference not only in the traits of different individuals but also in the dynamic organisation of the traits.*

Besides the difference in the individual traits or the organisation of these traits, persons differ also in the level of organisation of traits. The traits of some persons are loosely organised. They are not closely interrelated. The traits of other persons are closely intergrated. They form an interrelated system of traits. Within the system, the traits are also ordered. A few traits dominate over others. The other traits and characteristics of the person are subordinate to them. Such a person will be said to possess a highly integrated personality. Most persons do not manifest such a high level of unity of personality. Their personality consists of several trait systems some of which may also be unrelated. Only a few persons possess a highly integrated personality. Also, only a few persons have very loosely organised personality. In extreme cases we get a complete dissociation of personality. Such cases are abnormal and are found among a kind of mental patients; they have a double or even multiple personality. The same person may combine within him both the quiet and talkative, the shy and the sociable, the conservative and the liberal, the rigid and the flexible. At one moment one personality comes into the forc and the individual behaves in a manner determined by one set of traits. At another moment he behaves in an altogether different manner because the other set of traits get into ascendance. The famous novel of *Robert Louis Stevenson* gives a very good illustration of the double personality in *Dr. Jakyll and Mr. Hyde. There has been a very well-known case of a girl, Miss Beauchamp, who developed three independent personalities. Each personality was represented by its own set of traits.*

Personality is not only unique. It is also stable and enduring. It persists and generally remains very much the same. The traits of personality, as we saw, are enduring characteristics of personality. Once established, they do not undergo sudden or quick change. The organisation of traits also endures or persists through time. Successive events of behaviour of a person show the same patterning of his traits. The individual retains his uniqueness through time. If personality changed from moment to moment social life would be impossible. Man is a social animal. He lives in a society of other persons. These other persons influence his behaviour and he influences their behaviour. Such mutual influence has been called the process of social interaction. Most goals and purposes of the individual depend for their satisfaction on the process of social interaction. The type of influence one person exerts upon the other is very largely a matter of the personality of each person. A may be assertive, rigid and obstinate. If B also happens to be qualified by the same traits, A's influence on B may lead to a clash or even a regular fight. On the other hand, if B is submissive, flexible and considerate, the outcome will be conciliation and friendship. Imagine a husband and wife, both dominated by the same traits of independence, self-responsibility and impulsiveness. It will not be difficult for you to imagine the condition of the home and the family. It is very clear, therefore, that behaviour in interpersonal situations depends, in a very large measure, upon the personality of the individuals engaged in the interpersonal behaviour. A person can achieve his goal and purposes only when he is able to expect uniformity or consistency in the behaviour of those he has to deal with. His expectations are generally fulfilled, because an individual's personality, besides being unique, is also enduring. His traits generally do not undergo sudden or abrupt changes.

To sum up, personality is the dynamic organisation of the trait and characteristics of an individual. All characteristics which an individual possesses—his needs and wants, his attitudes and habits, his abilities and powers, his goals and aspirations, his patterns of behaviour to objects and persons—constitute his personality. They are all organised within him in a manner that makes him different from any other person. The traits and characteristics persist through time. Once formed and stabilised, they become enduring predispositions for behaviour. The traits of personality cannot be directly observed. They can be inferred from the observed consistency of the person's behaviour to a variety of situations. The traits of a person may be highly integrated or loosely organised. We can thus conceive of difference in the levels integration of personality. In a highly integrated person the traits form a unified and well-ordered system. When integration is poor, the traits form several unrelated subsystems.

Personality Types

The traits of person describe his personality. We may need to know several of his traits and characteristics to get an adequte description of the person. A much easier description is to classify a person under a type. There are such types as extraverted vs. introverted, dominant vs. submissive, inhibited vs. expressive, active vs. passive, and so on. We have also a classification of body types—the asthenic vs. the pyknic. The asthenic type has thin and narrow-chested body. The pyknic has fat and broad-chested body. The asthenic is "shy, sensitive, aloof and withdrawn". The pyknic is "jovial, lively, outgoing and moody". According to the classification by type every person has to be fitted into one or other type. He is either extraverted or introverted, dominant or submissive, inhibited or expressive, sociable or seclusive, asthenic or pyknic. But a person may not properly fit under any type. He may be neither extraverted nor introverted. In some situations he may act in a manner characteristic of the introvert. In others he may act in ways peculiar to the extravert. He may be sociable like the extraverted and unconventional like the introverted. His behaviour may show no consistency in related situations. No generalisation can therefore be made about his behaviour in order to place him under a type. Neither extraversion nor introversion fits as a label for his behaviour. Same may be the case with the other categories of classification. Individuals differ all the way between the extreme types. Most persons fall at the middle. Any attempt to force a person under a type may give a faulty description of his personality. To classify persons by types is to over-simplify the matter of personality description.

Personality is highly complex, and in describing a person one should never ignore this aspect. In fact it is not possible to achieve a complete description of personality because of the great variety of personality traits and characteristics and also because of the very different patterns in which they may be organised. Personality description is a difficult task which requires very skilful handling.

The Determinants of Personality

We use the traits of a person to describe his personality. His traits and the ways they are patterned make him different from other persons. They constitute what makes him a unique person. But we may ask how he came to possess the traits that make him different ? What factors made him what he is at a particular moment in his life ? These factors have been called the determinants of personality. They explain why a person is what he is today.

The determinants of personality may be classified into : (1) the biological or physiological determinants and (2) the social determinants. We will first consider the biological determinants. They account for those differences in personality that are not derived from the peculiar social environment in which a child is born and grows. They arise from the differences within the germ cell from which life starts.

Biological Determinants

Difference in temperament of persons is supposed to be determined by biological or genetic factors. From the moment of birth one child may be observed to be highly energetic, active and lively, another to be slow, sluggish and calm. There is a biological difference, therefore, in the total output of energy or physical drive at the disposal of a person. Similarly one child is more emotionally expressive than another from the moment of birth, more responsive, excitable and jolly. The general level of activity or energy and of emotional expressiveness in which persons differ from one another constitute their temperamental characteristics. The determinants of these characteristics are not social but genetic.

Difference in intelligence is also generally considered to be due to biological or hereditary factors. Intelligence is now generally accepted to be an innate or inborn capacity of a person. It grows and develops just like the body. No amount of learning can produce an increase in the inherent intellectual capacity of a person. Intelligence, however, is a very important element of personality. Difference in this aspect of personality is also, therefore, biologically determined. Genetic factors account for this difference also.

The endocrine glands or glands of internal secretion are considered to be important biological or physiological determinants of personality. As we have seen in Chapter II, these glands secrete a hormone which passes directly into the blood stream. It, thus, affects every part and organ of the body. Excessive increase or decrease in secretion influences the growth and development of the body and of its different organs. Increased secretion accelerates the growth of some organs. Decreased secretion retards their growth. The accelerated or retarded growth is accompanied not only by some peculiar bodily characteristics. It is attended also by some specific personality characteristics. Let us take the examples of the thyroid gland. When the thyroid is under-active there is all-round sluggishness in the activities of the person. His weight increases. He gets mental depression. His memory becomes ineffective and his thinking is slow. He cannot take decisions easily, loses initiative, and gets readily into anger. When the thyroid becomes over-active, there is an increase in the output of energy, the level of activity becomes high, blood pressure rises, body weight decreases. These effects are also accompanied by some personality characteristics. The person whose thyroid gland is over-active is dominant, aggressive, energetic and emotionally expressive. *While the person with an under-active thyroid is passive, docile, and submissive, wanting in emotional expressions and moody.* Similar differences in personality characteristics have been found to be associated with the unusually high or low activity of the other endocrine glands.

Difference in the build of the body is supposed to be another biological determinant of difference in personality characteristics. In respect of the build of their body, persons have been classified into three types, the *endomorph*, the *messomorph* and the *ectomorph*. The endomorph has a round body, with excessive fat and over-growth of the visceral system. He is a jolly, ease-loving, extraverted and sociable person. The messomorph has a square body, with developed bones and muscles. He is assertive, dominant, aggressive and adventurous. The *ectomorph* has a linear body, thin and frail. He is theoretical, idealistic, secretive, seclusive and emotionally inhibited.

Social Determinants

Differences in the characteristics of personality result also from the peculiarities of the social environment of persons. By social environment is meant the environment of other persons and social institutions. Among the social determinants of difference in personality, culture and the family are most powerful.

Studies have been made of the dominant personality characteristics of people who belong to different cultures. It has been found that cultural differences in personality are as remarkable as differences between the individuals in the same culture. Most of the studies have been made of the less advanced or primitive societies; they manifest more similarities in day-to-day behaviour of individuals than what is to be found in the more advanced and civilised societies. In some primitive societies, the people show a general lack of emotional warmth and responsiveness. They are generally self-centred and wanting in kindness and generosity. Other societies show entirely different cultural characteristics. The people are generally more cordial, kind-hearted, group-centred and co-operative.

Within the same culture also we can observe the cultural differences in personality characteristics. Every society is divided into high and low classes. The people in the lower class of society display certain characteristics of behaviour that make them different from those in the upper or the middle class. For example, the lower middle class people are generally more conservative, more conventional and less flexible in the observance of social norms and in their regard for moral values. They are also more patient and forbearing, though emotionally more insecure and tense.

The cultural factors, as we found, do not account for individual differences in personality. They explain the differences between social groups or social classes. Nevertheless, the study of these differences makes us appreciate the role of culture in the formation of personality characteristics.

The family, which is the smallest unit of the social group, is the most potent social determinant of differences in personality. The individual receives the earliest influence from his family. The attitudes, values, habits, practices, mode of behaviour of the family members, and pattern of relationships between them have considerable influence in favouring or obstructing the formation and growth of certain personality qualities in the child. Such factors as early or late weaning, early or late toilet training, cup-feeding or breast-feeding, feeding at regular intervals, interrupted feeding and so on, have been presumed to be of great significance in the formation of later personality traits. Such characteristics as emotional security and stability, independence, self-confidence, ascendance, responsibility, orderliness, sociableness, obstinacy, miserliness, etc., have been found to be associated with the practices followed in a family in serving the biological needs of the child. The parents' attitudes of rejection, indulgence, overprotectiveness, indifference, consistent or inconsistent discipline, make their own contribution to the patterns of emotional and social adjustment that the child develops. Excessive affection or fondling by parents may lead to self-centredness, egoism, obstinacy, impulsiveness and irresponsibility. Want of affection, on the other hand, may produce anxiety, emotional insecurity, lack of self-confidence, submissiveness, pessimism and other peculiarities of personality and character.

Such factors as the child's rank among his brothers and sisters, being the only child, the only male or female child, being an orphan, having a step-mother or a step-father, being brought up by a close or distant relative, and so on, have also been found to influence the types of attitudes, motives and other personality characteristics a person develops. The eldest, the youngest or the only child has been found to show a set of traits that make him different from other persons. The sibling position or rank, as it is called, does not, however, necessarily lead to a particular set of characteristics. Much depends upon the attitude and reactions of the other members in the family, particularly the parents. The youngest child may be a much-longed-for male baby or an unwanted burden on the family's too limited resources. The eldest, like-wise, may be a welcome addition to the family long awaited by the childless mother, or, he may be a much too early and unwelcome arrival who restricts the freedom of the young couple.

An understanding and affectionate woman may give more love and encouragement to her step-child than he got from his deceased, unbalanced, highly aggressive, and self-centred mother. The step-mother's behaviour will, then, have a wholesome effect on the development of the child's personality. All step-mothers are not alike. Some step-mothers are forced into the step-motherly pattern. Even their kindly behaviour is so perceived and interpreted as to be fitted into the conventional image of the step-mother. We have already discussed the influence of needs, attitudes, and interest on perception in an earlier chapter. Finding her positive feelings for the child unrewarded by her social environment, the woman, quite naturally, lapses into the attitude of indifference and want of concern for the child. The child is also encouraged to exploit the peculiar relation and makes excessive demands on the step-mother's indulgence. The failure to meet the demand is perceived as an evidence of negligence or ill-treatment.

We have seen that personality differences arise on account of both biological and social determinants. But we should not think that the biological factors play their part independently of the social factors. The high or low intelligence, the over-active or the under-active endocrine glands, the fatty, muscular, or thin body do not directly influence the formation of personality characteristics and traits. Much depends upon the type of reactions made by other persons to the mental or bodily peculiarities manifested by a person. Many highly talented children develop conceit, egoism, non-responsiveness, apathy, strong-headedness, irresponsibility, aggressiveness, and other undesirable characteristics because of their over-indulgent parents. The parents had unduly admired and excessively overrated the intellectual abilities of the children. On the other hand, a child of poor intelligence may develop the feeling of personal worth, self-reliance, responsibility, sociableness, co-operativeness and other socially valued characteristics, because his understanding and sensible parents gave him the love, sympathy and respect that should be the due of every child. They created in him a feeling of success and personal value by holding out expectations that were not inconsistent with his abilities. Favourable or unfavourable reactions from parents and other persons in the child's social circle will, likewise, contribute to the development of one or other set of traits and motives in the child whose physical characteristics are out of the common. If the attitude and behaviour of others do not make him feel different, if he is dealt with just other normal children, he too will develop the usual characteristics of a normal child, in spite of his physical handicap or peculiarity. It appears therefore that the social determinants are more important than the biological determinants; the latter influence personality development through the mediation of the social factors.

Like the personality characteristics that are interrelated into a system, the determinants of personality are also interdependent in exerting their influence on personality development. Individuals develop different sets of personality characteristics because each individual is exposed to a particular pattern of determinants. No single factor, social or biological, can explain by itself the formation of a particular characteristic. It is the interplay of several determinants, the pattern of their relationships, which has to be taken into account. We have seen how the social factors interact with the biological factors in producing difference in the personality of individuals. We can note similar interaction between the social factors themselves. One culture encourages in parents one set of attitudes toward their children. Another culture discourages the same attitudes. For example, putting restrictions on the youngsters' freedom of decision and action find favour in Eastern culture. In Western culture such restrictions are considered unwholesome. Similarly a behaviour for which the child is punished in one social class may be tolerated, and even rewarded, in another social class. Likewise the love and respect denied to the child in the family may be restored to him by the sympathy and consideration he receives in a modern advanced school.

The determinants of personality are highly interdependent. In influencing personality development several of them interact. This makes the interpretation of personality differences as difficult as their description. Each factor has to be taken note of. The possible relation of each to every other has to be examined. One factor may be supporting or counteracting another. The relative frequency and strength of each one in the life of the individual has to be determined. The child might have been exposed to a few factors more often. A few have been more dominant as compared to others. The determination of all this is evidently a difficult task. Only experienced psychologists can ascertain the value of each factor in making a person what he is found to be at the moment.

Measurement of Personality

We noted above that the personality of an individual is highly complex. *It is not possible, therefore, to measure the personality of an individual as a whole. All that one can achieve is to measure the elements or traits of personality.* We will deal later with the measurement of abilities and aptitudes. It is possible to measure needs, attitudes, interests, values and other personality characteristics also.

The following methods have been used for measuring personality characteristics :

1. *The Questionnaire Method* : This method involves the preparation of a list of questions or statements. Each one is concerned with some aspect of the feeling, attitude, habit, or mode of behaviour related to the personality characteristic which is intended to be measured. The person who is to be tested is required to indicate his agreement or disagreement, acceptance or rejection, affirmation or denial of each statement. The questions are so worded that the affirmation of some and the denial of others express the presence of the trait that is measured. Each question or statement is followed by "Yes", "No", "?", "True", "Untrue", "Doubtful", or other similar responses. The testee selects and underlines a response that shows whether the statement describes his behaviour or not. Each statement or question is called an item. Following is the type of items used:

1. When you have to make an important decision, do you prefer someone else to decide for you ?
2. When you have thoughtfully planned an activity, do you feel that others should follow it uncritically ?
3. In social gatherings, I like to be the centre of attention.
4. In a meeting, I prefer to occupy a back seat.

Supposing the above items are used in a test of dominance, the person who possesses this trait is likely to affirm or accept items 2 and 3, and deny or reject items 1 and 4.

A personality test contains a good number of items, say thirty or fifty. The person who responds to most items in a consistent manner, that is, accepts those that express the presence of the characteristic and rejects those that show its absence, gets high score in the test. Another person who consistently rejects most positive items and accepts most negative items will get low score in the test. Supposing the test is measuring dominance. The consistency of the responses made by the first person would enable us to infer that dominance is a strong trait of the person. The same consistency of responses in the second person would lead us to conclude that submission is the distinctive characteristic of this person. Those who do not make consistent responses to the items, that is, affirm some and deny other positive items and deny some and affirm other negative items will get intermediate scores. They will not be credited with the trait of either dominance of submission.

The questionnaire method of measuring personality is also called objective test of personality. It is objective because whosoever administers the test will give the same score to the person tested. There will be no difference from tester to tester. However, though the method is objective, it may not yield a valid result. A person's score in the test may not represent his real characteristics. The person may not be frank and truthful while responding to the test items. He may affirm statements which he should really deny and deny those that he should really affirm. His high or low scores in the test will be highly deceptive. This is more likely to occur when the characteristic that is measured is socially desirable or undesirable. For example, the traits of punctuality and self-centredness. One is highly desirable and the other is highly undesirable. Unless a person is very frank and truthful, he is likely to respond to each item in such a manner that his scores reveal him to be punctual and the opposite of the self-centred. In using the questionnaire method, it is very important to win the confidence of the testee so that he presents a correct picture of his behaviour.

2. *Projective Tests* : One does not encounter the above difficulty when one uses a projective test. The projective test is a device for measuring personality which the person tested does not recognise as such. He makes, therefore, spontaneous responses in the test. The test presents a highly ambiguous situation which the testee is required to perceive and describe. The situation has no definite characteristics and so different persons perceive it in different ways. We have seen how our perceptions are influenced by our individual needs, purposes, habits and attitudes (p. 91). The same fact is illustrated in the projective tests. In perceiving the ambiguous situation, also called unstructured stimulus, each person reflects his own needs, attitudes, habits, interests, feelings and behaviour patterns. His descriptions manifest these and enable the tester to get access to the characteristics of the person without his knowledge. The method is called projective because in perceiving and describing the situation, a person brings

into the open his personality characteristics. The stimulus functions as a screen over which his personality is projected.

Two projective tests have become very well known, as they have been very widely used. One was introduced by Hermann Rorschach and is named after him as the *Rorschach Test or RT. It consists of* 10 *cards, each one having an inkblot on it.* You have seen one such inkblot on p. 130. Similar inkblots were made by Rorschach. Some blots are coloured and some are in black and white.

The inkblot, as you see below, does not represent any object. It is an ambiguous or unstructured figure. The ambiguity of the blot results in the great variety of responses it produces. Such an inkblot is placed before the testee. He is asked to describe what he sees. He is also required to say in what portion he sees and what makes him see the object that he describes. His responses are noted and classified under different categories. A great variety of responses are made. These responses differ from person to person. Some testees respond to the whole figure, some to the parts of the figure. Some respond to form or shape, some to colour or the white space between the coloured or black patches. Some see moving and others stationary objects. Some see human figures or parts of human body. Others see animals or inanimate objects.

It has been found in a series of systematic investigations that *differences in the perceptions of persons are related to differences in their abilities, needs, feelings, attitudes, interests and other personality characteristics.* Classification of the responses made to the total of ten cards by a testee shows that certain types and categories of responses are made consistently. These responses are interpreted as indicating the personality characteristics that they are generally found to accompany.

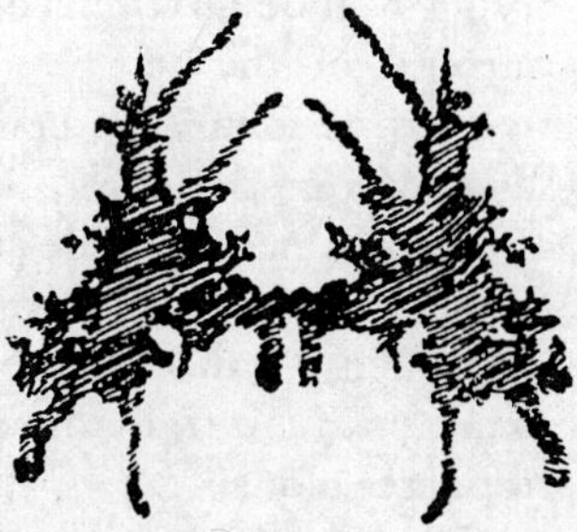

Fig. 35

Murray's Thematic Apperception Test, or TAT, is another projective test of personality. This test consists of twenty pictures. Each picture contains one or more persons in very ambiguous situations. For example, in one picture a very old woman with wrinkled face is standing behind a young woman looking very serious. In another picture a man is standing besides a bed on which a woman is lying. The testee is asked to write a story on each picture. The story should have a theme. It should say what is happening, what led to the happening, and what is going to be the outcome or result. In writing a story, the testee is expected to identify himself unconsciously with a character in the story. The story is thus built round his own needs and frustrations, feelings and attitudes, ideas of self and of others, real or imaginary, modes of meeting difficulties and resolving conflicts, and so on. However, one can get no clue about the characteristics of the testee from a single story. Only, when one finds the recurrence of the same or similar characters, expressing similar feelings and attitudes, encountering similar difficulties and conflicts, entertaining similar hopes and fears, etc., one may be led to think that the stories reveal the person's own characteristics. Here again, observed consistency of his behaviour becomes the basis for the inference of the person's characteristics.

As we stated above, the projective tests possess the advantage that the testee's are spontaneous and frank. He is not trying to hide anything or to make a show of himself. The real purpose of the test is disguised from him. He does not know that his personality is being tested. But, very unlike the personality questionnaire, the projective test has the disadvantage of being subjective. The same RT or TAT responses are likely to be interpreted in different ways by different psychologists. Not much reliance can be put on the description of the personality of an individual made on the basis of his RT or TAT responses alone.

The questionnaire method or the projective test makes use of the verbal behaviour or the person tested. The verbal behaviour gives an account of the person's perception of himself, of other persons or of the situation that he confronts. The first-hand data on which this account is based, specially in the questionnaire method, are drawn from the person's introspection or self-observation of his feelings, attitudes, interests, values, and modes of behaviour. The two other methods we will discuss below depend upon objective observation of the behaviour of the person tested. In one method the behaviour is observed in everyday situations. The other requires observation of behaviour in standard, or test situations. The first is called Personality Rating. The second is named as the Situational Test.

3. *Personality Rating* : In this method on person judges or rates the characteristics of another person. The person who judges is the rater and the person who is judged is the ratee. The basis of the rating is the rater's general impression drawn from his observation of the behaviour of the ratee in a variety of related situations. For example, a class teacher may be asked to judge such personality characteristics of his pupils as orderliness, punctuality, industriousness, co-operativeness etc. The teacher has known each pupil individually over a long time and has observed each one's behaviour in various situations. The teacher may be asked to express his rating on each trait by locating the position of each pupil on a so-called rating scale. The following is the example of a rating scale :

PUNCTUALITY

5	4	3	2	1
Always in time	Generally Punctual	Sometimes Punctual Sometimes Unpunctual	Generally Unpunctual	Never in Time

The above scale has five divisions, or points, numbered from 5 to 1. Each point is described separately. In rating the pupils on the trait of punctuality, the teacher has to decide where he should place each one. He may decide about a pupil to be highly punctual. He would place him at the left end of the scale and give him the sore of 5. Another pupil he thinks to be highly unpunctual. He locates him at the right end of the scale and gives him the score of 1. Another pupil has given equal evidence in his previous behaviour of both punctuality and unpunctuality. The teacher places him at the middle position and gives him score of 3. In this manner he locates each pupil on the scale at one point or the other from his knowledge of the previous behaviour of each one. He also assigns to each child the score meant for the point where he is placed.

4. *The Situational Test*: The situational test is slightly different from personality rating. In the situational test, a person is required to act in a situation which is specially arranged for the purpose of the testing. The tester observes the behaviour of the testee while he is acting in the situation. Genreally the testing is done in a group. Five to six persons, or even more, are placed in the same situation which involves some difficulty. Their behaviour in the situation is carefully observed and noted. The observer has a set of well-defined traits in which he proposes to test each person in the group. For example, a party of ten to twelve students is taken out and camps at the foot of a hill. The students collect together and are given some cash. They are asked to plan and arrange for preparing their lunch. They start discussing various plans so that they could come to a workable plan and set on getting busy about the preparation of the lunch. The teacher who accompanies them observes the behaviour of each one from the beginning to the end. He finds that a certain person comes forward with ideas and considers the possibilities of translating each one into action. A few others are listening to him and one or two are opposing him. Those who oppose do not seem to impress the listeners. When the decision is taken and the work starts, one person is found to offer himself for buying the needed articles from the neighbourhood. The first one gives direction and assigns duties to others. A few get busy doing things readily. Some move hesitatingly. One person is noticed to just watch others without lending a helping hand. He also passes critical remarks from time to time. Similar other aspects of behaviour manifested by each one are minutely observed by the teacher. On the basis of his objective observation of the behaviour of each student in the situation, the teacher rates each one separately on the qualities of leadership, initiative, tact, resourcefulness, co-operativeness, drive, responsibility, etc.

The situational tests have been used in assessing the personality characteristics of candidates for the war service. Special situations that involve a problem are devised for the purpose. The situational tests, however, do not form the only basis of the personality assessment. Other methods and tools are also used.

The personality rating, as well as the situational test, is subjective. The description of personality made on their basis depends upon the judgment of the rater. The judgment may not be reliable. Individuals differ in their capacity to judge the traits of other persons. There may be no agreement between two judges. They may give very different descriptions of the personality of the same person. It may be difficult to decide which one gives the more reliable description.

The situational tests have one advantage over personality rating. In the situational test two or more judges may be engaged in judging the same persons behaving in the same situation. In personality rating, each judge depends upon his observations of the behaviour of the ratee. The observations are not made at the time of rating. The rating actually depends upon the general impression of the ratee that past observations of his behaviour have produced in the rater. Two or more raters are not likely to have observed the ratee's behaviour in the same sets of situations. Their general impressions may very widely differ. The difference is not expected to be as large when raters observe the ratee's behaviour in identical situation.

Situational tests have, however, one disadvantage also. They require that special situations be provided for the testing. This is not always possible. It may also be quite expensive. Personality rating makes no special requirement. It can be utilized much more easily.

5. *Personal Data Schedule* : The methods of measuring personality provide information about the enduring characteristics of a person. A systematic account of the determinants of an individual's personality is also important. To understand an individual's personality we need both types of data. The Personal Data Schedule or the Personal Data Blank, as it is called, provides a scheme for collecting information about the determinants of personality. We have seen that the social determinants of personality are more important than the biological determinants. The social determinants are covered by the so-called background data. They consist of information about the person's family and include such facts as the economic

and cultural status of the parents and of the brothers and sisters, the pattern of emotional and social relationships within the family, the condition of physical and mental health of the family members, the individual's rank among his brothers and sisters, and so on. In addition, such facts are also included as the physical health of the individual, his educational history and status, his interests and hobbies, and some other matters that are not covered in the data provided by the measurements of personality.

Personality Assessment

We have seen that human personality is very complex. It consists of several elements. There are also several determinants of these elements. We have seen that the uniqueness of personality depends not only upon the peculiar elements that constitute it or the specific determinants that account for those elements. The pattern of interaction between the determinants, as well as the interrelation of the elements, is no less important. Mere collection of data from different sources or by different methods will not be enough. The data have to be integrated. They are to be looked at not in isolation. One has to understand the relation that one fact bears to every other fact. One has to assess the relative strength of the various factors. In other words, one has to construct a total picture of the individual's personality. In order to do this the psychologist sometimes finds it necessary to interview the person. The interview provides an opportunity to get a glimpse of the person in flesh and blood. It enables the psychologist to get a first-hand information of feelings, attitudes and behaviour of the person. The psychologist can verify the picture he has constructed on the basis of the data that he gathered. He becomes able not only to check his data, but also to fill up the gaps here and there. He may get new meanings of the facts.

A brief account of the method of interview is given below :

The interview is a face-to-face situation consisting of the interviewee and the interviewer. The interviewee is the person whose personality is assessed. The success of the interview depends upon the degree to which the interviewee makes free and frank responses in the interview situation. This requires special skill in interviewing. The interviewer has to so behave in the situation that the interviewee is enabled to make a frank and free narration of all relevant facts about himself and about his environment. The interviewer should be able to win complete trust and confidence of the interviewee. This is possible only if he can establish with the interviewee a relation of cordiality, warmth and responsiveness. Such a relation has been called 'rapport'. Without a rapport no psychological interview can be a success.

To establish rapport, the interviewer has to show genuine interest in the interviewee. He must listen to him attentively and patiently. He should not interrupt, criticise or pass any remark or judgment on what the interviewee says or does in the interview situation. If the interviewer is able to do this, he will win the trust and confidence of the interviewee. The interviewee would then bring into the open fearlessly and unhesitatingly all the hidden facts about his needs, feelings, attitudes, interests, values, and modes of behaviour. All forces of resistance that prevent him from doing this will lose their strength. He would even reveal such motives, feelings and attitudes that he may not be prepared to admit even to himself. He had so far been considering them to be too bad or too embarrassing. When he finds another person listening to them with interest and attention, without showing any annoyance or making any criticism, he comes to think that they are not really as bad. The feelings of guilt and shame associated with them are very much reduced. These feelings prevented him to bring them back to his memory. With these feelings gone, he can think of them more easily and narrate them freely and unhesitatingly.

The interview, as we saw, projects further light on the conditions of the person and on the factors that account for the peculiarities of his characteristics and behaviour. The interview enables the psychologist to know and understand the dominant needs, motives, attitudes and values of the person and the factors in his life and development that have contributed to their strength. All this, however, the psychologist could know from other sources as well. The interview has a special value which is peculiar to it. It enables also the person concerned to understand the dynamics of his personality, the forces that move him from within. He comes to appreciate his real needs and motives, his real attitudes and values, and his real goals and purposes. Many of these are concealed from him because they are repressed (p. 169). Many of them were also transformed by the defence mechanisms that operate in him (p. 168). In the free and permissive atmosphere of the psychological interview they come to the surface. The individual comes to know and accept them. This gives him a new insight into his personality. He gets a new understanding of why he is behaving in the way that he behaves.

The knowledge of the dynamics of his personality, of the forces that move him, give the person a power to control them. Knowledge gives power not only to deal with the outer environment. Knowledge gives power to control and direct the forces that influence one's own attitudes and patterns of behaviour. The interview is, thus, the most important tool in the hands of the psychologist to help a person in redirecting and even changing the dynamics of his personality—his motives and traits. Such a change becomes specially necessary for those individuals whose personality is maladjusted. They are the persons who cannot adapt themselves to the circumstances of their life and fulfil the demands of their environment. Mental illness is an extreme form of such maladjustment. The interview, in one form or other, is the principal psychological method to help persons suffering from mental illness. The interview is the technique used by the psychologist not only for dealing with cases of severe maladjustment. It has its value in all forms of maladjusted behaviour. It is the most effective device for helping people solve their personality problems.

Chapter XIII

INTELLIGENCE AND APTITUDES

Nature of Intelligence

We call one person intelligent, another dull. We expect the first one to learn difficult tasks and to learn them quickly. We expect the second one to learn only easy tasks and to learn them slowly. We believe that the first one would be able to adjust to new and unfamiliar situations. The second one will have difficulty in adjusting to such situations. The first one would be able to find solutions of a new problem. The second one will apply the solutions that he has learned but do not fit in the new situation. He cannot appreciate the difference between the new and the old unless the two are very different. The intelligent person can observe very minute differences. He can view the qualities of an object apart from the object. He can also view one quality in separation from other qualities. He has the power to think abstractly.

When he is required to act in a new situation, the intelligent person will be able to grasp the relationship between the parts and aspects of the situation. He will be able to appreciate the significance of each part or aspect in leading to the goal for which he may be working. He can imagine new relationships and the result to which they point. He will, thus, be able to anticipate the result of an action before performing the action. As he proceeds with a task in hand, he can look back and see the relationship that the step he has already taken bears to the step he is going to take.

The intelligent person is likely to be attracted more by difficult and complex tasks. Such tasks that require repetitions of the same activities over and again, without much change, will make an intelligent person feel bored and uneasy.

From the above account we find that we understand what intelligence is by looking at the various types of activities an intelligent person is able to perform. It will not be correct to say that itntelligence is a name for all these activities. We can only say that these activities are the marks of intelligence, that intelligence lies at the back of these and other activities; a person is able to perform these activities because of intelligence. *Intelligence is to be regarded, therefore, as a general ability which a person possesses in more or less amount.*

Intelligence is a general ability because it is expressed through the great variety of activities an intelligent person is able to perform. As we saw, the ability shows itself in learning, in adaptation to new situations, in making fine comparisons, in thinking abstractly, in grasping and imagining relations, in solving problems, in successfully performing difficult and complex tasks, and so on. Different psychologists have picked up different aspects of intelligent behaviour. They have defined intelligence accordingly. We have such definitions of intelligence as the 'capacity to learn or to acquire new capacities', the capacity to adapt to new situations', 'the capacity to do abstract thinking', 'the capacity to apprehend relations', and so on. Some psychologists have attempted a more comprehensive definition. They have included in the definition not one but several characteristics of the behaviour in which intelligence is manifested. *No definition, however, is a complete definition. The reason is that intelligence is the all-round ability of a person.* It expresses itself in mental activities as well as bodily activities, in performing a purely intellectual task as well as accomplishing one that requires complex bodily behaviours. A good engineer, a clever surgeon, a successful businessman, or an able administrator has to make as much use of intelligence as a good scholar, a famous scientist, a shrewd lawyer, or a distinguished novelist. *Intelligence is a general ability which manifests itself in a great variety of functions that different individuals are able to perform.*

Measurement of Intelligence

We saw above that the persons are not equally intelligent. Some are more intelligent, some are less intelligent. The difference in the intelligence of persons is a fact known not only to psychologists. It was known long before the psychologists discovered and proved it. But it was expressed in qualitative terms. A person was judged to be of high or of low intelligence, to be bright or dull, just as a person was judged to be tall or short, having a heavy body or a light body. One could, however, also measure the height or weight of a person and tell in exact terms how high or how heavy a person was. This was possible because a standard scale for measuring length or weight was already devised. But one could not say how intelligent or how dull a person was. All descriptions of intelligence were qualitative. Difference in intelligence could not be quantitatively expressed. There was no scale for measuring intelligence until Alfred Binet, a French psychologist, developed his so-called test of intelligence.

An intelligence test consists of a variety of tasks. The tasks sample intelligent behaviour. They are such that intelligence is required for solving them. As we have seen, several kinds of activities involve the exercise of intelligence. A test of intelligence, therefore, requires several tasks, not all of the same kind. Each one is called a test item. A test, thus, consists of several items; an item is a part of a test.

As we shall see later, intelligence grows with age from the moment of birth, very much like the size and strength of the body. We have distinguished learning from maturation (Chap. VI, pp. 97-98). We have seen that the growth of the body, the increase in its strength and in the capacity of the body to perform more difficult and complicated movements depends upon maturation. We have called maturation a natural process of growth and development. It takes place more rapidly at first, but slows down gradually; it more or less completes itself and stops on reaching the adult age. Intelligence also is influenced by the same process of maturation. Just as the strength of the body increases with age, the strength of intelligence also increases with age. The strength of intelligence is measured by a person's capacity to perform more and more difficult and complex tasks. In his early infancy, a child can do only very easy tasks. As he grows in age, he is able to solve more and more difficult and complex problems.

Let us understand how Binet developed his test of intelligence. Binet's test has not only been the first test for measuring intelligence in the manner intelligence came to be measured.

It has exerted the greatest influence on the methods of measuring intelligence that are known to us today. We will know about them when we will refer to the different types or classes of test.

Binet prepared several items for his test, each one involving a particular task. The items were graded in order of difficulty; items involving easier and simpler tasks were followed by items involving more and more difficult and complex tasks. The difficulty of an item was determined by the percentage of children of a particular age that could pass that item. An item that was passed by about 60 to 70 per cent of children of an age was assigned to that age. In this manner five to six items were assigned to each age. Each one of these was passed by about two-thirds of children of the age to which it was assigned, by a much smaller percentage of children of the age just below that, and a much larger percentage of children of the next higher age.

Having assigned different sets of tests to different ages, Binet determined what was called the mental age of the child to whom his test was administered. If a child passed, for example, all the items assigned to eight years, his mental age was considered to be eight years. If his chronological age was also eight years, the child was said to be of average intelligence; he possessed the intelligence of the average child of eight years. Chronological age is the age measured in months and years from the moment of birth. A comparison between the mental age and chronological age would tell whether the child was just average in intelligence, below average, or above average.

The comparison between mental age and chronological age was made later by finding a ratio between the Mental Age (M A) and the Chronological Age (C A). A ratio is found by dividing one number by another number. The result of the division is called a quotient. If 6 is divided by 3, the quotient will be 2, and if 3 is divided by 6 the quotient will be 5. Similarly when M A was divided by C A to find the ratio, a quotient was found. For example, if a child's M A was 9 years and his C A was six years, the quotient will be 1.5. If both were equal, the quotient would be 1. If C A were larger than M A, the quotient would be less than 1, i.e., a fraction of one.

A large quotient, i.e., more than 1, *will indicate superior intelligence. A small quotient, less than* 1, *would mean inferior intelligence.* The quotient of $\frac{MA}{CA}$ thus came to be called Intelligence quotient or I Q. A quotient that is less than 1 is a fraction. A quotient that is more than 1 may also not be a whole number. For example, M A=8 and C A=6; $\frac{MA}{CA}$ will be equal to 1.33. But it is always more convenient to deal with a whole number. It was, therefore, decided to multiply the quotient by 100. This led to the well-known formula for finding I Q, namely, $IQ=\frac{MA}{CA}\times 100$.

The Binet Tests were revised and adapted in various languages. By adaptation of a test is meant that the items of the test are modified to suit the background of the people for whom the test is meant. An item may include the name of an unfamiliar object or one that is not known to most people. A few items may be less difficult in one and more difficult in another region.

The most famous adaptation of Binet's Test was made by Terman, and later by Terman and Merril, in America. The Terman-Merril Test measures intelligence from the age of 2 years upward to the adult age. There are six items assigned to most ages. By passing each item one gets a credit of two months. The M A of a person is determined by first finding the age for which he passes all items. As there are less difficult items below that age, he will pass those items. He need not, therefore, actually try them at all. The person may be first given the items assigned to an age one or two years below his chronological age. If he passes all items for that age, he need not go further below that age. In case he fails them, or fails some items, he may be asked to try items for a still lower age. The person gets full credit for the age when he passes all items for that age. He gets additional credit for the number of items he passed above that age. Supposing, a 9-year-old child passes all items for this age as well as those for ten years. He passes 2 items assigned to 11 years and one item assigned to 12 years. He fails all items for 13 years. He gets a total credit of 10 years, or 120 months, plus 4 months and 2 months. His mental age will be 126 months. His C A is 9 years or 108 months. His I Q will be :

$$\frac{126}{108} \times 100 = 116.66 \text{ or } 117.$$

Within any age we get a wide range of I Q's. If the test is applied to a random sample of, say, 200 6-years-old children, the I Q's will be found to be widely scattered about the Mean I Q. The Mean is found, as usual, by totalling the I Q's of all persons in the sample and dividing the total by the number of persons within the sample. Most I Q's will be near the Mean I Q. Some I Q's will be farther from the Mean. A few will be quite far. In other words, the I Q's will be dispersed about the Mean, some near it and some far from it, both above and below the Mean. If you arrange the I Q's in an increasing order from the lowest to the highest, you will get a scale of I Q's. The scale can be represented by a horizontal line. It will be similar to a foot scale used for measuring length. The foot scale has 12 equal parts or units. Its extreme left value is 0, and its extreme right value is 12. Suppose your scale of I Q's extends from 60 to 147, i.e., the lowest I Q is 60 and the highest I Q is 147. It can be represented by a line having 60 at its left and 147 at its right end. It will be divided into 88 equal units. But you can divide the line also into 11 equal units. Instead of taking 1 as the size of a unit, you take 8 as the size of a unit. Each unit is called a step. There are 11 steps. The size of a step is 8. The size of a step is also called Step Interval. The following line illustrates such a scale :

You will find that the 200 I Q's will fall not the same number of times within each step. Say, you find two children having an I Q that falls in the first step from the bottom, i.e., between 60 and 67, and 13 children having I Q's falling between 76 and 83. In this way you can count the number of I Q's falling within each of the 11 steps. The number within a step is called the frequency of that step. You can express the frequency of each step as shown in the following Table :

TABLE OF FREQUENCY DISTRIBUTION

I Q's in Step Intervals	Frequency
140-147	2
132-139	6
124-131	13
116-123	24
108-115	35
100-107	40
92-99	35
84-91	24
76-83	13
68-75	6
60-67	2
	N=200

The above Table is called a Frequency Distribution Table.

You can also plot the following graph on the basis of the Table above.

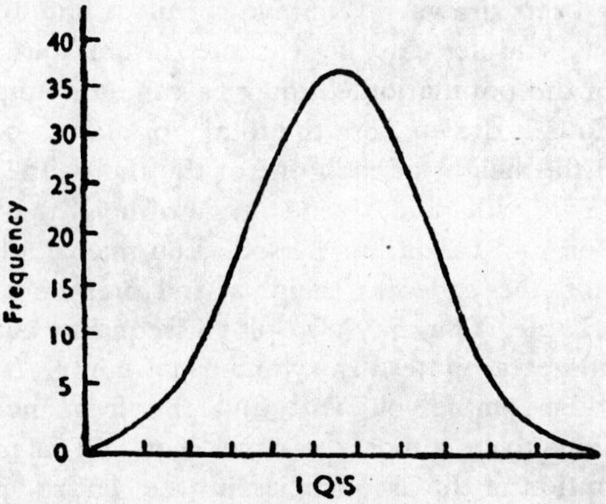

Fig. 36

In the above graph the base line is the scale of I Q's divided into 11 equal steps. The vertical line on the left is a scale of frequency. The maximum frequency is 40 and the minimum is 2. We have taken 0 instead of 2. The vertical scale has;

therefore, 40 units, if the size of each step is taken to be 1. Here we have taken 5 as the size of each step. The line has been divided therefore into 8 equal steps.

The graph on p. 205 is called a frequency polygon. It resembles a temple, or, church bell. Its both sides have the same shape. A figure whose right and left sides have the same shape is called a bilaterally symmetrical figure. Bilateral means both sides. Bilaterally symmetrical means both sides having the same shape. Intelligence test scores have frequencies that produce such a bilaterally symmetrical curve. This happens, however, only when the scores are found by administering the test to a random sample of not a small size. A random sample is also called a representative sample. The inclusion of a person in a random sample depends only upon chance. In other words, a random sample is drawn in such a way that the individuals who are included in the sample had the same chance of being left out as those that have actually been left out. There are different procedures for drawing a random or representative sample. It is called representative because it possesses all the important characteristics of the population from which the sample has been drawn. Whatever result is found in dealing with such a sample can be expected from other random samples from the population. Suppose a random sample of ten thousand adults is drawn from the total population of the State of Bihar and the height of each one of the thousand persons is measured. You will find a wide range of heights between the shortest person and the tallest person. You may find out the frequencies of the different heights and prepare a frequency distribution Table. You may also plot a frequency curve. Here also you will get a bilaterally symmetrical curve. If you draw another random sample you will find the frequencies of the different heights to be almost the same. You will infer that such is the distribution of the frequencies in the entire population of Bihar State.

It is not only intelligence test scores, or measures of height that produce a bilaterally symmetrical curve. This is expected of measures of most characteristics of man, and of other living objects.

When we look back at the Table on p. 205, we notice another feature also. We find that the frequency of the steps changes from step to step. It is minimum in the top and bottom steps. As we proceed from the two ends, it becomes larger and larger. When we reach the middle step, the sixth one, the frequency becomes the largest. Thus, we do not find equal distribution of the 200 I Q's from step to step. The distribution is unequal. But there is a systematic order. Larger and larger frequencies appear as we proceed from the bottom or the top. It is this feature which makes the curve in Fig. 36 a bell-shaped curve. Such a bell-shaped curve of frequencies is also called a normal curve. It is so called because the measures of most biological characteristics produce a curve of this shape. Normal means here the usual. The distribution in the Table on p. 205 will be called a normal distribution.

It has been found that I Q's are normally distributed. We can draw some important conclusions from this. It follows that in any population the number of persons whose I Q is very low, or very high, is very small. Most persons have an average I Q, i.e., they fall at the middle position. In other words, very few persons are very dull and very few persons are very bright. Most persons are neither dull nor bright; they have moderate intelligence. This also shows that it is not only very intelligent people who attain success in life. Many successful persons in different walks of life are of average general ability. For success, therefore, some other abilities are also needed. They are called special abilities or aptitudes. We will discuss them at the end of the chapter.

Interpretation of I Q's

I Q's have been classified in the following manner in order to estimate easily what level of intelligence a person has when his I Q is known :

TABLE

140 and above	Genius
130—139	Very superior
120—129	Superior
110—119	Bright
90=109	Average
80— 89	Dull
70— 79	Inferior
below 70	Feeble minded

Those whose I Q is below 70 are regarded as mentally deficient. They are classified into the following three groups according to the degree of mental deficiency :

50-70 Morons
20-50 Imbeciles
Below 20 Idiots.

The idiot cannot take care of himself. Even as an adult, his mental age is below 3 years. You can expect the same behaviour from him that you generally observe in an average child of 3 years. The imbecile has a mental age of 3 to 7 years as an adult. He can perform routine duties; can talk and learn simple skills. But he cannot profit from schooling. The moron adult has a mental age of 8 to 12 years. He can learn to read and write. He may take responsibility for himself and earn a living. But he is not expected to complete high school education.

Age Scale and Point Scale

The Binet type of test is an age scale. By passing the test items a person gets a mental age. We saw above how the mental age is determined. For most ages, a person gets a credit of 2 months for passing a particular item. The total credit that he gets is the mental age assigned to him. This becomes his total score. This may be called age score to distinguish it from what is called point score. A point score is the total number of points made by a person. Suppose a test has 50 items. If a person passes 35 items, he earns one point for each. His total score becomes 35. Sometimes a credit of 2 or 3, instead of one, may be given for each item passed. The score, however, will be the total credit a person earns. Other types of intelligence tests are point scales.

Limitation of Binet Type Tests

Though the Binet type test was the foremost test of intelligence, few tests of this type are now being developed. One reason is the difficulty in finding the I Q of persons older than 14 or 15 years. We will see that intelligence grows rapidly at first. It gradually slows down. We will also find that the growth of intelligence when measured by an intelligence test stops, on the average, at 14 or 15 years. Persons older than this age are likely to get the same score in an intelligence test as those of this age. Only a few will exceed this level. In such a case we cannot think of a mental age above 15 years. An average person of any age beyond 15 years will pass items of only such difficulty as passed by the average 15-years-old. Only a small percentage of persons above 15 years age will pass more difficult items. If 15 years is accepted to be the highest mental age then the older a person the lower will be his I Q. The I Q of all persons who are 20 years old will be 75. i.e., $\frac{15}{20}$ multiplied by 100. Each one will be a border-line case and definitely of inferior intelligence. This is ridiculous. To avoid such a result, for ages above 15, I Q. is calculated by substituting for C A in the formula not the real chronological age that a person has. The C A is allowed to remain at 15. The M A is determined by first trying him on the items meant for 14 years. He is then given 4 sets of tests of increasing difficulty. For passing each item he gets separate credits. If he passes all tests he gets the maximum M A of 23 years. This is, however, very very exceptional.

Tests of the Binet type are not altogether objective. An objective test or measurement is that in which the examiner plays no part in determining the result of the test. The usual school or college examinations are subjective in this sense. The same answers may be allotted different marks by different examiners. Even the same examiner has been found to allot different marks to the same answer on different occasions. The result of the examination, in such a case, does not depend entirely upon what the answer contains. It also depends, partly, on the examiner. He may be strict or lenient. He may have examined the answers carefully or carelessly. For these and other reasons we expect large differences between examiners. Psychological tests are objective. The result of the test does not depend upon the examiners. Whosoever acts as the examiner, the result or the test score will be altogether the same.

Binet type tests are not objective as other psychological tests, though they are much more objective than school or college examinations. Their answers are short. The answers in the school or college examinations are generally quite long. They cover pages. For this reason these examinations are called essay type examinations.

In the Binet Test the examiner is provided with a Key of alternative answers which he uses to check whether the answer given by the person who is tested is correct or incorrect. All this is possible because the answers are short. If the answer made by a testee, i.e., the person who is tested, tallies with one of the answers given in the Key, the scoring becomes objective. Anyone would know it to be correct and there will be no difference in scoring. But if the answer does not altogether tally with one of the keyed answers, the examiner has to exercise his own judgment. The wording of the answer used by the testee may be different from the wording of the answer in the Key. The examiner has to judge whether in spite of the difference in language the meaning or content is the same. He will give credit to the answer if he feels satisfied about the content. Otherwise, he will judge it to be wrong and will give no credit. This introduces an element of subjectivity in the scoring of the Binet type tests. If the judgment of the examiner is wrong, the tester may either get a credit which he should not get or lose a credit which he should get. The exact mental age of a person will, therefore, depend upon whether credit is given or withheld for answers that are not identical with the keyed answers. As we have seen, the I Q of a person will increase or decrease with increase or decrease in the mental age assigned to him.

We said that the Binet type tests are not very objective. This does not, however, apply to all items of the Binet Test, specially some of those items that are meant for the lower ages. Examples of such items are picture completion, naming objects from memory, repeating digits. But there are also other items whose scoring cannot be altogether objective. For example, for age four there is an item called comprehension which consists of two questions : (1) "Why do we have houses ?" and (2) "Why do we have books ?" The Key gives as many as fourteen correct alternatives for the first question and nine for the second. These, however, cannot exhaust all possibly correct answers. Room is still left for the examiner to exercise his judgment. At the higher age levels, such items predominate. Many of them require the use of abstract thinking, such as finding similarities or differences between two things, finding reasons etc.

Classification of Intelligence Tests

The Binet type tests are called Individual tests. They can be administered to only one person at a time. They are to be distinguished from Group tests of intelligence. They are so called because they can be administered in groups. More than one person, fifty to hundred, may take the test together and at the same time. However, if the size of the group is large, the tester will need one or two assistants. But one experienced tester can very well manage alone a group of forty to fifty.

The group tests are completely objective. Following is an example of an item from a group test :

Idea is related to mind in the same way as fruit is related to
Thought, Ripe, Taste, Tree, Vegetable ?

The item contains five alternative answers of which only one is correct. The testee has to identify the correct answer and underline it. The correct answer in this case is Tree. Fruit is produced in a tree as idea is produced in the mind. Hence, fruit is related to tree in the same way as idea is related to mind. The Key contains the correct answer. The examiner checks from the Key and fails the testee if he underlines any other answer.

Supposing, in the above example the alternatives were not given. The tester may then give plant or garden, instead of tree, as his answer. He may even say basket or fruit shop. One examiner may give credit for basket or fruit shop thinking that a basket or a fruit shop contains fruits, just as the mind contains ideas. Another examiner may accept only tree, plant, or garden, thinking that ideas grow in the mind as fruits grow in a tree, plant, or garden. When alternatives are given, as in the above example, so that only one is correct and others are incorrect, the correct choice can be only one. There is no scope for any difference between examiners.

Besides the difference between individual and group tests, tests may also be distinguished as verbal and non-verbal. The verbal tests use words or numbers. Words or numbers are signs or symbols. They stand for objects or relations of objects. The above example (p. 211) is an item of a verbal test. Non-verbal tests do not use words or numbers. They use actual objects. They are called performance tests. For example, we have what is called the Block Design Test. It is a performance test. The testee is supplied with several one-inch cubes. The six sides of the cube are differently coloured. Four sides are each coloured red, green blue or yellow. One side is coloured half red, half green, another half blue and half yellow. The testee is given a coloured design. The following is an example :

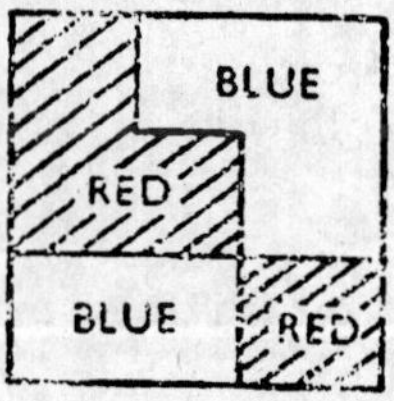

Fig. 37

The testee has to place the blocks together in such a manner that the upper surface of the joined blocks makes the design. In a performance test the testee has to manipulate, that is, to move, or put together in a certain relation, some given objects so that a desired result is produced. He has to solve a practical problem with his hand, using some objects.

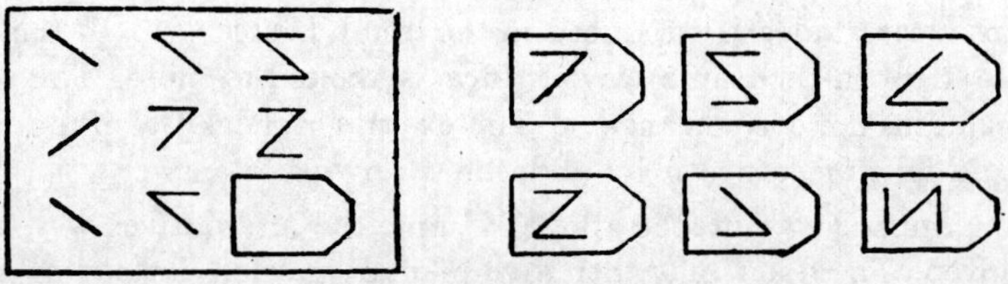

Fig. 38

There is another kind of non-verbal test that cannot be called a performance test. The above is an example.

Here we have a drawing which does not represent anything. It is not a sign or a symbol and, therefore, neither a word nor a number. It is not an object that can be manually manipulated. It is just a pattern of lines. The testee has to find out which one of the alternative designs at the right will fit into the pattern at the left.

The above type of tests has led to another classification of tests : (1) Paper-and-pencil test and (2) Performance tests. Both verbal and non-verbal tests can be paper-and-pencil tests. The tests contain printed materials and the testee has only to use his pencil in pointing out the correct answer. Performance tests form, in this sense, a distinct class. They consist of objects or parts of objects and the testee has to use his hand in manipulating them.

Test Scores and Norms

The mental age score or the point score that a person gets in a test of intelligence has no meaning. A person may be found to have the mental age of 10 years, or to get the total score of 73. We cannot come to any conclusion about his level of intelligence. i.e., whether he is of superior, average or inferior intelligence. To get a meaning we have to relate these scores to some other facts. Thus, a mental age as we have seen becomes meaningful when related to the chronological age. Similarly the total score of 73 becomes meaningful when related to the average score made by persons of the same age. For this reason a mental age score or the point score that a person obtains is called an absolute score. It is also called raw score. It has to be converted into what is called relative score or derived score. I Q, as we have seen, is a relative or derived score. We have already known how an I Q is derived. There are two other important derived scores. They are described below, one after the other.

Percentile Score

The percentile score indicates the position or rank of a person in relation to other persons in his age group. The rank or position is expressed in terms of percentage. We have seen how the scores in a test can be arranged along a scale (p. 204). We can similarly arrange or order the scores in such a manner that each score marks a point on the scale above and below which fall certain fixed percentage of scores. A score which has the 50th percentile position in such a scale is called the Median. Fifty per cent of the scores will be above the Median, and fifty per cent will be below the Median. Similarly, one can find the score that has 25th percentile position. This score sets the limit for

25 per cent of scores that fall below it and 75 per cent of scores that fall above it. Likewise the 75th percentile score will set the limit for 25 per cent above it and 75 per cent below it. Similar scores may be found that set the limits for 10, 20, 30, 40, 50, 60, 70, 80, or 90 per cent of scores. When the scores that mark off the various percentile positions have been found, they are set in a Table which has two columns. One column gives the percentile rank or position and the other the scores corresponding to each position. The following is an example :

TABLE

Percentiles	Scores
95	136
90	129
80	120
75	116
70	113
60	106
50	100
40	94
30	87
25	84
20	80
10	69
5	61

The above table is called a table of norms. It is so called because you can use the table for interpreting the raw scores obtained by a person. You can find his place in his group. You can know how many persons in a group of 100 are expected to be above him and how many are likely to fall below him. The table gives you the standard with which you can compare a score and find its meaning. Norm is another word for standard. A scale of intelligence is as useless without norms as is a scale for measuring weight without using the standard weights. It is always necessary, therefore, to develop norms also when one prepares a test of intelligence.

When we know the position of a person in his group, we can make some conclusion about him. Suppose a person gets a score of 68. Looking at the above table you know that 90 per cent of individuals in his group are above him. Only, a little more than 8 per cent will be below him. Such a person is evidently of very inferior intelligence. Another person gets a score of 130 in the same test. He is definitely of very superior intelligence. He excels 90 per cent of other persons in his age group.

Standard Score

We have seen that we can arrange the scores in a test along a scale (p. 204). We also saw that the scale may be divided into several equal units or steps. Below we have a scale of test scores that extends from 10 to 130. The scale is divided into 12 steps, the size of each step is 10. We also have a frequency distribution curve (p. 204) and our scale is the base of the area under the curve. The distribution is the bell-shaped normal curve (p. 205).

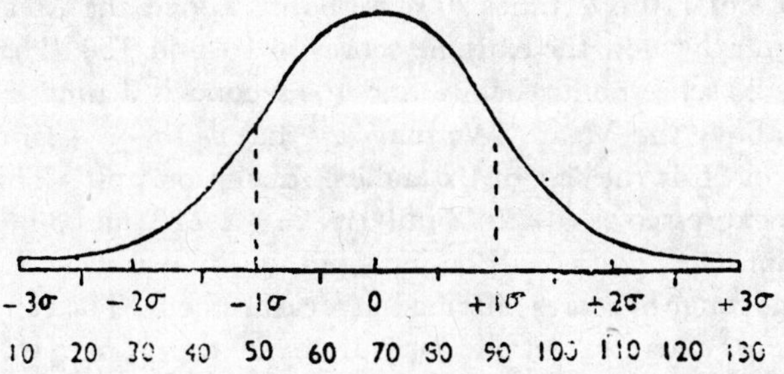

Fig. 39

Suppose we divide the scale into 6 instead of 12 equal units. In this case each unit or step will cover 20 successive scores. The first step from the left will extend from 10 to 29, the second from 30 to 49, and so on. Instead of starting from the left end of the scale, we may start from the middle position. The middle position in a normal distribution is occupied by the Mean. We will then have 3 steps on the left and 3 steps on the right of the Mean. When the base line of the area under a normal curve is thus divided, the unit of division is called standard unit. It is called standard because this kind of division has been found useful for the purpose of statistical calculations. It has been accordingly adopted as the standard unit of division. The standard unit is called the standard deviation unit. It is so called because each unit becomes a measure of distance or deviation from the Mean. In the above scale the Mean is 70. Starting from the Mean and moving to the left, the first unit ends at 50. Hence 50 is at a distance of 1 standard unit from the Mean. Similarly 30 is at a distance of 2 standard units, and 10 at a distance of 3 standard units. Same will be the case when we move to the right, i.e., above the Mean. The first standard deviation unit is called I SD or just SD. We use the Greek letter σ, small sigma, for standard Deviation. The second standard deviation unit is called 2 SD or 2σ, and the third is called 3 SD or 3σ. The units above the Mean are given plus sign; the units below the Mean are given minus sign. These are shown in Fig. 39.

In the above scale a score of 50 is 20 score points below the Mean, while a score of 90 is 20 score points above the Mean. Likewise the score of 30 is 2 times 20 score points below and the score of 110 is 2 times 20 score points above the Mean. We can similarly view the extreme scores of 10 and 130. The first is 3 times 20 score points below and the second is 3 times 20 score points above the Mean. We may say that -1σ or $+1\sigma$ is equal to 20, or 20 is the size of 1 standard deviation unit. This may also be expressed as $\sigma = 20$. Similarly, $2\sigma = 2 \times 20$; and $3\sigma = 3 \times 20$.

What score points will be included within a unit will depend upon the range of scores obtained in measurement. The range may be wide or narrow. In one measurement the range of scores obtained may be, say, from 16 to 35, or 20, in another it may be, say, from 5 to 52, or 48 and in still another from 46 to 173, or 128, and so on. The extent of the score points within a standard deviation or σ unit will thus vary from measurement to measurement. In each case, therefore, it has to be specially determined. Suppose for a certain set of scores you obtain a Mean of 50 and standard deviation of 8. In this case the first σ unit or/1σ will extend to 58 above the Mean and 42 below the Mean 2σ to 66 above and 34 below the Mean, and 3σ to 74 above and 26 below the Mean. The standard deviation or σ is called a measure of variability. It shows the average extent to differences between scores as measured from the Mean.

When you look at Fig 39 you will find that a large area below the curve is covered by the perpendicular lines drawn at $+1\sigma$ and -1σ. The area covered is 68.26 per cent of the total area, i.e. a little more than two-thirds. A little less than one-third of the total area falls outside. The area covered between $+2\sigma$ and -2σ is 95.44% of the total area. Only a little less than 5 per cent falls beyond $+2\sigma$ and -2σ. Outside $+3\sigma$, and 3σ, there is practically no space left, since 99.73 per cent of the total area is covered this far.

The standard deviation unit is also the standard score unit. The standard score is thus a measure of distance from the Mean expressed in terms of the standard deviation unit. Any raw score can be converted into a standard score by finding the difference between the score and the Mean, and dividing this difference by the standard deviation. In Fig. 39 we have found the scores of 90 and 50 to be at a distance of 1σ from the Mean, which is 70. The size of the σ is 20. (p. 216). We can arrive at the same result by finding the difference between 90 and 70 and dividing the difference by 20. The difference is plus when the raw score is larger than the Mean. It is minus when the raw score is smaller than the Mean. The standard score in one case is $+1\sigma$; in the other case it is -1σ. The scale in Fig. 39 has also been shown as a standard score scale. We may divide this scale into 12 steps, rather than 6, by taking $\frac{1}{2}\sigma$ or ·5 as the unit of division. The standard scores will then be separated not by 1 unit but by half sigma unit. Starting from the left, we will have -2.5σ next to -3σ, -1.5σ, next to -2σ, and $-·5\sigma$ next to -1. We will have similar scores above the Mean. Only, this time each score will have a plus sign.

The standard scores can be reconverted into the raw scores by a reverse process. We have to multiply each standard score by the obtained standard deviation and add the obtained Mean to the product. Thus $+1\sigma = 1 \times 20 + 70 = 90$; $-2\sigma = 2 \times 20 + 70 = 30$.

We saw above that the area bound by the perpendiculars drawn at $+2\sigma$ and -2σ covers about 95 per cent of the total area under the distribution curve. Only 2.5 per cent of the total area on each side is left out. This means that a person who gets a standard score of $+2\sigma$ is inferior to only 2 persons in a group of 100 persons; he exceeds 97 persons. He must be of very superior ability. Similarly a person whose standard score is -2σ has 97 persons above him and only 2 persons are below him. He must be of very inferior ability. It seems therefore that the standard scores of $+2\sigma$ or $-2\ \sigma$ gives us a limit ability beyond which we need not go. For practical purpose, therefore, the standard score scale may end with $+2\sigma$ and -2σ. If we take $\frac{1}{2}\sigma$ or $\cdot5\sigma$ as the standard score unit, we will then have the following standard score scale which has four steps above and four steps below the middle or zero score value :

-2σ -1.5σ -1σ -0.5σ 0 $+0.5\sigma$ $+1\sigma$ $+1.5\sigma$ $+2\sigma$

Including the middle step, the scale has a total of 9 steps.

The standard score scale as we saw, has plus and minus values, and some steps have also decimal values. Again, the scale has zero value at the middle. It is more convenient to have plus scores and in whole numbers. This can be very easily done. Take the middle value, which as we have seen is the Mean, to be other than zero. You may take it to be 100. You may further take the standard deviation to be 20. You could have as well selected any other value for the Mean or the standard deviation. You will get a standard score scale which begins with the lowest value at the left end, and goes on increasing along the scale in whole numbers. This will be a transformed standard score scale. To obtain this, all that you have to do is to multiply each one of the scores in the standard score scale by 20 and add hundred to the product. Your transformed scale will be the following :

60 70 80 90 100 110 120 130 140

This scale too has nine steps. It is a standard scale with nine steps. The above scale has score values that are indentical with those in the IQ scale. (p. 207). The Mean is 100 in both cases. An IQ of 100 and the standard score of 100 have the same meaning. The other values above or below 100 too have the same meaning for both scales. There is no harm then if we call the values in the above scale also as IQ's We have only to remember that these IQ's have been derived by a different method. They belong to a point scale and not to an age scale. To avoid this confusion, these IQ's have been called deviation

IQ's. They are so called because they indicate different units of deviation from the Mean, and not the ratio of the mental age to the chronological age.

The deviation IQ has been used by Wechsler in his individual test of intelligence. Wechsler has developed two tests. One for measuring the intelligence of children. Another for measuring the intelligence of adults. The first one is the Wechsler-Bellevue Test for Adults; second one is the Wechsler Intelligence Scale for Children. Like the Binet type tests, these tests of intelligence contain both verbal and performance items. In the Binet test the two types of items are mixed up. Wechsler's tests have 5 sets of verbal items which are separate from 5 sets of performance items. The test can, therefore, provide separate verbal and performance scores, besides the full test scores.

Marks of a Good Test

You will find that there are hundreds of tests of intelligence. All of them are not good tests. How then would you select a good test if you need one ? There are three characteristics of a good test. It is reliable, valid and practicable. We will describe each characteristic separately.

Test Reliability : When you use any measuring instrument, you feel sure that you will get the same result whenever you use it. A standard foot scale will measure the same length whenever used. For this reason, you do not have a measuring tape or scale made of rubber. Rubber stretches; the length that a rubber scale would measure should vary from measurement to measurement. It will not give you a reliable measure of length. Before buying a thermometer you test whether it records the same temperature when applied to the same body at quick intervals. If it does not, the thermometer is unreliable. A test also is unreliable if it does not give the same result for the same persons when administered under similar conditions. It is reliable if it gives consistent results. An unreliable test, like an unreliable thermometer, is not well constructed.

Three methods have been generally used for estimating the reliability of a test. They are described below :

(1) The test is administered to a sample. It is then divided

or split into two halves. The odd-numbered items i.e., 1, 3, 5, 7, etc., form one half. The even-numbered items, i.e., 2, 4, 6, 8, etc., form the other half. Separate scores are found for each half of the test. Two sets of scores are thus available. If the test is reliable those who obtain high scores in the first half obtain high scores in the second half also. Similarly those who obtain low scores in one half obtain low scores in the other half. If you arrange the scores in each half test in rank order, you should expect that the person who gets first rank in one gets first rank in the other. He who occupies the second position in one should occupy the second position in the other. In other words, each person should have the same position in both halves of the test. There may be minor deviations here and there, but, generally, there should be a close correspondence. If there is no close agreement, you should be doubtful about the reliability of the test.

The agreement between the two halves of a test can be expressed by a value which is called the coefficient of correlation. The size of this value will tell you how close the agreement is. If the agreement is perfect, the correlation coefficient will be 1 or unity. For example, you measure 50 serially marked wooden sleepers of different lengths and record the length of each against its number. Let someone also measure the same and keep a separate record. When you campare the two sets of measures, you will find perfect agreement. You can calculate the correlation coefficient by using a formula given in any book on statistics. The correlation will be 1. Let us take another example. Suppose you measure the chest of 100 persons and also measure the length of each one's foot. You expect no correspondence from measurement to measurement. Some persons may have a broad chest with small feet and some with large feet. Others may have a narrow chest in some cases with large feet and in some cases with a small feet. You will observe no relationship between measurement of chest and length of foot. If you calculate a correlation coefficient between the two sets of measurements, i.e., of chest and of foot, the value you will get will be zero or near zero.

Perfect correlation is expressed by 1; zero shows no correlation. Between 0 and 1 there will be different amounts of correlation. Those that are near zero will show poor agreement.

Those that are near 1 will show strong agreement. The values between 0 and 1 will be less than 1. A value that is less than 1 is a fraction or part of one. It is, therefore, expressed in a decimal form. For example, it has been found that there is a correlation between intelligence test scores and examination marks. Those who get high marks in examination generally get high scores in an intelligence test. Those who get low test scores generally get low examination marks. The relation, however, is not perfect. Quite a few persons achieve better in examination with low test scores. They are called over-achievers. Similarly, quite a few with high intelligence test scores show poor achievement. We call them under-achievers. The correlation coefficient value, therefore, is expected to be near about 5.

Besides differing in amount, the correlation may also differ in direction. The value of correlation may be positive or negative, i.e., a plus or a minus. The correlation between intelligence test scores and examination marks is positive. The two sets of measurements generally increase or decrease in the same order; when one increases the other also increase and when one decreses the other also decreases. Correlation has been found between intelligence of parents and size of the family. But the correlation is negative in this case. More intelligent parents, generally, have a smaller family than less intelligent parents. Here increase in one is accompanied by decrease in the other. There is a relation between parents' intelligence and family size, but the relation is inverse or negative. Negative correlation should not be confused with zero correlation. Zero correlation has a negative sense. It means no correlation. Negative correlation has a positive sense. Like positive correlation, it shows the presence of correlation. It differs from positive correlation in the direction or sign of the relationship. The relationship is inverse. A negative correlation between two sets of measurements indicates that when one rises or increases, the other falls or decreases.

We saw above that the extent of agreement between the two halves of a test can be expressed by the coefficient of correlation. The value of the correlation coefficient, thus, becomes a measure of reliability. It may, therefore, be called the coefficient of reliability. As it is found by dividing the test into two halves, it is called split-half or odd-even reliability. The correlation coefficient found gives the reliability of the half test. It is possible to estimate, from this knowledge, the reliability of the full test by using a simple statistical formula.

(2) Reliability can be estimated also by another method. The test is administered twice, at a certain interval of time, to the same group of persons. The coefficient of correlation is then found between the scores obtained in the two administrations. If the correlation is high, the test is judged to be reliable. The reliability thus determined is called retest or repeat-test reliability.

(3) A third method is to administer equivalent forms of the test to the same group of persons. Some tests are developed in two or more equivalent forms. Equivalent forms of a test produce the same Mean and the same standard deviation when applied to the same group of persons. If there are more than two forms, equivalent tests would also have the same amount of correlations with each other. When the two forms are administered to the same group, the correlation between the two sets of scores becomes a measure of reliability of each form. The reliability is called equivalent forms or two-form reliability.

The reliability of a good test of intelligence should be near perfect. The correlation coefficient obtained by any method should be above 0.9. The coefficient of reliability has often been found to be near 0.95.

Validity of Tests

A good test of intelligence must be valid. By validity of a test we understand that the test is measuring what it is intended to measure. A test of intelligence is intended to measure the all-round ability of a person. If we find that a certain test of intelligence consists of items which really explore the interests and values of persons, we will not call it a valid test of intelligence.

To estimate the validity of a test we require another mark or criterion of the ability that the test is measuring. For example, we know that intelligence grows with age during the early years of life. We expect that, on the average, older children are more intelligent than younger ones. Age is therefore a good criterion for estimating the validity of an intelligence test. Suppose, there is a test of intelligence that can be applied to children from the age of say 6 to 14. If the test is valid, you should expect that the Mean scores in the test obtained by older children will be considerably larger than the Mean scores obtained by younger children. Another criterion may be examination marks. Success in examination partly depends upon the general ability to acquire knowledge and skill that a pupil possesses. Those who are of superior intelligence are, therefore, likely to secure higher marks than those who are of inferior intelligence. If you find a good correlation between intelligence test scores and examination marks, you consider the test to be valid. However, you should not expect a very high correlation. There are other factors, like academic interest, satisfactory study habits, facilities for home study, besides industriousness also, which matter for good or poor results in examination. Still a good verbal test of intelligence should have a correlation of 0.5. or more with examination marks.

A common criterion is another established test of intelligence. The Terman-Merril Test has been used as a criterion for estimating the validity of a new test of intelligence in English. A verbal test of intelligence in the English language should have a correlation of at least .5 with the IQ's found in the Terman-Merril Test.

Practicability of a Test

A good test of intelligence must be one that can be easily administered, scored and interpreted. The administration of a test, or its scoring, may be difficult, or very time consuming. Only highly trained and experienced psychologists are able to administer or score the test satisfactorily. Or the cost of the test may be high. The test can be administered only individually and not in group. Such tests involve practical difficulties. Other reliable and valid tests that are easy to administer and score, and are less costly in time and money should be preferred.

Constancy of Intelligence

Individuals differ in the amount of intelligence that each one possesses. This difference can be measured from the very early years of life. We have seen that the Terman-Merril Test can measure the intelligence of children from the age of two years. We have also seen that we can interpret the score obtained by a child by relating it to the scores made be other children of his age. It has been found that the relative position or standing of a person remains about the same as he grows in age. The high or low intelligence with which he starts persists through time. The amount of his intelligence remains more or less constant. This fact has been proved in many studies of the so-called Constancy of IQ. The IQ's of children have been obtained at regular intervals during the process of their growth from early infancy to adult age. It has been consistently found that the IQ's obtained by a person at different ages do not show much difference. Under normal circumstances, generally, the change in IQ has been found to be within 3 to 4 points only.

The fact that IQ remains constant shows that an individual maintains his difference to other individuals in intelligence. It is important to discover this difference early. In the education and trainning of a child, this difference has to be kept in view. The child's educational programme should be so planned that he is likely to achieve success. We will see that intelligence is not the only ability that matters for success. But intelligence is very important for academic achievement. We have said earlier that a person whose IQ is below 70 is not likely to complete high school. It is no use forcing him to do this. A person with IQ between 90 to 100 at high school is not likely to succeed in college, and so on. The IQ of a person alone does not tell us whether he is of inferior or superior intelligence. We can know this from his score in other tests also which do not give IQ. Percentile norms, or standard score norms, as we saw above, will enable us to know his relative position in intelligence. If the test is administered at different times and his percentile score or standard score remains constant, we can draw a more or less definite conclusion about his intelligence.

ORIGIN AND GROWTH OF INTELLIGENCE

How does a person come to possess the intelligence that he has? Does he acquire it as he acquires knowledge and skill as a result of experience and training? Is it inborn and shows itself like one's body by a natural process of growth? There has been no definite answer to these questions. But psychologists are generally of opinion that genetic, and not so much the environmental, factors account for the origin and growth of intelligence. The life of an individual starts from the germ cell. The germ cell possesses the potentialities for future development of the body and of its different parts. The germ cell also possesses the potentialities for the growth of intelligence. In this sense the factors that account for intelligence and its growth are called genetic.

Controlled studies have been made of the development of intelligence in identical twins. Identical twins develop from the division of the same germ cell in the mother's womb. Ordinarily, the division of the cell is repeated and more and more cells are produced. These, however, form part of the same body. In the case of the identical twins, when the first division or duplication takes place, each one grows separately to form two independent bodies. Identical twins, thus, have identical heredity. For this reason, their physical characteristics are almost the same. It is difficult to identify one from the other. All twins are not identical. They develop from separate cells in the mother's womb. Generally, only one cell from the father, called the sperm, fertilizes a single cell of the mother, called the egg. The result is the formation of a single body. But sometimes more than one sperm may independently fertilise more than one cell of the mother. In such a case, more than one body grows in the mother's womb and twins, triplets or quadruplets are born. Such twins are called fraternal twins. As each one starts from a separate germ cell each has a separate heredity. They have no more resemblance than siblings have. Siblings are the children born of the same parents.

In the study of twins, the intelligence of identical twins has been measured and compared at different ages. Similar measurement of the intelligence of fraternal twins, and of unrelated children has been taken. All categories of children studied were of the same age. Identical twins showed minimum difference in intelligence test scores at different ages, as compared to fraternal twins or unrelated children. Studies were also made of twins separated after birth and brought up in foster homes. A foster home is one in which a child is adopted and grows and lives. The foster homes in which the twins lived were culturally and economically very different; the environment of the two homes was dissimilar. In spite of the difference in the environment, the identical twins were much close in their intelligence as compared to fraternal twins or unrelated children. These results support the general conclusion that genetic factors play much more important part in the origin and growth of intelligence than do the environmental factors.

Studies of the intelligence of children at different ages have shows that the growth of intelligence is very rapid at first. It gradually slows down and reaches its highest level, on the average, at the age of 14 or 15 years. The following graph presents a picture of the growth of intelligence from the moment of birth to the age of 15 years.

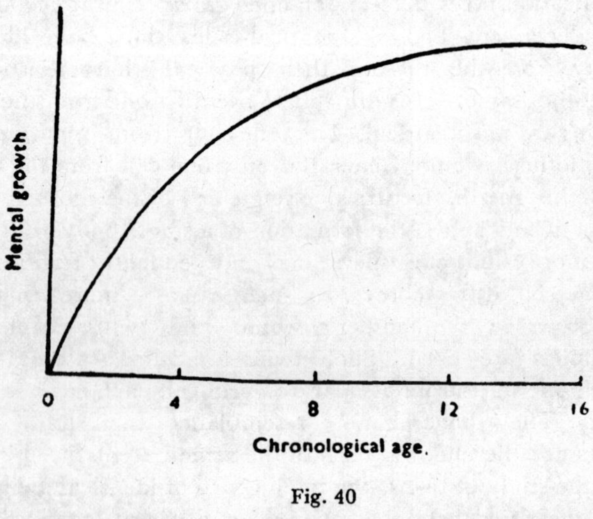

Fig. 40

The above curve has been called the mental growth curve. The curve shows that the rate of growth is very rapid at first. A child of one year may be said to be twice as intelligent as a child of 6 months and a child of two years to be about two times as intelligent as a child of 1 year. But the difference in the increase of intelligence between any two successive years becomes very small when we go beyond seven or eight years. The difference between 12 years and 13 years, or between 13 years and 14 years is almost negligible.

Aptitudes

We have described intelligence as the general ability which is manifested in a great variety of activities and functions that individual persons are able to perform. Intelligence sets a limit to the knowledge and skill a person is likely to acquire. It also determines at what level of difficulty and complexity of a task an individual can function successfuly. Intelligence, however, cannot determine what kind of knowledge and skill a person will be able to acquire, or what type of tasks he will be able to perform. Besides the general ability that a person has, we have also to think of a set of special abilities or aptitudes. You come across many persons who are very highly intelligent, e.g., a physician or a scientist, but they cannot compose or even appreciate poetry, write a novel, or create any other form of literature even if they have the time and desire to do so. Their capacity for literary creation or appreciation is poor. They lack what is called literary aptitude. Similarly a person may be known for his high intelligence, but he may lack the ability to become a painter, photographer, sculptor, or architect. His artistic ability is poor. Likewise, to become an engineer one should be strong in mechanical aptitude, besides having a strong mathematical aptitude. Mere high level intelligence will not be sufficient. There are several such special abilities or aptitudes. Some of these have been specially identified as mechanical aptitude, scientific aptitude computational aptitude, clerical aptitude, literary aptitude artistic aptitude, and musical aptitude.

Both general ability and special ability are necessary for achievement of success in any field. Aptitude for a kind of task can alone enable a person to perform the task. Possession of superior intelligence will enable him to attain high level success in the task. For example, a good artisan or craftsman should possess strong mechanical aptitude. But a good engineer should possess superior intelligence also. If a person knows his strong aptitudes, he can decide in what direction he can go, i.e., for what functions or vocation he might prepare himself. If he knows his level of intelligence, he can foresee how far he can go in the chosen direction, i.e., how high he can climb in the vocation for which he prepares.

Intelligence and aptitude are important but not sufficient for success. Strong motivation and drive are as much needed. We have seen that besides ability, motivation is another basis of learning (pp. 95-96). It is the need, drive or motive that moves a person from within to make effort. If the motive is weak, the effort will also be weak. The individual will not apply his full energy to the task. Or, he will not make sustained effort in the performance of the task. Capacity to make strong and sustained effort is called industriousness.

Strong motivation is also accompanied by strong interest in the activity aroused by the motive and in the goal to which the motive is directed. We have understood the nature of motivation in an earlier chapter. An interesting activity can be performed without voluntary or forced attention (p. 75). Interest in the task performed is, therefore, still another important factor that contributes to success.

Like the measures of intelligence that we described above, we have tests of aptitudes also. The more widely used tests of aptitudes are the tests of mechanical aptitude, tests of clerical aptitude and tests of artistic aptitude. Tests of mechanical aptitude are used for the selection of suitable persons for the various types of technical training courses. Tests of clerical aptitude are used for the selection of typists, stenographers, and other categories of clerical workers. A good aptitude test also should be reliable and valid.
